Fightb

MANCHESTER
1824

Manchester University Press

Critical Labour Movement Studies

Series editors
John Callaghan
Steve Fielding
Steve Ludlam

Already published in the series

John Callaghan, Steven Fielding and Steve Ludlam (eds), *Interpreting the Labour Party: approaches to Labour politics and history*

Fightback!

Labour's traditional right in the 1970s and 1980s

Dianne Hayter

Manchester University Press

Published by Manchester University Press
Altrincham Street, Manchester M1 7JA, UK
www.manchesteruniversitypress.co.uk

British Library Cataloguing-in-Publication Data
A catalogue record for this book is available from the British Library

Library of Congress Cataloging-in-Publication Data applied for

ISBN   0 7190 7270 0 *hardback*
EAN   978 0 7190 7270 3

ISBN   0 7190 7271 9 *paperback*
EAN   978 0 7190 7271 0

First published 2005

This edition first published in 2016

Typeset
by Northern Phototypesetting Co. Ltd., Bolton, Lancs.
Printed in Great Britain
by Lightning Source

To David

Contents

Series editors' foreword

The start of the twenty-first century is superficially an inauspicious time to study labour movements. Political parties once associated with the working class have seemingly embraced capitalism. The trade unions with which these parties were once linked have suffered near-fatal reverses. The industrial proletariat looks both divided and in rapid decline. The development of multi-level governance, prompted by 'globalisation' has furthermore apparently destroyed the institutional context for advancing the labour 'interest'. Many consequently now look on terms such as 'the working class', 'socialism' and the 'labour movement' as politically and historically redundant.

The purpose of this series is to give a platform to those students of labour movements who challenge, or develop, established ways of thinking and so demonstrate the continued vitality of the subject and the work of those interested in it. For despite appearances, many social democratic parties remain important competitors for national office and proffer distinctive programmes. Unions still impede the free flow of 'market forces'. If workers are a more diverse body and have exchanged blue collars for white, insecurity remains an everyday problem. The new institutional and global context is moreover as much of an opportunity as a threat. Yet, it cannot be doubted that compared with the immediate post-1945 period, at the beginning of the new millennium, what many still refer to as the 'labour movement' is much less influential. Whether this should be considered a time of retreat or reconfiguration is unclear – and a question the series aims to clarify.

The series will not only give a voice to studies of particular national bodies but will also promote comparative works that contrast experiences across time and geography. This entails taking due account of the political, economic and cultural settings in which labour movements have operated. In particular this involves taking the past seriously as a way of understanding the present as well as utilising sympathetic approaches drawn from sociology, economics and elsewhere.

John Callaghan
Steve Fielding
Steve Ludlam

Preface and acknowledgements

This book started with my reading Philip Gould's book about how the modernisers 'saved' the Labour Party.[1] 'That's not true' I shouted to an empty room – three years' research later, and this book is the result. There has been a conundrum in the party's recent history. Controlled by the left for a decade to the extent that in 1981 the party's right flank felt they had to leave, how was it that within a few years the remaining right – reduced in number and internally unpopular – had wrested control from the left and set about changing the character of the National Executive Committee (NEC)? The numbers did not appear to add up, and the left-wing Leader, Michael Foot, was no friend of those who slowly won this internal battle.

It is sometimes difficult – even for a small player in this story such as myself – to recall the bitterness and sectarian hostility within the movement, which was daily played out in TV studios and in the press. Having lost the 1979 general election after the Winter of Discontent, the Labour Party descended into internal turmoil, as the left-dominated NEC and conference sought revenge on the centre-right Parliamentary Labour Party (PLP) for its alleged failures in government. Then, in 1981, the Social Democratic Party split from Labour, leaving the Labour Party facing possible electoral extinction.

What happened then, virtually ignored by the press and largely by academic observers, was that the trade unions – founders of the Labour Party – came to its rescue. They were led by a small group of dedicated general secretaries and staff who set out to regain the NEC for the moderates, and to return the Labour Party to what they termed 'sanity' and electability, by expelling Militant, safeguarding the position of Deputy Leader Denis Healey when challenged by Tony Benn, and delivering for Neil Kinnock (the Leader they helped install after the 1983 election) an NEC committed to supporting him in changing the party.

This is the story the book tells. It is of the 'stayers', those who, despite being deeply unhappy about the state of the party, not only stayed after 1981 but organised the fightback. What I had no idea of as I started on this venture was the amount of sheer organisational hard work undertaken to achieve change and to assist in Labour's re-emergence as an electable party. As Neil Kinnock said to me: 'without organisation, politics is pleasant but it's only poetry'.

In order to set this organisational fightback in context, the book first summarises the background to 1981, reaching back into 1974–79, and outlining the environment faced by the right. It describes the non-policy battleground fought over within the party: Militant, One-Member-One-Vote and the 1981 and 1983 leadership contests. It then moves on to the real substance: the organisational response; firstly the less successful (the Manifesto Group and Labour First) and then the more successful: the internal party groupings which led the post-1981 fightback of the traditional right (the St Ermins Group of trade union leaders, the Labour Solidarity Campaign and *Forward Labour*).

The book draws on extensive private papers and archives, together with over 70 interviews with key players. As will be obvious, the research owes an enormous debt to the time given by these interviewees and the loan of archives and personal papers. The Rt Hon. John F. Spellar MP and Roger Godsiff MP have produced both in abundance, without which the story could never have been told. Lord (Alan) Haworth (until recently Secretary of the PLP), Sir David Bean, Nick Butler, Bob and Helen Eadie, Mrs John Grant, John Gyford, Mike Parker, Greg Rosen, Charles Turnock, David Webster and Sir Ian Wrigglesworth have all been particularly generous with their papers as well as with advice and information. The Rt Hon. Lord (Roy) Hattersley kindly allowed me full access to his papers at the University of Hull whilst Stephen Bird, the archivist of the Labour History Archive, supplied knowledge and advice in addition to access to the Manifesto Group and Labour Party's papers. Lord (Giles) Radice – my first ever boss – gave me access to his then unpublished diary whilst Baroness (Llin) Golding and Paul Farrelly MP let me see the manuscript of John Golding's wonderful book before it was in print, allowing me to take advantage of its contents at an early stage of my research.[2] The real debt, of course, is to those whose names appear in the book, who worked desperately to save the party they loved, and now have given of their time to allow me to re-tell the tale.

Despite this abundance of material, I could not have undertaken this work without Professor Lewis Minkin having said 'excellent idea' when I first tentatively suggested I might do a PhD so as to write a worthwhile book. Not only did he encourage me, but at every step of the way he read, advised and helped the research take shape. Thus encouraged, I asked Professor Peter Hennessy to supervise the thesis, and without hesitation he generously agreed, taking on the difficult task of turning a sociologist into a contemporary historian, and a participant into an observer. His diligence and humour, not to say his gossip and information, helped enormously. The resulting PhD thesis, which contains far fuller references and detailed notes and appendices, is available at Senate House, London.[3]

However, despite the efforts and generosity of all the above, nothing would have come of this without the patience, tolerance, computer skills, desk-building ability, grammatical eye, support and encouragement of Professor David Caplin. To him, my husband, my greatest debt is owed.

Notes

1 Philip Gould, *The Unfinished Revolution* (Little, Brown, 1998).
2 Both have subsequently been published: Giles Radice, *Diaries 1980–2001: The Political Diaries of Giles Radice* (Weidenfeld & Nicolson, 2004) and John Golding, *Hammer of the Left* (Politico's, 2003).
3 Dianne Hayter, 'The Fightback of the traditional right in the Labour Party, 1979 to 1987' (PhD thesis, University of London, 2004).

Abbreviations

ACTT	Association of Cinematographic, Television and Allied Technicians
AGM	annual general meeting
ASLEF	Associated Society of Locomotive Engineers and Firemen
APEX	Association of Professional, Executive, Clerical and Computer Staff
ASTMS	Association of Scientific, Technical and Managerial Staffs
AUEW	Amalgamated Union of Engineering Workers
CDS	Campaign for Democratic Socialism (1960s)
Clause IV	soft left non-parliamentary grouping and newsletter
CLP	Constituency Labour Party
CLPD	Campaign for Labour Party Democracy
CLV	Campaign for Labour Victory (1977 to 1981)
COHSE	Confederation of Health Service Employees
EETPU	Electrical, Electronic, Telecommunication and Plumbing Union
FBU	Fire Brigades' Union
GMC/GC	General Management Committee (later called the General Committee) of local Constituency Labour Parties
GMWU	General and Municipal Workers' Union
IMF	International Monetary Fund
IMG	International Marxist Group
ISTC	Iron and Steel Trades Confederation
LCC	Labour Co-ordinating Committee
LSC	Labour Solidarity Campaign
NAC	(Solidarity) National Advisory Council
NCC	(Labour Party) National Constitutional Committee
NEC	(Labour Party) National Executive Committee
NGA	National Graphical Association
NUJ	National Union of Journalists
NUM	National Union of Mineworkers
NUPE	National Union of Public Employees
NUR	National Union of Railwaymen
NUS	National Union of Seamen
OMOV	One-Member-One-Vote
PLP	Parliamentary Labour Party (comprises Labour MPs)
POEU	Post Office Engineering Union
PPS	Parliamentary Private Secretary
SDA	Social Democratic Alliance
SDP	Social Democratic Party

TGWU	Transport and General Workers' Union
TSSA	Transport Salaried Staffs' Association
TUC	Trade Union Congress
TULV	Trade Unions for a Labour Victory
TUPO	Trade Union and Political Offices Group
UCATT	Union of Construction, Allied Trades and Technicians
UCW	Union of Communication Workers
USDAW	Union of Shop, Distributive and Allied Workers

Part I
Background

1

Introduction

As late as 1993, Margaret Thatcher was able to write that 'on 28 March 1979, James Callaghan's Labour Government, the last Labour Government *and perhaps the last ever*, fell from office' (emphasis added).[1] Whilst such a premature obituary from this source could have been penned more in hope than anticipation, it nevertheless might have looked prescient in 1980 or 1981. At that time the Labour Party, reeling from its 1979 defeat, faced disillusion from unions and party activists, infiltration from the Trotskyist Militant Tendency, a dysfunctional party apparatus, policy divides (especially over Europe) and a campaign to rewrite the party's constitution to transfer power from the Parliamentary Labour Party (PLP) to the conference and constituencies. Meanwhile the left-controlled National Executive Committee (NEC) appeared at war with the record of the last Labour government, vindictive towards MPs, tolerant over Militant and unable to turn the party's infantry or big guns on its opponents in the House of Commons.

In 1978, the lesson one reviewer drew from a study[2] of the left's take-over of the party was that 'those opposed to the left must organise and be as assiduous as the left'.[3] The present book relates how this advice was heeded and how Labour's traditional right, weakened and tested by defections to the new Social Democratic Party (SDP) in 1981, nevertheless set about its objective of reclaiming the Labour Party to make it electable. It is an untold story: 'The campaign . . . to restore a moderate NEC and put the Labour Party back on the rails deserves a full study to itself. It came before red roses and mattered more.'[4]

In embarking on this campaign in the aftermath of the 25 January 1981 Limehouse Declaration (which led to the SDP), Labour's 'traditional right' exhibited very different characteristics from those of its predecessor elements. The Labour Party, founded by unions and funded by them, reflected in both its structure and its mores a division of roles between the party's constituent parts, the deference then common in society and a deeply loyalist tradition. Thus the unions would (until the late 1960s) rarely criticise a Labour government in public and, in their policy-making role in conference (where they wielded some 90 per cent of the votes), work to persuade rather than mandate the elected representatives. Similarly local party members, having selected (with union input) their parliamentary candidates, largely respected MPs' decisions, concentrating on campaigning and supporting them within the constituency.

The 1960s saw the break in this 'settlement' which had until then left MPs fairly independent both of the unions and of the membership. Conference voted for unilateralism against its Leader's wishes, and so the Gaitskell-supported Campaign for Democratic Socialism (CDS), the first organised right-wing caucus, was formed to overturn this, which was achieved in short order. Hitherto, it had been the left which organised (in the Tribune Group) against the PLP's right-wing majority. The other change in the 1960s and 1970s was the passing away of right-wing leadership in many trade unions, which was to impact on the Labour Party for over a decade.

In the 1960s and 1970s, as Europe became a divisive issue, the right again organised around a policy issue although its proponents were also increasingly working together against the left who, in addition to winning seats year by year on the party's governing NEC, were increasingly vocal in their criticism of Labour governments. Their demands for control over MPs, the manifesto and the choice of leader were aimed at weakening the hold of the right-wing parliamentary leadership over the party, and at redistributing power to the rank-and-file, with MPs individually and collectively accountable to local activists and conference delegates. Chapter 2 summarises the pre-1981 position.

After the SDP split, the traditional right's response changed. Solidarity (bringing together MPs and party activists) never engaged in policy, whether on incomes policy, Europe or defence. The St Ermins Group of trade unionists set itself a more limited and focused task – to regain control over the NEC by disciplined use of its voting strength. Only this, the Group reasoned, could provide an NEC supportive of the parliamentary leadership and one willing to create an electable Labour Party – by returning it, in their words, to 'sanity'. The St Ermins Group members largely came from strong loyalist, even deferential, working-class backgrounds. Some had served as Labour Party agents or councillors; all were committed to the party as the route to improving the lives of those they represented. Their experience of the inner sanctums of the party, however, and their fear of the electoral oblivion threatened by the SDP[5] led them to put policy differences aside and to work together to produce change within the party. Others who shared many of their political standpoints (such as David Basnett of the General and Municipal Workers' Union (GMWU)) favoured a different, less interventionist approach, whereby policy differences would be held at bay by keeping them out of the public eye and making some common cause with the left, so as to win an agreement to live with their differences and not make any further changes to the party's structure.

The right described in this book wanted no such compromise with the left, largely because polling evidence showed the electorate's rejection of the left's policies and behaviour. There was an urgency to their task, as the SDP notched up by-election victories, and they foresaw the possibility of being eclipsed by them in the general election. They were thus driven by electoral, rather than sectarian, considerations. In Neil Kinnock's words, speaking of the trade unionists, 'the fact of the matter is, and this took me quite a time – perhaps as much as a year – to recognise, that these people were not organising for classic right-wing hegemony in the Labour Party. But they were organising in favour of the Labour Party. They were immensely irritated by the nutters, and frustrated by the extended weakness of the Party.'[6]

The trade unionists also had doubts about the parliamentarians' reliability. It was, after all, MPs (not the Electoral College) who had chosen Michael Foot as Leader (under whom the SDP defected and who was proving an electoral liability). The unions had witnessed a lack of courage in MPs in standing up both to Tony Benn and to their local activists. The hard men of the unions thus took the lead in changing the composition of the NEC, whilst encouraging Solidarity to campaign against Militant and working with them to preserve Healey's deputy leadership position.

Meanwhile MPs in Solidarity found themselves in an unusual position. Coming from a loyalist tradition, they were torn between that instinct and their doubts about the ability of the leader for whom few had voted. How that affected their success is detailed in chapter 11 on Solidarity. Here we might note some of the characteristics of the right as it faced the post-Limehouse future, bereft of some of its leading lights.

Firstly, this traditional right was effectively leaderless throughout the 1980s. Solidarity was headed by Roy Hattersley and Peter Shore, whilst campaigning for Denis Healey as deputy leader. The St Ermins Group of trade unionists were unknown to the public and even to the great majority of party members. Given the evidence of the success of these groups, this absence of a strong leader contradicts the academic literature on change within political parties. Frank L. Wilson, for example, maintains that political parties do not respond with changes unless ordered to do so by their leaders.[7] This book demonstrates that, far from being the project of the Leader, the work of the St Ermins Group took place without Michael Foot's knowledge. Only after he became Leader did Neil Kinnock become aware and subsequently supportive of the group. However, under neither leader were the changes the result of initiatives launched from the top.

Secondly, despite the importance of policies to a political party, both the St Ermins Group (and its smaller cousin, *Forward Labour*) and Labour Solidarity were effectively policy-free zones. They had strong views on internal party matters (particularly Militant and One-Member-One-Vote, or OMOV) but took no positions on the big policy issues – in contrast to the effective pro-European stance of the earlier Campaign for Labour Victory (CLV). Whilst this enabled the groupings to encompass a wide spectrum of opinion, it reflected the absence of an articulated philosophy – a role filled in earlier times by Evan Durbin, Tony Crosland and other Fabians.

Thirdly, in contrast to CDS, Solidarity had neither patronage nor encouragement from Michael Foot, the party Leader. CDS was an overtly loyalist organisation, motivating those who favoured unity behind the party's elected Leader, Hugh Gaitskell. Solidarity supporters had largely supported Healey over Foot, yet grouped traditional loyalists whose instincts remained 'pro-leader'. Initially, many senior MPs held back from organising within the party, in deference to Foot's plea that there should be no groupings.

Fourthly, these right-wing groupings had to fight a war on two fronts (quite apart from the Conservatives): against the left in the Labour Party and against their former colleagues now in the SDP. The SDP split weakened internal opposition to the party's move to the left, and for some time there remained suspicion that Solidarity members would defect. Roy Hattersley felt that any pro-European sentiment could be taken as the first step to defection.[8]

Fifthly, for virtually the whole period of the union-led 'fightback', there was probably no majority for this within the activist membership of the party. Right-wing MPs mostly believed the battle could be fought solely in the PLP and failed to comprehend the penetration of the left's arguments within the party. It would be for a later generation, especially Neil Kinnock and subsequently Tony Blair, to re-establish a moderate majority amongst activists. Nevertheless, the moderate groups described here always believed that they spoke for Labour voters and for the wider Labour membership – and took succour from the evidence of OMOV ballots.

Finally, the difficulty in terminology even for this book reflects an unease within a left-wing party for anyone to be labelled 'right'. For all party members, the Conservatives were the real 'right'. Within the party before 1981, the pro-Europeans, particularly around Roy Jenkins, were fairly commonly identified as Labour's right wing, and the Manifesto Group could be labelled that way. It is more difficult after the SDP split, when many of Labour's right departed, to continue with that term for the remaining non-left. The key players themselves used different terms. John Golding called his group 'The Loyalist Group' or 'the Mods' (Moderates). Trade unionists referred to each other as 'friends' or 'mainstream' colleagues. To Kinnock they were 'not right-wingers but certainly die-hard anti-ultras'.[9] Furthermore, as he now acknowledges, this very categorisation of left and right was a part of the problem:

> Big mistake that a lot of us made including me, even though possibly I got over it a bit earlier than one or two others, was to draw up a category of left and right. Which had as major definitive considerations – not sole, but major – where you stood on the European Community, and where you stood on the Bomb. And some people were very left wing and very pro-European. Others were on the right and very CND. And many in both cases so as to make the line a bloody zig zag! And we all were massively misled by these definitions.[10]

The post-1981 anti-left groups are in this book labelled 'traditional right', which reflects a union-based, loyalist tradition, mostly in the centre on policies (though with notable anti-Common Marketeers and some unilateralists, policies seen as left), deeply wedded to parliamentary democracy and loyalty to the leadership. This is not wholly satisfactory, particularly as, over the years, some on the soft-left joined its ranks. Even from 1981, it is hard to define Peter Shore as right in any sense that he would have accepted; yet he is key to this 'traditional right'. For convenience, therefore, the term 'moderate' is used as an abbreviation for 'traditional right' post-1981 (and centre-right to encompass both the post-split moderates and the pre-split right). Hopefully the story, despite shortcomings in labelling, will explain the 'anti-far-left' cohesion of this otherwise disparate grouping, whose motivation speaks for itself.

The story – despite Thatcher's premature obituary for the Labour Party and despite, initially, a leadership unwilling to challenge the left in the party – is of moderate trade unionists and parliamentarians winning control of the NEC and gradually implementing reforms which helped make the party electable. For the whole of his period as Leader, Kinnock had a majority on the NEC (sometimes wafer-thin) which was provided by continuous and intense union organising and bargaining behind the scenes. This book describes this manoeuvring and assesses its successes and failures. Apart from John Golding's recently published memoir,[11] virtually none of this organisational story has been documented. Although some of the Manifesto Group papers are available, no history of it has been written, which is also the case for those groups described in this book whose archives are not available at all.

Notes

1   Margaret Thatcher, *The Downing Street Years* (Harper Collins, 1993), pp. 3–4.
2   Michael Hatfield, *The House the Left Built* (Victor Gollancz, 1978).
3   George Jones, 'A left house built on sand', *Socialist Commentary*, November 1978.
4   Edward Pearce, *Denis Healey: A Life in Our Times* (Little, Brown, 2002), p. 557.
5   The SDP and Liberal Parties' joint opinion poll rating, for example, in November 1981 was 43 per cent, to Labour's 28 per cent and the Conservatives' 25.5 per cent; Jim Claven, *The Centre is Mine* (Pluto Press, Australia, 2000), p. 38.
6   Neil Kinnock interview. (Dates and places of this and all other interviews are listed in the Appendix.)
7   Frank L. Wilson, 'The sources of party change: the social democratic parties of Britain, France, Germany and Spain', in Kay Lawson (ed.), *How Political Parties Work*, (Praeger, 1994), p. 275.
8   Roger Broad, *Labour's European Dilemmas: From Bevin to Blair* (Palgrave, 2001), p. 145.
9   Neil Kinnock interview.
10 *Ibid.*
11 John Golding, *Hammer of the Left* (Politico's, 2003).

2

The scene the right faced

The 1979 Labour Party conference sapped the strength of its leader, James Callaghan,[1] who indicated to Neil Kinnock that he was at the point of resigning. Votes for mandatory reselection of MPs, calls for control of the manifesto to pass to the NEC, distrust of the parliamentary party, and moves to widen the franchise for the election of the leader had the right feeling defensive, depressed and insecure. Meanwhile, on the left, a strong band of organised supporters, receiving succour from unions and party activists, campaigned to change the constitution and the leadership itself.

The May 1980 special conference, with its attacks on David Owen and fellow right-wingers, heralded a likely split in the party whilst the 1980 annual conference in Blackpool witnessed a major assault on the record of the Labour government – by one of its own members. Tony Benn's attack on his erstwhile Cabinet colleagues and the PLP, as well as his 'impossibilist' programme for a government, simultaneously epitomised and sharpened the fissure between the party in the Commons and the party in the country.

The response of the right was muted. Within parliament the Manifesto Group secured majorities in internal elections but had little dialogue with the NEC. It had no cheerleader and no shared view on Europe, defence or economic policy – the rallying cries within the wider party. The right-wing activists' Campaign for Labour Victory was outgunned. Unbeknown at the time, it also had within it a small group preparing to split from the party and launch a new political movement. Superficially the impending battle looked like those of the 1960s. Indeed, most of the surviving members of CDS, both inside and outside parliament, were active in the Manifesto Group or in CLV. Some therefore expected that a similarly managed, targeted effort could achieve its required ends. However, the 1980s were different for Labour's right.

Firstly, they were leaderless. In comparison to Gaitskell's towering impact on CDS members, the 1979–80 Leader of the Opposition (Callaghan) offered little attraction for younger members. Denis Healey did not run a 'court' and there was no intellectual lead. Shirley Williams was outside the House, as was Roy Jenkins (in Brussels). Neither David Owen nor Bill Rodgers fitted the bill and Tony Crosland was already dead. Peter Shore's anti-Europeanism ruled him out. Roy Hattersley failed to attract personal loyalty either within the PLP or outside and was not yet an heir-apparent.

Secondly, there was a range of policy positions within the right. They were united more against the left's agenda (especially on constitutional reform and PLP/party relations) than on any one policy. Neither Europe nor defence united all the anti-hard-left, unlike earlier battles in the party.

Thirdly, the charges of 'betrayal' levelled against the 1974–79 governments, which were part of the *cause célèbre* of the left, came not after a long period in opposition with its attendant frustration at repeated election defeats (the CDS experience), but close on the heels of a period of government and when there appeared to be a prospect of returning to power.[2]

Fourthly, the right's opponents had an agenda of apparently democratic constitutional reform, making the *status quo* harder to defend. Age and class splits made the 'accountability/radical/change' agenda attractive to newer, younger members whilst the older and working-class members had difficulty defining their opposition to apparently reasonable demands. Early calls for OMOV initially found little favour amongst unions and it was only on the agenda long after it could be a rallying cry for the right.

The right's major problem was its distance from the party's activists. It is therefore important to understand its roots. Labour's vote was concentrated in urban areas where many councils were Labour dominated. The MPs, councillors, Justices of the Peace, school governors were all party and union stalwarts, in touch with their community but unable to respond to social change. Such change came quickly to the industrial cities, with the closure of engineering, wholesaling, manufacturing, textile and printing companies. Manual work declined and professional residents moved in. The migration in the 1950s–60s of working-class families to the new towns, followed by local government reorganisation (which increased council size, making it less likely that councillors or employees lived cheek by jowl with those they served), saw a severing of party–community links.[3] Many blue-collar trade unionists, the bedrock of local parties, found the new breed of university-educated party members difficult to manage and felt themselves frozen out of the activists' agenda. The former were predominantly white, male and over 40, largely unmoved by Vietnam demonstrations, abortion debates, feminism or the public sector unions' disillusion with the Callaghan government. Small local parties sufficed when the co-operatives, unions, Catholic Church, Labour clubs or the pubs offered a constant dialogue between party activists and their locality. They were a major problem when the membership no longer reflected its community.

The major discord between activists and the PLP was over the interpretation of the record of the 1974–79 governments. This was not the first time that a Labour government had been found wanting. Evaluation of earlier governments had documented insufficient moves towards equality.[4] Seminars had debated how ministers had become distant from the party. The emergence of state-funded political advisors was just one attempt to retain party/government dialogue. However, the conflicting appraisals of 1974–79 lay at the heart of the subsequent hostilities and help explain the delay in the usual solution of the-unions-riding-to-the-aid-of-the-party.

In the public mind, the unions hampered the government. Yet, despite Callaghan's view during the Winter of Discontent that 'this great trade union movement in this great crisis . . . has nothing to say. It is completely leaderless',[5] the unions refused to accept any blame for the disaster. Success in overturning *In Place of Strife* had led both Callaghan (the leading dissident) and union leaders to assume a government–Trade Union Congress (TUC) dialogue would carry the unions with it. But just as the 1960s generation in the constituencies was challenging assumptions of local parties, so the new shop-steward movement meant that union leaders could no longer carry their members. The Cabinet's failure to heed the general secretaries' warnings that they could not continue with the pay policy led to the 1978/79 industrial disputes.

After the 1979 election, differing conclusions were drawn. Union members, along with constituency activists, blamed the leaders for not listening to the led. An existing mood for constitutional change and greater accountability turned into the belief that it was no longer enough just to win policy resolutions in conference. Until elected leaders were accountable to the party, they would continue to betray the movement and fail to deliver party policy. The left-wing Campaign for Labour Party Democracy (CLPD) was set up to work for constitutional changes to overcome these problems, through the introduction of mandatory reselection, NEC control over the manifesto and the election of the party leader by an Electoral College (or conference). These demands became central to party debate. After the 1979 fall of the Labour government, 'democracy and power in the party became dominant almost to the point of making substantive issues secondary', with a forceful and effective attempt by the left to bring the parliamentary party under the control of the Labour Party outside the House of Commons.[7]

The mood within the PLP turned to despair. Individually under threat because of impending reselection and feeling abandoned by the NEC,[8] MPs saw local activists favour the solutions advocated by Tony Benn. The party turned in on itself, just at the point when the Conservative government's policies were adversely affecting many Labour voters, who became frustrated that the party appeared more interested in its internal rows than in their predicament. The 269-strong PLP was unable to defend the record of the previous Labour governments with any confidence. The left's attacks hurt long-serving MPs who had trooped through the lobbies late at night to sustain a Labour government – especially as they had seen left-wing MPs miss votes 'to salvage their consciences' whilst the 'loyalists' did their duty.[9] These feelings were described in CLV's 'Roll of Honour' of the 17 MPs who died 'whilst keeping our government in power . . . Those strains are still showing in prematurely shortened retirements . . . We should honour not abuse those who night after night fought the good fight.'[10] The toughest attacks on the Callaghan government came from his own party and particularly the NEC.

Labour MPs were not popular with the party after 1979. The Manifesto Group was unable to attract one new member from the 1979 intake of new MPs. Although still commanding a controlling vote in the PLP, it lost the debates on reselection, election of the leadership (which removed the PLP's only seats on the NEC) and control over the manifesto. It was out-gunned in the newspaper and TV debates about the future of the party. As the traditional leader of the right, the PLP failed to offer any leadership against the left. Right-wing activists were frustrated at the absence of personalities willing to battle for them. CLV complained that few Shadow ministers would grace their platforms[11] and a deputation to Healey about the situation in the party saw him patronisingly reassure them to leave it to him.[12] Right-wing MPs continued to believe the battle would be fought solely in the PLP and underestimated the penetration of the left's arguments within the party. Even the soft-left misunderstood the trends. For example, when John Silkin later stood for deputy leader, he was amazed and disconcerted to discover that the new Electoral College required him to spend time courting Constituency Labour Parties (CLPs) and unions rather than simply his fellow parliamentarians.[13]

Both the Manifesto Group and CLV had been founded before 1979. The Manifesto Group was formed to ensure the right's natural majority was organised for PLP elections. CLV was created to counter CLPD, work for a Labour victory, increase party membership and activity, and to make the NEC more representative. At its founding meeting in Central Hall, Westminster on 19 February 1977 (the day Tony Crosland died), CLV passed a resolution which regretted 'the negative attitudes of the [NEC] towards the Labour Government'. Whilst the first issue of the CLV newsletter (in May 1977) concentrated on the general election and the electorate's concerns, by issue two it was leading on the need to reform the NEC, reject moves to widen the franchise for the leader and to take action against Militant. It had acknowledged the fight had moved to within the party. These preoccupations were later reflected in a joint Manifesto Group/CLV publication following the 1979 defeat.[14]

Neither the Manifesto Group nor CLV were well positioned to resist the onslaught from the left. The MPs were identified with a tired and latterly ineffective government. Two natural leaders (Roy Jenkins and Shirley Williams) were out of the Commons. And the unpopularity of MPs led CLV to select a solid but unknown figurehead (Clive Wilkinson, Leader of Birmingham City Council) for what was meant to be a high profile campaign. Equally damaging for the right, there was no concerted union effort to ensure the party responded constructively to its electoral defeat. New general secretaries had emerged in some of the major unions, the left's grip on the NEC was complete and, as important, the activities of the new Conservative government focused union attention on the interests of their members.

During 1979 and 1980, whilst CLV and the Manifesto Group struggled to motivate and mobilise the right, there was little union input (the Electrical, Electronic, Telecommunication and Plumbing Union (EETPU) being the main exception)[15] and they were hampered by a potential split. This was floated as early as November 1979 in an internal CLV paper. From Roy Jenkins' hint of a new political movement in his 22 November 1979 Dimbleby lecture,[16] a number of CLV members covertly mobilised to set up an alternative organisation (possibly a new party).

Former Labour MPs Colin Phipps and Michael Barnes were involved, whilst Jim Daly and Clive Lindley set up an organisation (the Radical Centre for Democratic Studies) to keep Brussels-based Jenkins briefed on the UK political scene. They opened talks with the Liberals, two-day conferences being held at least twice, with other seminars on voting trends and policy, the first taking place near Monmouth in January 1980. Meanwhile, some of the Manifesto Group officers (John Horam, Mike Thomas and Ian Wrigglesworth) were beginning to see that there might be an alternative to Labour as the solution to the current situation. The effect of such moves was to undermine the parliamentary and extra-parliamentary groupings on the right.

Some discussions did take place between leading lights of the CLV/Manifesto Group and trade unions, as a number of union leaders began to realise the importance of taking action to refocus the party on electoral matters, whilst simultaneously persuading those who were later to become the Gang of Three that the party was rescuable. Prior to the 1980 conference, CLV concentrated on putting the case for social democracy (publishing a 'Gang of Thousands' advertisement in the *Guardian* on 26 September 1980 to support the 'Gang of Three' letter from David Owen, Bill Rodgers and Shirley Williams in the same paper on 1 August) and on the composition of the women's section of the NEC. A CLV conference in Birmingham in May rehearsed the party's problems and possible remedies. Tellingly, all the speakers were to defect within a year.

The 1980 conference was a dismal failure for the right. Not only were the hoped-for gains not made in the NEC, but the conference voted for an Electoral College to select the party leader. Perhaps as important for subsequent events, the atmosphere in the hall was poisonous. Delegates speaking – or sometimes even voting – contrary to the 'Benn hegemony' were barracked or slow-handclapped. MPs as a species were in the firing line, alongside those judged likely to defect. Responding to the debate on reselection, trade unionist Sam McCluskie turned on the MPs' bank of seats and said, in relation to what one MP had called the 'penance' of their subscription to the party: 'They [the MPs] have been doing penance for years to keep the Prentices[17] in power, and it is ... underlined when you get Joe Ashton [MP] coming on that rostrum and telling us that Roy Jenkins, if he starts a middle party, would have 25 MPs who are already members of the Labour Party. Why don't you join them?'[18] This was loudly applauded – taken by the right as a signal that they were not wanted in the party. Later, a known Militant delegate (later an MP) Dave Nellist returned to the theme – to similar acclaim – stating that, 'If there are 25 Labour MPs ... who want to join Roy Jenkins and the so-called Centre Party, the sooner they do it and give us the chance to replace them with genuine Labour Party MPs, the better party we are going to have for it'.[19]

The main event, however, for much of the subsequent story, was the speech delivered by Tony Benn on transferring responsibility for control over the manifesto from a joint Cabinet/NEC meeting to the sole prerogative of the NEC. The debate had been opened by Patricia Hewitt (a CLP delegate), who claimed that members were 'angry about much of what the last Labour Government did and a great deal of what the last Labour Government failed to do'. This was met by applause, as was her call for the constitutional changes to get rid of 'the divide between the policies that we as a party decide on, the policies on which we fight the election, and the policies which the Labour Government implement in office'.[20] Benn's response to the debate was a *tour de force* on the iniquities of the Labour government (of which he was a member) and its influence on the 1979 manifesto. His speech, later reproduced by the right with the 'factual inaccuracies' clearly marked, became a symbol of all they believed was wrong with his campaign.[21] The EETPU even used videos of the speech to show shop stewards the 'fallacy' which lay at its heart. But it was ecstatically received in the hall, except by most MPs. David Lipsey, lately a political advisor at Number 10, heard it with increasing bitterness, muttering 'liar' at least five times in its duration.

Despite Benn's urging, the NEC's amendment giving it control over the manifesto was defeated. There were also early indications of the role unions would take in changing the party. David Basnett, GMWU General Secretary, introduced the report of a Committee of Enquiry not from the rostrum but from the platform – at that time, highly unusual. He was followed by Clive Jenkins, General Secretary of the Association of Scientific, Technical and Managerial Staffs (ASTMS), also not an NEC member, yet speaking from the hallowed platform. The report gave notice that the party's paymasters were taking a close interest in the way their money was spent.

The most immediate issue, however, was the Electoral College, agreed in principle on 2 October but without any particular method (or percentage splits between the three parts of the movement) being agreed. Attention had to turn to the make-up of the College as there were already rumours that Callaghan would resign, triggering a leadership contest. Transport and General Workers' Union (TGWU) research officer, Jenny Pardington, making an off-the-cuff remark that night to the GMWU's research officer, Larry Whitty, that a special conference would be the normal way to resolve such issues, saw him speed off to relate this to his boss. Pardington found herself hearing Basnett propose this in an emergency motion the next day – and hence the Wembley special conference was born.

Before that could take place, however, the old system for electing the leader was brought into use one more time. Callaghan resigned on 15 October and, despite calls from the NEC that the selection of his successor be delayed until a new system was established, the PLP decided (in a determined assertion of its own role) to proceed to elect a leader. The left were deeply unhappy about a new leader being selected under old rules and tried unsuccessfully to get candidates to agree to resign and stand for re-election later under the new system.

The right assumed Healey would be elected and that a new chapter in the party's fortunes could begin. They had calculated without their candidate's personality. Even his own team acknowledged that he fought a dreadful campaign, though in truth he did not fight, assuming MPs knew him well enough. However, he grossly underestimated both the pressure on MPs facing reselection to back Michael Foot, and the desire of many for a quiet life which they mistakenly thought would accompany a Foot leadership. Furthermore, MPs Tom Ellis, Neville Sandelson and Jeffrey Thomas – who were subsequently to defect – voted for Foot to hasten the party's demise.[22] For whatever combination of reasons, Michael Foot won on 10 November 1980, to the horror of the right.

The period between November 1980 and the January 1981 Wembley special conference saw a flurry of activity. Foot worked to get an NEC proposal for at least half of the College votes going to the PLP. The left wanted less for the PLP. Meanwhile, CLV and the Gang of Four were deep in debate as to whether the party had a future. A Fabian New Year School at Ruskin College heard their Vice-Chairman, Shirley Williams, warn of the electoral challenges but understood her as seeing the party remaining viable. However, the reality was that at the same time – and within hours of leaving Oxford – she was deep in discussion with Roy Jenkins, Bill Rodgers and David Owen. They had agreed to give Labour one last chance, and to remain if the Wembley special conference agreed to OMOV for the Electoral College. On 24 January, Owen was to make as strong a case as any (until John Prescott's in Brighton a dozen years later) for OMOV but the union votes were already stacked against him.

Meanwhile, the unions concentrated their efforts on patching majorities together for particular formulae for the College. A briefing paper by the research officer of the Association of Professional, Executive, Clerical and Computer Staff (APEX), Roger Godsiff, for his general secretary laid out the options and the support each attracted. The detailed work behind this was crucial for the unions' subsequent response to Wembley. Its research avoided wishful thinking and meticulously calculated numbers. It showed that, correctly marshalled, unions sympathetic to the moderate cause could command a majority. This became central to the soon-to-be-created St Ermins Group.

In the meantime, the 24 January 1981 Wembley conference produced a result no-one wanted. The decision to set up an Electoral College to elect the leader having been taken, the NEC favoured half of the College votes going to the PLP; with a quarter each to the affiliated organisations and the constituency parties. The EETPU and the Owenites wanted an OMOV ballot of all party members, whilst the left supported the College being divided into thirds – with equal shares for the PLP, the affiliates and the CLPs. Initially, little consideration had been given to the Union of Shop, Distributive and Allied Workers' (USDAW's) proposed composition: 40 per cent for the affiliated trade unions and 30 per cent each for the PLP and the CLPs. However, as the Amalgamated Union of Engineering Workers (AUEW) was committed not to vote for any proposal which did not give more than 50 per cent to the PLP, left-influenced votes were switched to USDAW's 30:40:30 proposal (which had only been tabled to keep USDAW's sponsored MP, the left-wing Audrey Wise, happy and without any intention of pushing it). With the moderate USDAW then having to support its own formula, and the AUEW unable to vote for the NEC's preference of only 50 per cent for MPs, it was the left who won the day.

This Wembley result could not have been better for the potential defectors. Instead of having to launch their party on the unpopular cause of Europe, they had their ready-made and popular cause – that the leader of the Labour Party was henceforth to be elected with the votes of distrusted unions which, two years earlier, had fuelled the Winter of Discontent. In the long run, the Wembley decision was in fact to bolster the case for OMOV, greater internal democracy in both unions and the party, and the rise of a populist leader. However, in the immediate aftermath of the Wembley conference, two things happened. One – the high profile creation of the SDP – was drastic for the Labour Party and for a time threatened its very existence. The other – almost clandestine – would in time move the Labour Party back to the centre-right and to electability. The story of the first of these, the January Limehouse Declaration and the March creation of the SDP, has been told elsewhere.[23] But the fightback of the traditional right within the Labour Party has not been documented. It started secretly in one case (the St Ermins Group) and sorrowfully in another (Solidarity) but first the old organisations had to die. CLV and the Manifesto Group both contained 'stayers and goers', and thus had to go through the process of splitting before a single new organisation of the moderate wing, the Labour Solidarity Campaign (LSC), could be created on 17 February 1981 to cover both parliamentary and constituency membership. Meanwhile, on 10 February, the St Ermins Group was born in the Charing Cross Hotel.

This book tells the story of these post-SDP split 'fightback' groups. To put this in context, a brief description of the main issues and events of the period from 1981 to 1987 is given, followed by the history of the Manifesto Group of Labour MPs which tried, but failed, to hold the right in the PLP together.

Notes

1 His speech to conference followed an attempt by a delegate to move 'a vote of no confidence in Mr. Callaghan'; *Report of the 1979 Annual Conference of the Labour Party*, p. 225.
2 Labour nearly won the Southend East by-election in March 1980 and, in her first year in office, Thatcher's standing in the polls suggested she could be beaten.
3 Sue Goss, *Local Labour and Local Government* (Edinburgh University Press, 1988); John Gyford, *The Politics of Local Socialism* (George Allen & Unwin, 1985); John Silkin, *Changing Battlefields: The Challenge to the Labour Party* (Hamish Hamilton Ltd, 1987); Peter Tatchell, *The Battle for Bermondsey* (Heretic Books, 1983).
4 Peter Townsend and Nick Bosanquet (eds), *Labour and Inequality* (Fabian Society, 1972); Nick Bosanquet and Peter Townsend (eds), *Labour and Equality: A Fabian Study of Labour in Power, 1974–79* (Heinemann, 1980).
5 Bernard Donoughue, *The Heat of the Kitchen* (Politico's, 2003), p. 266.
6 The January 1969 White Paper which sought to regulate industrial relations, particularly unofficial strikes (Cmnd 4327, HMSO). It was defeated by union, NEC and parliamentary pressure.
7 Lewis Minkin, *The Contentious Alliance: Trade Unions and the Labour Party* (Edinburgh University Press, 1991), p. 192.
8 Joe Haines, *The Politics of Power* (Coronet Books, 1977), p. 14.
9 Jim Wellbeloved interview.
10 *Labour Victory*, October 1980, p. 2.
11 A November 1979 CLV internal document complained that MPs and those who had been associated with Jim Callaghan had not been very supportive whilst the right's prominent spokesmen had only rarely helped CLV.

12 Jim Daly interview.

13 Silkin, *Changing Battlefields*, pp. 49–50.

14 'Reform and democracy in the Labour Party', *Labour Victory*, CLV, 1979.

15 The EETPU put resources into CLV. Other general secretaries, especially from the Amalgamated Union of Engineering Workers, the Association of Professional, Executive, Clerical and Computer Staff, and the National Union of Railwaymen, made helpful interventions (Terry Duffy in *Labour Victory*; Sid Weighell in *The Times*) and a number placed advertisements in *Labour Victory*, helping to defray expenses.

16 Reprinted in Wayland Kennet, *Rebirth of Britain* (Weidenfeld & Nicolson, 1982), pp. 9–29.

17 A reference to former Labour MP Reg Prentice who had 'crossed the floor' in the Commons, becoming a Conservative MP.

18 *Report of the 1980 Annual Conference of the Labour Party*, p. 142.

19 *Ibid.*, p. 145.

20 *Ibid.*, p. 143.

21 Michael Cocks MP, Chief Whip, Speech to GMWU conference, 7 June 1981; 'The Last Labour Government and the 1974 manifesto'.

22 Pearce, *Denis Healey*, p. 543.

23 Bill Rodgers, *Fourth Among Equals* (Politico's, 2000); Ian Bradley, *Breaking the Mould? The Birth and Prospects of the SDP* (Martin Robertson, 1981).

Part II
Events and issues

3

The 1981 deputy leadership contest

The 1981 deputy leadership election is now recognised as the high water mark of Bennism but at the time it was viewed by many as another step to a more left-wing party. Few would have predicted that Benn would be out of parliament and thus unable to contest the leadership only two years later. Indeed, his nomination for the deputy leadership was viewed as the forerunner of a challenge for the leadership. Similarly, most commentators failed to note that, within days of Benn's defeat, the right snatched five gains on the NEC, so increasing Foot's authority there and beginning their trek back into ascendancy.

The deputy leadership vote was the first use of the Electoral College, and it produced for Healey a victory which would have been denied him had the College been segmented into thirds. The unions voted 25:15 for Healey – their 40 per cent tranche helping to provide his final 0.852 per cent[1] winning margin. (Had all the unions voted according to their members' wishes, his victory would have been more emphatic. If the TGWU had cast its 1.25 million votes – 8 per cent of the entire College – according to its consultation, Healey would have polled 57.5 per cent to Benn's 42.5 per cent, a 15 per cent majority.[2])

There were to be implications for union democracy from such block voting, but the interest of the contest is what it did for the St Ermins Group and for Solidarity. For the former, the events demonstrated the accuracy of Godsiff's predictions and the role the group could play in marshalling votes. For the latter, it strained the moderate/centre-left coalition as many could not stomach open support for Healey. Even Solidarity's Co-chairman, Peter Shore, whilst voting for Healey, never endorsed him publicly.

More broadly, the contest demonstrated the gap between many union leaders and their members. The National Union of Public Employees (NUPE), for example, whilst circulating statements from all 3 contestants (the third being John Silkin), expressed a clear preference: both assistant general secretaries together with 12 officers signed the Benn advertisement.[3] The NUPE leadership expected to cast their votes (4 per cent of the College) for Benn and were surprised that their branch ballot favoured Healey, leading Healey's team to claim: 'it was the dinner ladies what won it for us'.[4] (NUPE's increased affiliation to the party, from 150,000 to 600,000 over six years,[5] also contributed to Healey's success.) Other unions found similar results, though sometimes more closely allied with their leadership. The Confederation of Health Service Employees (COHSE) voted Healey 57 per cent:Benn 33 per cent; the Post Office Engineering Union (POEU) 72 per cent:20 per cent. The unions' membership votes, where tested, favoured the incumbent.

For some unions, the contest provided the opportunity to air their views on Tony Benn. The EETPU, in particular, had long been campaigning against him, using material culled from his 1980 conference attack on Callaghan over the 1979 manifesto to highlight discrepancies between his allegations and the printed documentation. Replying to Benn's request for EETPU support, General Secretary Frank Chapple's three–page letter of 7 September 1981 rehearsed the union's objections, especially that he was unsympathetic to trade unions and that 'you also dismiss the views of the great bulk of members and shop stewards, blaming the media for brainwashing them. We reject this attitude of aristocratic disdain'. He detailed their difficulties with Benn as employer (when a minister at Industry and Energy) before concluding: 'We will, therefore, not be supporting you for the deputy leadership of the Party'.

Organisationally, the St Ermins Group set to work at local and national level, circulating lists of potentially sympathetic CLPs to friendly unions to get branches to nominate Foot and Healey to their General Committees (GCs) – although only Healey faced a contest, this made the request more palatable locally. The closeness of the contest put enormous pressure on every MP, especially those from left-wing constituencies (with reselection looming) – despite CLPs having their own vote for the first time under the Electoral College. John Grant MP urged colleagues to stand firm, although 'the long-held principle of the secret ballot, free from intimidation, has been thrown away' with MPs' votes being recorded. He emphasised that it would not only be their GCs who would see these but 'their wider electorate. It will be known and stressed at meetings and on the doorsteps … They may succumb to pressure now – and find it backfires on them when they ask the ordinary voters, who have the last word, to return them to Westminster'.[6] Even Peter Archer felt the need to explain his vote for Healey to his moderate and normally loyal GC, emphasising that it was 'the express wish of Michael Foot' that his deputy should be supported as he had 'made it clear he can work well as a team with Denis Healey'.[7] Others went more public. The left-wing Janey Buchan MEP published an Open Letter to Benn in *Labour Weekly* on 7 August as to why she could not support him, criticising his campaign's stance of 'those who are not for us are against us'. Healey was more blunt in his rebuttal of these pressures, claiming that forcing MPs to be programmed to follow the wishes of CLPs – ignoring both voters and their own consciences – would turn MPs into zombies.[8]

Silkin's manifesto, favouring 'the complete withdrawal of Britain from the Common Market' and nuclear disarmament,[9] would not attract any votes from the right but was aimed at the non-Bennite left. Whilst his candidature attracted 65 soft-left MPs[10] in the first round, it offered no respite from the Benn–Healey choice at the critical stage, leaving 35 MPs the only option of abstaining.[11] Kinnock, who had opposed the contest and disagreed with Silkin's candidature, abstained on the second ballot. Sitting on the platform awaiting the result, he confided to Joan Lestor that he then wished he had voted for Healey as he thought a Benn victory would be a disaster for the party. The impact of the abstentions was to hand victory to Healey but it also marked a major split on the left. Kinnock was attacked within hours (aggressively in the gents' toilet;[12] verbally at the Tribune rally) but the long-term consequences were seismic. It caused the split on the left which led to the creation of the Campaign Group of Labour MPs and with it the rightward shift in the Tribune Group. Henceforth, the parliamentary left was split, the so-called 'hard left' Campaign Group maintaining an 'oppositional' role to the front-bench.

The contest consolidated the organisational push of the St Ermins Group, and forced other unions to take more heed of their members' views. The unsatisfactory nature of the unions' consultation – some undertaking none at all – added impetus to demands for OMOV, with Hattersley and others supporting this.[13] Similarly, party members not on GCs began demanding that their views should be sought before their CLP's vote was cast. Where constituencies balloted the membership, they all favoured Healey over Benn. This added to the pressure for extending democracy to individual members. Whilst the left had long supported an Electoral College, they had not anticipated its role in buttressing the right's demand for OMOV.

At the start of the contest Benn thought it would be 'unifying for the Party . . . [and would] consolidate our support' amongst the electorate.[14] Immediately after his defeat, he claimed he had 'achieved the politicisation of the trade union movement' whilst accepting that in 'the non-politically conscious unions, and among the non-politically conscious members of unions, there is a hell of a lot of work to be done'.[15] This assumption that all politically conscious trade unionists would support him was diametrically opposite to the St Ermins Group's conclusion that the more their members were consulted, the more they backed Healey.

The 1981 contest was Benn's last chance of high office (he lost his Shadow Cabinet place in November) and led to the Tribune–Campaign Group split. For the traditional right, it demonstrated (and rewarded) their organisational effectiveness (which had been lacking in the late 1970s). It boosted the case for OMOV and for internal union democracy. Solidarity was adversely affected because it was unable to wage a strong pro-Healey campaign even though its members viewed a Benn victory as disastrous. Electorally, Labour Party support dropped 17 per cent between July and December as the party fought the contest.[16]

Notes

1 George Cunningham has argued that, had the abstentions been discounted first and the votes actually cast then been counted, Benn would have won: George Cunningham, 'Was Tony Benn the true winner against Healey?' (unpublished, 1983); Dianne Hayter, 'What if Benn had beaten Healey in 1981?', in Duncan Brack and Iain Dale (eds), *Prime Minister Portillo and Other Things That Never Happened* (Politico's, 2003). However, the results were never questioned by Benn. Furthermore, they confirm that each section retains its allotted quota regardless of how few of its members vote.

2 *Forward Labour*, November 1981. Alex Kitson – Acting General Secretary – opposed Benn's challenge and stopped the union nominating him, despite Benn's claim that he would have their support (*Financial Times*, 22 September 1981; Brian Nicholson interview).

3 *Labour Weekly*, 19 June 1981.

4 Roger Godsiff interview, 4 December 2001.

5 Minkin, *The Contentious Alliance*, p. 199.

6 John Grant MP, Speech to the EETPU, Brighton, 26 September 1981.

7 Peter Archer, letter to his GC, 3 September 1981.

8 *Labour Solidarity*, July 1981.

9 John Silkin, deputy leadership leaflet, 1981.

10 More accurately, 64 and John's brother, Sam Silkin, MP for Dulwich.

11 Thirty-seven actually abstained but two had voted for Healey in the first round. One appears to have missed the vote; the other was moving towards the SDP (*The Times*, 1 October 1981).

12 David Warburton interview.

13 *Financial Times*, 25 September 1981; Phillip Whitehead, *New Statesman*, 16 October 1981.

14 BBC TV news, 2 April 1981.

15 *Morning Star*, 1 October 1981.

16 N. Webb and R. Wybrow, *The Gallup Report 1981* (Sphere, 1982), p. 192.

4

The 1983 leadership election

The first use of the Electoral College to choose the party leader – where the unions would cast 40 per cent of the votes – was triggered, within 48 hours of the 9 June 1983 general election, by the unions, which then effectively decided the outcome within weeks. Most notably, many of the St Ermins Group unions – which had worked closely with Roy Hattersley's Solidarity – delivered their votes for left-wing Neil Kinnock. This chapter looks at how they did this, and at their reasons for supporting him.

The first blow struck for Kinnock was prior to the election when, through the EETPU's and John Golding's efforts in Bristol South, where boundary changes had altered the political make-up, the unions secured the winnable parliamentary seat for Chief Whip Michael Cocks MP.[1] When Benn lost Bristol East on 9 June he was out of contention for the leadership, giving Kinnock a clear run on the left. Kinnock has since said he would have preferred to fight – and defeat – Benn then,[2] but at the time it allowed a clear break with the Bennite legacy. The second blow came in the immediate aftermath of the election defeat. On Saturday 11 June, the left-wing trade unionist Clive Jenkins visited Michael Foot at his Hampstead home, resulting in the Labour Leader supporting ASTMS' proposal to nominate Kinnock.[3] On Sunday, Jenkins announced that ASTMS would back Kinnock[4] – making public Foot's retirement decision[5] and triggering the unions' round of decisions. The General Council of the TGWU (Kinnock's own union) quickly agreed to back him but then a different group of unions entered the fray. Clive Jenkins, Moss Evans (TGWU) and the moderate Alan Tuffin (Union of Communication Workers; UCW) met and agreed tactics over a barbecue at the US Ambassador's residence. Tuffin invited Kinnock to fly over to his union conference on the Isle of Man the following Saturday. Kinnock won a standing ovation and a vital nomination, Hattersley's request for support having been gently rebuffed.[6] The UCW was the first of the moderate unions to plump for Kinnock, but others followed: COHSE, the National Union of Railwaymen (NUR) and the St Ermins' stalwart, the Iron and Steel Trades Confederation (ISTC), which encouraged other unions to follow suit.[7] Kinnock had addressed the APEX conference – and received a standing ovation – prior to the election, and its branch consultation now supported him. The EETPU, abstaining on the grounds that the election should be 'conducted by an individual ballot of party members',[8] further deprived Roy Hattersley of an anticipated block-vote. By the end of June, Kinnock had 3.8 million union votes pledged to Hattersley's 1.8 million.[9]

Equally unanticipated (at least in June) was that the majority of MPs would vote for Kinnock,[10] including Tony Blair and all but one of the 1983 intake.[11] Kinnock's victory thus comprised majorities in all three sections of the Electoral College,[12] bestowing on him the authority he would need – and use – in remodelling the party. It is noteworthy that a right-of-centre PLP and a moderate union movement joined the left-wing CLPs in supporting Kinnock over the right's standard-bearer, Hattersley. The unions also helped ensure a rancour-free contest by championing the notion of a 'Dream Ticket' – that the only viable option was Hattersley–Kinnock or Kinnock–Hattersley as leader and deputy, with each agreeing to serve under the other, and that everyone should support that duo, whatever their preference between the two (the other contenders being Peter Shore and Eric Heffer). David Warburton claims credit for this 'Unity Ticket' notion, with the press renaming it 'Dream Ticket'.

The moderate unions and Kinnock were subsequently to collaborate closely on reforming the party, expelling Militant and working towards OMOV. Little of this was evident in 1983. So why did these unions, working to root out the left from the party, line up behind this unlikely candidate? It has been assumed that Kinnock's near absence from parliament in 1982, in favour of visiting constituencies and unions,[13] was part of his build-up to a leadership bid.[14] As such, it paid off: where unions consulted their members, Kinnock mostly won by a wide margin.[15] For some, it left a bad taste in the mouth: 'Kinnock, for some time prior to the election on some pretext or other, had devoted a major part of his time touring the country making himself known to union branches and constituency parties which must have been to the detriment of his duties in the House of Commons'.[16] Such campaigning – if that is what it was – continued during the 1983 general election, when he barnstormed his way around 100 constituencies, delivering 90 speeches (including to the EETPU conference), and spending only 2 out of 21 days in London.[17] However, two other factors contributed to the moderates' support for him. One was their lack of enthusiasm for his opponent. The second was the real respect they developed for Kinnock from their personal exposure to him.

Outside of parliament, Roy Hattersley was not seen as fighting against the left and many on the right recalled that he had never joined CLV when the going was tough. Former CLV Chairman and Leader of Birmingham Council, Clive Wilkinson, complained that the Birmingham MP 'was never there. He never turned up except for advice surgeries. We could never rely on Roy Hattersley to give support'. With hindsight, Wilkinson thinks Hattersley 'couldn't have made the changes' that Kinnock achieved.[18] Former party staff member Jim Cattermole felt Hattersley was 'never involved in anything – not prepared to put his head on the chopping block. When he was a minister he let me down a few times.' Despite the help given to Hattersley when he was looking for a seat, when Cattermole later asked the minister to help form a Trade Union Lunch Club, 'three times Roy

Hattersley promised to come; three times he cancelled'. Furthermore, he never 'made any political sacrifice'.[19] More publicly, the right-wing Frank Chapple declared: 'I wouldn't vote for Hattersley at any price, not if he was the only candidate'. He called him a disaster 'whose compromise with the left embarrassed those who wanted to fight for moderation in the party . . . he harmed the party by giving in to the left'.[20]

However, it was not simply antagonism to Hattersley that won over the moderates. Kinnock's campaigning brought him into contact with union officials – in their roles of attending meetings and chauffeuring politicians. In Kinnock, they saw a kindred spirit who, like them, believed returning Labour to power was the over-riding objective, taking precedence over intra-party wrangling. For Chapple, he had 'got balls'.[21] This had been evidenced by his courage in not voting for Benn in the deputy leadership contest in 1981. 'That changed the geography quite a bit – the degree of mutual understanding changed exponentially after that'.[22] Kinnock's personality also helped. Tony Clarke met Kinnock in the mid-1970s, when they addressed a May Day rally in Torbay, and their dialogue started then. Roy Grantham and Kinnock spoke at an aerospace meeting during the 1983 election and spent two hours in Grantham's car afterwards, when they both agreed the party had to change. This key St Ermins Group general secretary recognised the moderates would need to support Kinnock and then work with him to make those changes. Warburton's support stemmed from his desire to jump a generation, whilst Tuffin, who had also been on the campaign trail with Kinnock, felt he was 'prepared to have a go at things and tear down some of the things that made us unwinnable'.[23] Not every right-wing union supported Kinnock[24] but the St Ermins Group had found they could do business with him and saw in him someone willing to do the hard work. Without referring to his opponent for the leadership, Kinnock describes the unions' attitude to some of their political soul-mates:

> The trade unions were really bloody irritated by the fact that they knew that a lot of the battle had to be conducted by infantry officers that were willing to walk with their men. And some MPs would get to a TV studio but they wouldn't to a GC or regional conference. They were seriously brassed off about that. That's one of the reasons I got on with the union lads.[25]

There were other candidates for the leadership: Solidarity's Peter Shore had begun to plan his bid soon after the 1981 conference,[26] whilst Eric Heffer ran from the left (attracting only 7 per cent of the CLP vote – compared with Benn's 83 per cent in 1981[27]). There was a second major ballot – for the deputy leadership, where the unions' commitment to the Dream Ticket saw 35 per cent of their 40 per cent share go to Hattersley, with under 5 per cent to Michael Meacher, helping to provide the new Deputy with a 67.3 per cent to 27.9 per cent victory over his closest challenger.[28] However, the night of Sunday 2 October belonged to Kinnock, whose words in his acceptance speech echoed the unions' desire to win. Calling for unity, not just then or during a campaign, but 'here and now and from henceforth', the new Leader pleaded: 'remember how you felt on that dreadful morning of 10 June.

Just remember how you felt then, and think to yourselves: "June the Ninth ...
never ever again will we experience that".[29]

Notes

1 Robert Harris, *The Making of Neil Kinnock* (Faber and Faber, 1984), p. 193; Martin
   Westlake, *Kinnock* (Little, Brown, 2001), p. 208. The EETPU started work in Bristol early
   in 1982, in preparation for the boundary changes which would leave Benn without a
   winnable seat. By August it had increased its General Management Committee representation from 7 to 12, with more to follow; extensive work, including visits by head-
   office staff, ensured Cocks won the nomination for the safe seat. Benn was aware of this
   at the time: Tony Benn, *The End of an Era: Diaries 1980–90* (Hutchinson, 1992), p. 182.
2 *The Battle for Labour*, BBC 4, 30 October 2002.
3 Westlake, *Kinnock*, p. 217.
4 Giles Radice, *Friends and Rivals* (Little, Brown, 2002), p. 312.
5 Alan Sked and Chris Cook, *Post-War Britain: A Political History, 1945–1992* (Penguin,
   1993), p. 434. It had been assumed Foot would 'announce his intention to go this
   autumn' (private note by Nick Butler for Peter Shore, 10 June 1983).
6 Alan Tuffin interview; Richard Heffernan and Mike Marqusee, *Defeat from the Jaws of
   Victory: Inside Kinnock's Labour Party* (Verso, 1992), p. 36; *Guardian* 20 June 1983;
   Harris, *Making of Neil Kinnock*, p. 215.
7 Harris, *Making of Neil Kinnock*, p. 224; Bill Sirs, *Hard Labour* (Sidgwick & Jackson,
   1985), p. 130.
8 Letter from Frank Chapple to John Smith (Hattersley's Campaign Manager), 11 October 1983, in response to Smith's request of 29 September for the union to reconsider its
   decision to abstain in the deputy leadership contest; Frank Chapple, *Sparks Fly! A Trade
   Union Life* (Michael Joseph, 1984), p. 191.
9 Westlake, *Kinnock*, p. 218.
10 Kinnock won 14.778 per cent in the PLP section, to Hattersley's 7.833 per cent (*Report
   of the 1983 Annual Conference of the Labour Party*, p. 29). The Shadow Cabinet, by contrast, supported the runner-up, only 3 of the 13 non-candidate members voting for
   Kinnock; Westlake, *Kinnock*, p. 240.
11 The exception being Stuart Bell; Stuart Bell, *Tony Really Loves Me* (Spen View Publications, 2000), p. 11.
12 The figures were: Kinnock 71.272 per cent; Hattersley 19.288 per cent; Heffer 6.303 per
   cent; Shore 3.137 per cent (*Report of the 1983 Annual Conference of the Labour Party*,
   p. 29).
13 Kinnock claimed he had done 'over 200 Labour movement meetings in each of the last
   3 years'; *Broad Left Alliance Journal*, October 1982.
14 He also declined Shadow Cabinet promotion to 'avoid a damaging controversy with the
   right of the PLP'; Westlake, *Kinnock*, pp. 178, 216.
15 *Ibid.*, pp. 219–20.
16 Charles Turnock, 'Rigorous route by rail and river' (unpublished, 1995), p. 226. Unlike
   his union, the NUR, Turnock supported Hattersley.
17 Westlake, *Kinnock*, pp. 205–6.
18 Clive Wilkinson interview.
19 Jim Cattermole interview.
20 Chapple, *Sparks Fly!*, p. 191.
21 *Observer*, 4 September 1983.

22 Neil Kinnock interview.
23 Alan Tuffin interview.
24 The AUEW and GMWU voted for Hattersley – the latter finally only thanks to John Smith. Its ballot favoured Hattersley but on the eve of the vote Basnett phoned Hattersley and, on the grounds that his union always supported Labour leaders and, as Kinnock was going to win, asked if he could switch the union's vote. Smith promptly visited him and protested it made a nonsense of the balloting. The union cast its vote accordingly (Roy Hattersley interview).
25 Neil Kinnock interview.
26 Private briefing paper for Shore by Nick Butler.
27 Leo Panitch and Colin Leys, *The End of Parliamentary Socialism* (Verso, 2001), p. 210. The left was divided. The Labour Co-ordinating Committee and Clause IV supported Kinnock. CLPD, Socialist Organiser, Socialist Action, Campaign Group, Benn and the staff of *Tribune* supported Heffer (Report from CLPD Secretary to the 1984 CLPD AGM).
28 *Report of the 1983 Annual Conference of the Labour Party*, p. 29. Denzil Davies and Gwyneth Dunwoody polled 3.5 per cent and 1.3 per cent respectively. Hattersley won greater support from the CLP section than Healey in 1981. This may have reflected the increased number of CLPs balloting their members (at least 64) rather than a rightward shift.
29 *Report of the 1983 Annual Conference of the Labour Party*, p. 30.

5
Militant

> If the Executive will not act [on Militant], the party's centre and right-wing will conclude that the composition of the Executive must be changed. With the assistance of one or two big unions . . . it can be done – and probably will be.[1]

Labour's traditional right, in despair after the 1981 split and at the NEC's ineffectiveness in tackling infiltration, set about restoring a moderate balance to the NEC. This chapter does not retell the story of Militant (which has been told elsewhere[2]) but describes the NEC's role in tackling infiltration and the right's determination to make the party face up to this challenge. It then highlights the right's role in expelling Militant – including its lengthy struggle with the soft-left.

Militant was not new to the Labour Party, being formed in 1964 as successor to the Revolutionary Socialist League (which started its work inside the party in 1953). Whilst the NEC's role in suppressing the Underhill Report on Militant from 1975 was a key element in the right's desire to change the composition of the NEC, there was another dispute between the NEC and the right in the PLP in 1976/77 over the appointment of Andy Bevan, a known Militant supporter, as the party's youth officer. Ron Hayward (the party's left-leaning General Secretary) used his casting vote for Bevan in September 1976. This was an early test of the authority of the new Prime Minister, Jim Callaghan, as he sought to stop the NEC ratifying the appointment.[3] He failed. Bevan was confirmed by 15:12 in December and started work in January 1977.

There followed a major argument. The Tribune Group of MPs had backed Bevan[4] but the party's agents' trade union, the National Union of Labour Organisers, objected on the grounds that this post should go to a former agent.[5] Meanwhile, the right-wing Manifesto Group of MPs objected on political grounds, one of its members having equated Militant in the Labour Party with the National Front in the Tory Party.[6] Forty MPs joined the anti-Bevan campaign, supporting a resolution condemning his appointment to the PLP.[7] This incident, which inserted an active Militant supporter into the party's headquarters, reflected both Callaghan's weakness at the NEC and the gulf between many MPs and the NEC.

Meanwhile, the party's National Agent, Reg Underhill, who had disclosed that 6 out of 11 members of the Young Socialists' national committee were 'under

Trotskyist influence' as early as 1964,[8] submitted a dossier to the NEC in November 1975 from which he concluded: 'there is a central organisation associated with Militant with its own membership and full-time organisers'.[9] He was severely disappointed that the NEC would not even consider it, leaving it 'lying on the table'.

Although not published, the subject of the report was well covered in newspapers.[10] A campaign to expose Militant developed, with Shirley Williams attacking Trotskyist infiltration. The matter pressed on the NEC so that it set up a sub-committee of five, including Michael Foot, Eric Heffer and Ron Hayward, to consider Underhill's documents, whilst recalling its opposition to witch-hunts and McCarthyism. The sub-committee's report, although accepting that secret meetings existed, was similarly against witch-hunts and believed that 'Trotskyist views cannot be beaten by disciplinary action'. It recommended that party members be made aware of Militant's aims and claims (and therefore the report should be circulated), alongside a membership drive, political education and improved meetings (which would not drive members away).[11] This was approved by the NEC on 25 May 1977 but Frank Chapple immediately wrote asking for the documents, not just the report. The request was refused, the NEC deciding that the background documents should not be circulated in any way.[12] Therefore none of the ten documents was seen other than by the five sub-committee members.

Underhill retired to the Lords in 1979 but received ten more documents which were covered in the *Sunday Times* and the *Guardian*[13] and as part of a six-page supplement on 'The Labour Party's Militant moles'[14] – each detailing the degree of infiltration. Still the NEC refused to publish although it invited Underhill to publish any documents himself.[15] At his own expense, Underhill mailed his report to all CLPs, unions and the NEC.[16]

The NUR's Sidney Weighell had criticised the NEC's failure to act, and outlined a way forward, suggesting that Militant be asked to provide details of its constitution, internal structure, aims, publications, finances, membership and links with foreign organisations – with any failure to provide leading to expulsions.[17] Underhill sent more information when the party's organisation committee (chaired by Eric Heffer) was considering a recommendation that no action be taken against Militant (at the same time agreeing that the right-wing Social Democratic Alliance (SDA) be expelled for planning to oppose Labour candidates).[18] The committee was satisfied that there was nothing incompatible in Militant with party membership as it was not fielding candidates, but Underhill again wrote showing Militant was in breach of the constitution as it acted as a 'party within a Party'.[19] This long-standing party servant received a four-line reply stating that the NEC had decided to take no action.[20]

The issue rumbled on with a Fabian Society pamphlet on Trotskyism in the party[21] – published despite a strong attempt to suppress it led by Frances Morrell, Benn's former political advisor.[22] In November, Chief Whip Michael Cocks MP complained to the party's general secretary about the treatment of Liverpool's five MPs, with one having been deselected and three having defected – the odds of this happening he estimated as 1:1,830. In vain he requested an enquiry.[23] The

Manifesto Group wrote about extremist infiltration, labelling Militant 'a cancer in the body politic . . . a party within a party', urging the NEC not to endorse Militant supporter Pat Wall as a candidate, and 'to declare the activities and organisation of the Militant Tendency as incompatible with the constitution of the Labour Party'.[24]

At a two and a half hour PLP meeting, speaker after speaker insisted that something be done to curb Militant. However, Leader Michael Foot vowed he would not support expulsions or proscriptions[25] and reiterated his opposition to expulsions at the NEC, which reaffirmed its rejection of any investigation into Militant.[26] Tony Benn confided to his diary that, having learnt that 60 members of the Manifesto Group would leave Labour unless Militant were expelled, 'I wouldn't be sorry to see [the 60] go.'[27] However, he was shortly to be isolated on this when, in December, 'Foot wins call for inquiry on militant'.[28] The Leader's change of heart can probably be attributed to a 'Group of Ten' MPs who had been meeting for some months in various people's flats.[29] They felt Foot was in denial, failing to see any 'connection between Trots and Militant'. So, they

> went to see Michael in the Leader's Room before PM Questions – things were so absolutely desperate – and said, unless he denounced Militant and recognised it was a deep cancer in the party, the parliamentary party was on the verge of deeply splitting and was going to come apart. Just as the Benn deputy leadership vote was a turning point, this meeting was also absolutely critical to events. And Michael was shaken to the core. This was a frank speaking meeting. He faced a range of people in party terms – Ann [Taylor] was on the right; I was not in Manifesto Group; [Martin] O'Neill ran with Tribune, as did Jack Straw; Jeff [Rooker] not in either. Rooker told him as it bloody was: 'It's no good you just putting your head in the sand'. Michael was as white as a sheet. We were not taking no for an answer. This was not a plea, but an ultimatum. If you don't act, there is going to be a war. And you'll lose a lot of people.[30]

Whatever happened to change his mind, on 9 December 1981 Foot called for an enquiry and was supported 10:9 in the Organisation sub-committee (Kinnock's vote providing the majority).[31] Benn opposed, pledging to 'fight like a tiger' against expulsions, but Foot admitted he had underestimated Militant and now believed they were dangerous. The committee instructed Ron Hayward and David Hughes (Underhill's successor as National Agent) to investigate whether the activities of Militant were in conflict with the constitution.[32] There was widespread press coverage of Militant – including by Militant's Peter Taafe in the party's own paper, *Labour Weekly*.[33] Copious evidence was submitted, including a large amount of documentation from Solidarity.[34]

The Hayward/Hughes report became the hook on which subsequent action against the Tendency was taken. Turning its back both on outlawing members for their beliefs, and on any return to the Proscribed List,[35] Hayward/Hughes proposed a Register of organisations deemed compatible with party membership, but simultaneously stated that Militant was not eligible to be included on the Register. Even going this far, the authors had to genuflect to Foot's line by writing: 'We fully support the sentiments contained in the Party Leader's New Year Message 1982 against proscription lists, witch hunts and expulsions. Nevertheless the National Executive Committee has the right and the duty to safeguard the Party Constitution and

Rules'. It is hard to see how – without expulsions – they imagined Militant could be tackled.

For many on the centre and right, the report was a severe disappointment. Not only was the evidence to Hayward/Hughes again not published, but it merely supported a Register, not expulsions. Furthermore, other groups might refuse to register – as CLPD was already threatening. However, Solidarity recognised that immediate moves to expulsion could not be got through the NEC without Foot's support.

The NEC agreed the report[36] and the new General Secretary, Jim Mortimer, wrote to non-affiliated organisations (apart from Militant) in July 1982 asking them to register. The following year, the NEC ordered that no facilities be accorded to Militant (including selling *Militant* at meetings or letting rooms to them). A resolution at conference condemning this was lost by 1,754,000 to 5,049,000.[37] The left continued to oppose the ban, mobilising identical resolutions from 26 CLPs to the NEC.[38]

The NEC first tackled the Editorial Board of Militant, whose members were expelled in February 1983.[39] In 1984/85 CLPs began their own expulsions. The St Ermins Group supporters on the NEC wanted more and in December 1984 Ken Cure called in vain for a wider enquiry.[40] A year later, after Kinnock's crucial Bournemouth speech attacking Liverpool's Militants, and following letters from the GMWU's David Basnett and the left-wing General Secretary of the TGWU, Ron Todd, demanding action,[41] the NEC (by 21:5) suspended the Liverpool district party and launched an enquiry. The Enquiry Team was heavy with St Ermins Group nominees, the left having failed (by 9:17) to add Heffer to the team.[42]

The majority Liverpool report, which recommended action against unnamed members for involvement with Militant, was endorsed by the NEC on 26 February 1986 and circulated throughout the party in printed form. A minority report by Margaret Beckett and Audrey Wise rejecting any expulsions was defeated by 18:9 but nevertheless published by the party. The expulsions took a long time as the left fought every step. The Court having ruled that the 8 Enquiry Team members could not sit on the NEC to hear the charges,[43] 7 left-wing members walked out of the NEC meeting on 26 June 1986, making it inquorate – as only 14 remained (the quorum being 15). So on 18 May the full NEC (by 18:4) changed the quorum to 50 per cent of those eligible to participate in the business. Eventually the hearings took place and eight Liverpool Militants were expelled, the decisions overwhelmingly endorsed by the conference.[44]

Soon afterwards, the party set up a National Constitutional Committee (NCC) which thereafter heard all the Militant cases, though it was a number of years before the Militant MPs appeared there. Throughout, many on the left fought all such action. There was a small minority on the left who took a different view, such as Walter Kendall, who wrote: 'allegiance to *Marxism* is one thing, allegiance to *Leninism* is quite another', asking Militant whether they fitted the latter.[45] Similarly, Bryan Gould (a parliamentary candidate and former MP) claimed that the party's spirit of tolerance did not mean that no-one should be refused membership because of their ideas. He thought that any notion that the party had no ideological boundaries was specious, and argued that Militant was beyond the boundaries.[46] Kinnock used similar arguments when, defending his vote for the Hayward/Hughes report, he maintained that Militant had exceeded boundaries, was a 'party within a Party' and supported 'democratic centralism' which was 'arrogant and anti-democratic and absolutely contrary to the ideology of the Labour Party'. However, he still employed the left rhetoric in asserting: 'There is no question of a witch-hunt'.[47]

Support for any action remained a minority position on the left, partly because of the memory of the right's intolerance in the 1950s and 1960s; partly as it was believed that Militant was just the start and that the right would then move on the rest of the left. In 1976 the editor of *Militant* described the Andy Bevan exercise as the start of a witch-hunt – blocking his appointment would give a green light to the right wing to return to the 1950s' expulsions.[48] Despite his dislike of Trotskyites, Foot's long-time friend and colleague, Dick Clements, recalling the MP Konni Zilliacus' 1949 expulsion as a victim of the right's intolerance, pledged 'It must not happen again.'[49]

The left-wing Labour Co-ordinating Committee's (LCCs) 1981 AGM unanimously agreed: 'We should unequivocally oppose attempts to launch witch-hunts against any section of the left.'[50] CLPs started passing 'Opposition to the witch-hunt' resolutions.[51] Local groups became active, the Dulwich Labour Party newsletter calling on members to defend Militant as, if the attack on Militant succeeded, CLPD, LCC and then Tony Benn would be next in line. In Benn's words: 'There must be no registration of socialism.'[52] Over 200 CLPs supported the 'Defend Militant' campaign, with a Labour movement conference on 11 September 1982 (a Scottish circular claiming over 2,500 delegates attended) whilst only the right-wing rump of the Labour Party, 'the camp followers of John Smith, Donald Dewar and George Robertson', supported expulsions. Over 300 delegates in London's County Hall formed 'Labour Against the Witch-hunt' on 30 October 1982 and 'Southwark Labour Parties Against Expulsions' held a rally on 11 December 1982, with Peter Tatchell, Reg Race (Chair, Labour Against the Witch-hunt) and MEP Richard Balfe.

NEC member Tom Sawyer wrote in the *Labour Against the Witchhunt Bulletin*.[53] By April 1983, 55 CLPs had affiliated. The thrust of the work was to get the Greenwich Amendment – a resolution to scrap the Register – on the party's annual conference agenda. CLPD circulated model resolutions opposing witch-hunts and supporting the Greenwich Amendment. By August, a large number of resolutions from CLPs had been received by the NEC. In the debate at conference, Jack Straw was slow-handclapped when he called the term 'witch-hunt' 'a smokescreen for those who wish to claim immunity from the terms and conditions of our rulebook'.[54] Nevertheless, the unions felt differently from the CLP activists and the demand for an immediate halt to all witch-hunts was lost by 4,868,000 to 1,913,000.[55]

Pressure against expulsions continued, with the 1984 CLPD AGM voting by 150:77 to continue to campaign against the NEC's 'witch-hunt', and to overturn the proscriptions and expulsions. When resolutions came to NEC (for example, from Islington South, the CLP of Chris Smith who signed the March 1984 Campaign Group statement against the witch-hunt), the NEC would reassure the CLP that protecting the constitution of the party was not witch-hunting.[56]

The flow of anti-expulsion resolutions to the NEC continued throughout 1984 and 1985, at a time when Militant could gather 4,000 supporters in the Royal Albert Hall.[57] *Witch Hunt News* was launched by Labour Left Co-ordination, CLPD and the Campaign Group (the grouping included David Blunkett and Peter Hain).[58] CLPD's 1987 AGM again agreed (by 82:2) to campaign against expulsions by promoting an amendment to the party constitution which would provide a legal basis for groups of members holding minority views to campaign within the party, and to take up individual cases where there were no grounds for their expulsion.

This chapter has sought to describe how the right – both in the PLP and the unions – were frustrated in trying to deal with Militant. One of their number attributed the poor 1987 election result to this and to the 'constant pussy footing around by the leadership to placate the extreme left'.[59] This was the reason that the unions became so determined to alter the composition of the NEC and then play a role in expelling Militant. As one MP subsequently wrote: 'For what seemed like an eternity, the NEC simply equivocated on countering the Trotskyist takeover bid. When Neil Kinnock finally had an executive with the bottle, it took action'.[60]

Notes

1 Joe Haines, 'The rape of Labour', *Daily Mirror*, 25 January 1977.
2 Michael Crick, *The March of Militant* (Faber and Faber, 1986).
3 *Daily Telegraph*, 25 November 1976.
4 *Daily Telegraph*, 30 November 1976.
5 *Observer*, 21 December 1976; *Daily Telegraph*, 11 January 1977.
6 Alan Lee Williams, *The Times*, 14 December 1976.
7 On 7 December 1976.
8 *Daily Mail*, 27 January 1977.
9 'Entryist activities', known as the Underhill report; Paper to 26 November 1975 Meeting of the NEC; *Guardian*, 15 December 1976.
10 As a 'revolutionary plot' inside the party; *Observer*, 31 August 1975.
11 Appendix to 1977 *Annual Report of the Labour Party*.
12 Reg Underhill, letter to Frank Chapple, 27 July 1977.
13 On 16 December 1979 and 11 January 1980.
14 Tom Forester, *New Society*, 10 January 1980.
15 Minutes of the 27 February 1980 meeting of the NEC.
16 Lord Underhill, letter, March 1980.
17 1980 AGM speech.
18 *Daily Telegraph*, 15 December 1980.
19 Underhill letter to Hayward, 11 December 1980.
20 Letter of 19 December 1980.
21 David Webster, *The Labour Party and the New Left* (Fabian Society, 1981).
22 The current author, who was General Secretary of the Fabian Society at the time, was put under enormous pressure to stop the publication.

23 Charles Turnock, 'Mersey militants' (unpublished, 1987), p. 19.
24 Letter to Hayward, 2 November 1981.
25 *The Times*, 19 November 1981.
26 *The Times*, 26 November 1981.
27 Benn, *Diaries 1980–90*, p. 164.
28 *The Times*, 10 December 1981.
29 The ten MPs comprised a grouping of centre-right and soft-left: Andrew Bennett, Jack Cunningham, Robert Kilroy-Silk, Martin O'Neill, Giles Radice, Jeff Rooker, Jack Straw, Ann Taylor, Phillip Whitehead and Ken Woolmer. They were later to discuss getting rid of Foot as Leader (a cause ended by Labour's Darlington by-election victory on 24 March 1983).
30 Ken Woolmer interview. Foot also told Benn about this meeting; Benn, *Diaries 1980–90*, p. 183.
31 The ten comprised Michael Foot, Denis Healey, Eric Varley, John Golding, Betty Boothroyd, Russell Tuck, Neville Hough, Syd Tierney, David Williams and Neil Kinnock – some put on the NEC by the St Ermins Group only two months earlier. The result was endorsed at the 16 December NEC by 19:10.
32 *The Times*, 10 December 1981.
33 15 January 1982.
34 'Militant Tendency report' (known as the Hayward/Hughes report), NEC paper, 23 June 1982.
35 The Proscribed List, removed from the rulebook in 1973 (*NEC Report to 1973 Conference*, p. 11), had debarred anyone belonging to any organisation on that list from party membership. In ending it, the NEC stated there were sufficient rules to safeguard the constitution and asked members to refrain from associating with political organisations whose objectives were not consistent with those of the Labour Party.
36 Which was endorsed by the annual conference, 5,173,000:1,565,000; *Report of the 1982 Annual Conference of the Labour Party*, p. 275.
37 *Report of the 1983 Annual Conference of the Labour Party*, p. 75.
38 NAD 6/11/83, 23 November 1983.
39 *NEC Report to Labour Party Conference*, 1983, p. 22. The expulsions were confirmed at conference by majorities of approximately 5 million to 1.5 million.
40 Turnock, 'Mersey militants', pp. 26–7.
41 *The Times*, 28 November 1985.
42 Charles Turnock (Chair), Betty Boothroyd, Tony Clarke, Eddie Haigh and Neville Hough, with Margaret Beckett, Tom Sawyer and Audrey Wise from the left. Turnock, 'Mersey militants', p. 27.
43 Something which Kinnock had been warned about by barrister James Goudie. It was for that reason he had held back some 'reliables' from the Enquiry Team, and allowed some of the left on, so that he could still produce a majority at the NEC without the Enquiry Team's votes (Neil Kinnock interview).
44 *Report of the 1986 Annual Conference of the Labour Party*.
45 *Tribune*, 19 March 1982. Kendall was a socialist historian and activist, founder of the journal *Voice of the Unions* and author of *The Revolutionary Movement in Britain, 1900–21: The Origins of British Communism* (Weidenfeld & Nicolson, 1969).
46 *Guardian*, 26 July 1982. Despite these views, one Militant MP voted for Gould for the Shadow Cabinet elections, 'Dave Nellist MP Parliamentary Report', Summer 1987.
47 *Broad Left Alliance Journal*, October 1982.
48 Letter to *Daily Telegraph*, 17 January 1977.

49 *Tribune*, 25 September 1981.
50 Undated letter from Michael Meacher, Audrey Wise and others to LCC members.
51 *Militant*, 11 December 1981.
52 *Dulwich Labour Party Contact*, July 1982.
53 Number 4, May 1983.
54 *Report of the 1983 Annual Conference of the Labour Party*, p. 73.
55 *Ibid.*, p. 75.
56 Paper NAD/69/3/84, 28 March 1984 NEC meeting.
57 *Guardian*, 13 November 1985.
58 *Guardian*, 20 January 1986.
59 Turnock, 'Mersey militants', pp. 268, 273.
60 Frank Field, *Guardian*, 10 June 2003.

6

One-Member-One-Vote

In order to appreciate the importance of OMOV, a brief history of its development is outlined. There were two aspects of OMOV: initially – and partly in response to the left's reselection campaign – as the method of selecting parliamentary candidates (giving all local party members a vote in place of selection by general committees); and secondly, as the way of deciding how CLPs and unions should decide their votes in the Electoral College for the choice of leader and deputy leader. In both cases, the campaign was hard fought, and the issue used as a marker to label members 'left' (opponents) or 'right' (supporters).

Whilst it was resisted by most on the left, OMOV was not simply a device invented by the right in the 1980s to frustrate the left's attempt to wrest power from MPs. Its origins go back further, with proposals for a wider franchise being discussed in the 1960s.[1] However, any move to OMOV raised serious questions for the movement's constituent parts. The selection of parliamentary candidates was the responsibility of the local parties' management committees, where union delegates played a large role. It was possible in many seats (especially, as in mining areas, where one trade union was pre-eminent) for one or more unions effectively to select the candidate – in Labour areas, the MP. This could also work within a region, where perhaps one seat would be accepted as the TGWU's, the neighbouring one falling to the GMWU. Any move to OMOV, with only individual members voting and not the affiliated unions, jeopardised the role and power of trade unions.

In the case of the leader, similar forces were at play. Since 1906, Labour MPs had elected their own parliamentary leader (who was *de facto* – and later *de jure* – leader of the Labour Party). The majority of MPs wanted to retain this position. OMOV was proposed by the right only when a wider franchise was inevitable – and then only within the two new sections of the Electoral College, the PLP still retaining some input.

A number of unions had employed OMOV for internal elections for years – notably the EETPU and the AUEW. In the latter case, when postal ballots for officers had been under attack by the Communist Party (in favour of branch ballots) in 1975, a paper for the AUEW Insight Group (which was defending individual balloting against moves to branch ballots) set out the comprehensive case for OMOV by postal ballot. The EETPU also played a key role in the achievement of OMOV, by arguing the case and by funding local party ballots, a hitherto unreported, but significant, intervention.

OMOV for parliamentary candidate selection

The 1975 *How the Labour Party Works* by the National Agent set out how parliamentary candidates were selected by GCs on a majority vote after an eliminating ballot, yet intra-party warfare was about to erupt over this issue following the left's campaign for mandatory reselection – whereby sitting MPs had to go through a full reselection by the GCs after each general election. Hitherto, once elected, MPs were simply re-endorsed at each election unless the local party put up a very determined fight. However, even before reselection was on the agenda, a Fabian Group (which included Anthony Wedgwood-Benn[2] and Reg Race[3]) produced a 1971 pamphlet in which its editor and another group member favoured opening up candidate selection to all party members.[4] Jim Daly started supporting members' participation in 1976 and, by 1977, OMOV was favoured by the centre and right of the party.[5] CLV's February 1977 founding meeting resolved to campaign for 'the fullest possible democratic involvement of the party membership', which soon became a call for membership involvement in candidate selection.[6] There were some – particularly MPs – who supported this in response to the left's demands for reselection. For others it was a simply a logical extension of democracy. However, no sooner was it articulated than it was attacked by CLPD in, for example, a piece against 'Why can't all members select their parliamentary candidate?' in *Labour Leader* in August 1978.[7] *London Labour Briefing* called on the left to expose 'those who seek to "extend democracy" by introducing a primaries system for the reselection process'. Even worse, it whispered, 'Some members of CLV, not content with advocating that all members should be involved in the final selection, are calling for a postal ballot of all members to decide the candidate.'[8]

Daly took his OMOV ideas to a CLV meeting early in 1978 where they became CLV policy. In 1979, CLV and the Manifesto Group called for the selection of parliamentary candidates to be opened up to all party members of two years' standing.[9] Within the PLP, John Golding proposed that, if reselection were introduced, the vote should be by all members of the local party, not just the few who got on the General Management Committee.[10] This betrays OMOV's partial origins in diluting reselection. Thereafter it was seen as a right-wing ploy, making it difficult for anyone on the left to support it. Increasingly, as many of its proponents moved towards the Gang of Three (later Four and eventually the SDP), OMOV's chances of success correspondingly fell. The NEC set its face against OMOV, whereas the Manifesto Group began to see it as a central issue. Twelve of its number (the 'Dirty Dozen') supported OMOV[11] and, following Callaghan's 1980 resignation, the Group prepared ten questions for the leadership contenders, including 'Are you in favour of one member one vote in selections and reselections?' However, once Foot was elected Leader and opposed it, the campaign stalled.

The EETPU's submission to the party's 1980 Enquiry into Organisation recommended an individual postal ballot with a single transferable vote for all members to choose a parliamentary candidate, its second preference being a ballot at a meeting of all members of the CLP.[12] The union's evidence set out the proportion of members participating in reselections – from 3 per cent in Norwood to 18 per cent in Fife Central. Although the proportion reached 22 per cent in West Dunbartonshire, this was from an extremely low membership. The union concluded that the selectorate was unrepresentative of membership – and even less representative of Labour voters or the wider electorate (with just 0.05 per cent of Benn's electorate in Bristol South East participating in his selection).

After 1981 Labour Solidarity took up the cause, with Frank Field then deciding to concentrate solely on this objective. His support for OMOV pre-dated Wembley, having urged that selection be by more than just super-activists.[13] He wanted to maintain union involvement through the formation of party factory branches, favouring OMOV for selection and leadership elections. Two years later he established 'Labour Franchise', published a letter in *Labour Weekly* on a 'One person one vote' campaign and put together a 'pack' of supporting arguments for local parties and friendly MPs. In the run-up to the 1983 leadership election, Field asked the four candidates their views on OMOV for selection. It was then that Kinnock agreed to it, so Field expected it would happen once he was elected. But Field had calculated without the unions; it would take another decade for them to deliver. There is an interesting postscript to Field's long commitment to OMOV. On leaving the Blair government in 1998, his resignation speech mentioned 'initiating the one member, one vote campaign'.[14] Kinnock's former Head of Office, Charles Clarke, immediately disputed this in a 'robust conversation' with Field.[15] But Clarke was mistaken. Field was indeed one of the first MPs, and the first of the non-defectors, to back OMOV, and he went public long before Kinnock – or any of his staff – supported it.

One union was consistent in its support. The EETPU took on the left's opposition to OMOV. Its *Political Bulletin* confronted the 'Elitist arguments against extending the franchise', contending that

> Those who argue that the average Party member . . . is not well enough informed about the issues to make a mature judgement, would find ample support from the Earl of Rutland, who in 1867 said 'I do not think the state of education in the Country is sufficiently advanced to enable the Government safely to propose so large a measure as that of household suffrage'.[16]

A paper circulated to friendly MPs included the GCs' voting figures for reselection of Campaign Group MPs (those most opposed to OMOV) – such as 28:26 for Margaret Beckett, 64:36:27 for Tony Benn and 15:9 for Clare Short, with the numbers voting as a percentage of average CLP membership (respectively 13 per cent, 29 per cent and 6 per cent). Tribune Members' figures were little different, with 34:28 for Gordon Brown (14 per cent of average CLP membership), 18–0 for Robin Cook (4 per cent) and 23:19 for Harriet Harman (10 per cent).[17] For the EETPU, this amounted to a clear case for involving all party members.

Solidarity's first OMOV leaflet, 'One person, one vote – true democracy', was produced in 1983, when Hattersley believed the pressure for change was irresistible, whilst acknowledging that union support would be needed for their loss of control over selection.[17] As its supporters geared up for the campaign, the left worked equally hard – and more effectively – to resist it. The 1984 AGM of CLPD decided 'to give high priority to opposing the misleadingly named campaign for "one member one vote" . . . its propaganda gives the illusion that it would be an extension of democracy'.[19]

Simultaneously the St Ermins–Kinnock majority on the NEC was moving inexorably towards OMOV, John Evans writing in support, partly as a recruiting tool: 'Join the Labour Party and choose your MP'.[20] Kinnock echoed these views, publishing his letter to MPs which favoured giving GCs the choice of whether to give all members a vote in selection. He asked opponents to 'explain how in the name of democracy they can deny the chance to vote to the people who make up the party' and challenged their views that only GC members could decide on the candidate, that there were difficulties in organising ballots and that OMOV posed any danger to the union link. He pointed to the tiny average number of GC delegates (37) voting in the latest 206 selections and stressed the potential of opening up this decision-making to 100,000 members. 'Do those who oppose the proposals for direct membership voting really think that the great majority of party members cannot be trusted to make a judgement? If they do, they . . . had better admit it . . . [and] tell the people of the Labour Party that it's their membership that is wanted, not their opinion, that they are a respectful audience, not a movement'.[21] This was strong stuff for a founding member of CLPD, and he was roundly attacked by the left[22] which began organising union resistance to OMOV, on the grounds that it would reduce their role in selecting candidates. The National Union of Mineworkers (NUM) argued that, as a sponsor of 15 MPs, it should be specifically consulted and that the proposed change should be delayed a year to allow for such discussion.[23]

The Tribune Group wrote to unions criticising the move to OMOV as 'highly divisive', difficult to implement and seriously weakening the party–union link.[24] John Evans responded in the *Guardian*, defending the proposal (of which he was the author) to permit GCs to allow members the right to participate in selections.[25] By now the Leader, NEC and local members supported the rule amendment. It was defeated by the unions in conference, though Kinnock claimed 'We won the argument but lost the vote'.[26] Solidarity similarly took comfort, saying it was 'now irresistible. It is not so much a question of "if", but of "when" victory comes'.[25] The campaign continued, with resolutions reaching the NEC (for example, from Epping Forest and West Gloucestershire CLPs in favour of OMOV, and Southampton against – on the grounds that 'the one-member-one-vote system would mean party members not attending meetings would come under the influence of the Capitalist press, rather than being involved in the democratic processes of the Labour Party').[28] CLPD took a strong line against OMOV, resisting any widening of the franchise and seeking to retain power within GCs,[29] though the LCC made a brave move towards membership participation, arguing that at least a debate should take place on the left.[30] This was the first breach in the left's almost unanimous hostility to OMOV.[31] With five pro-OMOV resolutions on the 1985 conference agenda (including from the EETPU), CLPD worked to ensure their defeat, arguing they 'would certainly not lead to a greater involvement even of individual party members' whilst they would reduce union input.[32] Two resolutions were debated, with the EETPU's (calling on the NEC to table a rule amendment) being remitted to the NEC.

The campaign continued. Solidarity produced a leaflet, 'One person one vote: they say it can't be done', rebutting their opponents' arguments ('The Press will put pressure [on party members]'; 'It's a vote for sleeping members'; 'It will exclude local unions'; 'It will be too difficult to administer') and extended their demand to giving all members a vote for a CLP's delegate to conference.[33] Meanwhile, the NEC established a Working Group[34] and issued a consultation document on 'Party franchise for selection and reselection of parliamentary candidates', which attracted 372 responses. By 73:10, the CLPD February 1987 AGM reiterated its belief that 'the GC is the nucleus of Labour Party democracy and will continue to fight any adulteration of this principle whether by OMOV or any other future manipulations'. Its newsletter argued against 'so-called "one member one vote"' and urged supporters to submit its model resolution to halt OMOV.[35] The other left-wing group, the LCC, had meanwhile turned to embrace OMOV (which it had helped defeat in 1984), an OMOV ballot of its own members giving it a 2:1 majority.[36] Solidarity continued its long-standing campaign, offering speakers for meetings to build support for the case.[37]

John Evans, a staunch Kinnock supporter, author of the failed 1984 attempt and now Chair of the Working Group, continued his proselytising:

> I believe that the present method of re-selecting sitting Labour MPs is an enormous albatross which the Party has inflicted upon itself . . . There are no inherent grounds for arguing against the principle of extending the right to every individual member . . . of a vote in selecting and reselecting the . . . candidate . . . the time for 'one member one vote' has come; . . . it will rejuvenate the Party . . . the overwhelming majority of Party members, weary of narrow sectarianism, agrees with me.[38]

The Working Group produced a range of Options, from mandatory balloting to the *status quo*, rehearsing the arguments for and against each (and setting out the percentage of members participating in selections – an average of 8.4 per cent).[39] The EETPU quickly prepared its response, outlining how reselection had failed to extend involvement to members, with often fewer than 20 participating in the vote. Reviewing the suggested Options, the union favoured mandatory ballots. It was, said its submission, no more than the one-person-one-vote which the party supported for all other forms of election.

Most attention in this period, however, focused on the 1987 general election, which produced few extra seats. Immediately after the defeat, OMOV was on the agenda as a new round of reselections would start within 18 months. Some remained cautious; at an LCC conference, Robin Cook maintained that whilst OMOV was a good idea, it was not a panacea to provide a better image for the party.[40] However, at his first meeting of the left-wing Campaign Group of MPs, Bernie Grant, newly elected for Tottenham, caused a storm by giving his support to OMOV.[41] Undeterred, CLPD urged its members to reject the pseudo-democratic option of OMOV.[42] Former General Secretary Mortimer similarly argued that representative democracy was a sign of maturity and used the old 'guilt by association' by linking OMOV with David Owen before falling back on a welter of administrative difficulties, including the careful checking of records.[43] The 1987 conference voted to expand the franchise for selection, but a composite motion moved by the EETPU's John Spellar in support of OMOV was defeated in favour of a local Electoral College. This retained a 40 per cent input from unions although it did extend voting for the other 60 per cent to party members who either attended a meeting or, if they had good reason for non-attendance, applied for a postal vote.

After the 1988 conference, CLPD, recognising the importance of union votes, went direct to the unions, circulating a model resolution for 1989 union conferences which, whilst acknowledging OMOV had been agreed for the choice of leader, called on each union to oppose any further extension of non-participatory voting.[44] The CLPD executive tabled a resolution for its own AGM deploring the NEC's decision to take an OMOV amendment to the 1989 conference and calling for a campaign to retain decision-making at the GC.[45] Later, CLPD had to gear up to resist the extension of balloting to the choice of conference delegate, circulating a model resolution against postal ballots.[46]

Full OMOV for candidate selection still had some time to wait. The Labour First organisation – Solidarity's successor – set up a 'One member one vote now' campaign in December 1992 (with John Spellar as co-ordinator) and everything geared up to John Smith's mammoth battle at his first conference as Leader, in 1993, when – helped by John Prescott – the decision was finally taken, not without the twisting of a large number of arms. Union delegations were turned around, some at the very last moment, whilst others (such as the present author) with just a couple of votes to their mandate, were summoned to the Leader and warned he would resign if the conference defeated OMOV. His 18 July 1992 leadership acceptance speech had committed the party to OMOV in place of block votes and he believed he had to deliver.

OMOV for leadership elections

Whilst OMOV for candidate selection took until 1993 to be agreed, it came earlier for the choice of leader – not least because of media attention on how unions cast their massive block votes, and because of the importance of this choice for the whole country, not just one seat. Much earlier, the 1972 conference had remitted two resolutions calling for the election of the leader by conference, but it was 1976 before a motion was passed asking the NEC to set up a working party to consider widening the electorate for the choice of leader.[47] Of the evidence received, 1 affiliate and 18 CLPs favoured selection by individual party members.[48] However, MPs remained firmly of the view that they alone should retain the sole rights of election.[49] The report to the 1977 conference and the accompanying resolution confirmed the MPs' role in the election of leader (who would, for the first time, become the leader of the party, not just of the parliamentary party).[50] Two amendments extending the franchise beyond MPs were lost. However, the campaign to change this was to continue each year, with the 1980 Commission of Enquiry and the Bishop's Stortford meeting seeing the party Leader and former Prime Minister, Jim Callaghan, acquiesce in an Electoral College, to the despair of the right which saw it open the door to a Tony Benn leadership. The wider franchise was narrowly adopted in October, its composition being decided at the 1981 Wembley conference.

Immediately after the 1980 conference, when MPs had lost their monopoly, CLV called a meeting of its 100 key activists, which (unintentionally) took place between Callaghan's resignation and Foot's election. The meeting agreed (with David Owen dissenting[51]) that CLV remained in favour of selection of the leader by the PLP; only if that failed would their choice be full OMOV. It was much too late to start a campaign for that option.

At Wembley, Chapple spoke from the rostrum: 'The Labour Movement has always fought for the principle of one person one vote . . . we should uphold that principle today . . . firstly because it is right in itself; next because it enfranchises the entire membership and gives each and every supporter an equal right in choosing the leader'.[52] The case against OMOV was articulated by Militant delegate Pat Wall, who claimed that 'one man one vote' would give the four millionaires who control the media the biggest influence in the ballot.[53] The proposal was bound to fail. It had only been grasped, late in the day, by MPs after failing to keep the decision firmly in their own hands – and they were chided by local delegate Mo Mowlam for their 'impudence' in wanting more say.[54] Furthermore, being supported by the Gang of Three (David Owen, Bill Rodgers and Shirley Williams – who were to defect the following day) and CLV, OMOV was opposed not just by the left but by many whose political instincts warned them off such association.

Outside the confines of the party, others saw more than just the birthpangs of the SDP, one armchair observer noting:

> What was so startlingly clear from these television pictures . . . was the sincerity with which some constituency Labour Party delegates oppose the principle of one-man-one-vote. From the gleam in the eye to the finger in the air their every mannerism shows that when it comes to privileged voting rights, no 19th century totalitarian Tory demanding them in the name of the abnormal extent of his lands could outdo a 20th century totalitarian CLP delegate demanding them in the name of the abnormal extent of his activity.[55]

The left would oppose this extended democracy for another eight years (and until 1993 for candidates), with few breaking ranks (although Michael Meacher argued that union members should vote in their section, whilst GCs should decide locally, albeit mandated by branch meetings[56]).

The biggest incentive on the party to change the working of the new Electoral College was its first airing – for the 1981 deputy leadership, with the image of unions casting large tranches of the vote, often without consideration of their members' views. On television and in large spreads in the press, descriptions of the workings of delegations and executives shone unwelcome light on union decision-making.[57] The CLP figures were not much better, with few consulting their members. Twenty-two CLPs did undertake some sort of ballot, with turn-outs averaging 73 per cent for postal ballots, 89 per cent for personal delivery and collection of ballot papers, and 36 per cent for branch ballots.[58]

In mid-1982, the NEC had yet to be convinced, judging: 'It would be impractical to lay down a constitutional procedure for a one person, one vote election' in every CLP. It did however propose that members could be involved by a ballot either at branch meetings or at a mass meeting at CLP level, or (the favoured option) by a postal ballot. It was for each GC to decide; but few would give up power to the membership.[59] After the right took the chairmanship of the NEC Organisation Sub-committee, they continued to face left opposition to OMOV but were able to encourage full membership participation.

By the 1983 leadership election, the demand for OMOV was taking root. Many unions and CLPs decided to determine their voting choice by OMOV,[60] contributing to Hattersley's notable 40–point victory over left-wing Meacher for deputy leader (309 CLPs supported Hattersley with just 280 for Meacher). Hattersley won easily in most CLPs that conducted individual ballots: of 54 parties using a postal ballot, no fewer than 49 supported the victor. Meacher had a 2:1 lead where GCs took the decision.[61] A third of the GCs in London kept the decision to themselves, 40 per cent opting for a ballot of members, with a further 20 per cent using a branch ballot.[62] Where a ballot was open to all members, the percentage poll ranged from 21 per cent to 82 per cent, with an average of 52 per cent. With a ballot at branch meetings, the percentage poll ranged from 12 per cent to 35 per cent, with an average of 24 per cent.

Whilst slow progress was being made on all-member ballots for selections (where vacancies were appearing), the debate went quiet for the leadership after Kinnock's 1983 emphatic victory ruled out any challenge. That was to change after the 1987 election. Early in 1988 MP Frank Field returned to the fray, suggesting full OMOV for the choice of leader.[63] Meanwhile the left were contemplating a challenge to Kinnock[64] which emerged when Benn and Heffer challenged Kinnock and Hattersley for their respective positions. While the incumbents were always bound to win (although Prescott's nomination for deputy leader raised some doubts), the contest again shone a spotlight on how union members and local parties were consulted.

It was at this time that the EETPU swung into action. For any CLP where the union was affiliated, it offered to pay the postage costs of a full postal ballot to decide the CLP leadership vote.[65] Thirty-four CLPs took up the offer, the union reimbursing a total of £2,449. The results overwhelmingly favoured the incumbents but of more interest was the high number of ballot papers returned – up to 545 in one constituency. As the union guessed, once party members had exercised this right, they were unlikely to let it go. The following year, when the NEC began encouraging CLPs to involve members in the election of conference delegates, the EETPU repeated its funding offer to CLPs.[66]

Support for full participation grew. The principle of OMOV in elections for leader and deputy leader was agreed at the 1988 conference, with the appropriate rule amendment adopted the following March.[67] Later, when OMOV was extended to the election of NEC members in 1992, MPs Gordon Brown and Tony Blair immediately took advantage of this, getting elected on their first attempt.[68]

It had been a long battle, fought by Solidarity and its supporters, and by the EETPU, which argued the case, tabled resolutions and funded exemplary ballots. For many, it was a struggle to wrest control from left-dominated GCs. For some it was to show the public that the party's leader would not be selected by a handful of union leaders wielding unrepresentative block votes.

What the story of OMOV for both candidate selection and in the Electoral College shows, however, is how the right in the party had to struggle against the left throughout, taking on the hostility of local party activists as well as the vested interests of some trade unions which wanted to maintain their grip over the selection of MPs. It did not make right-wingers popular and meant it took courage as well as belief to pursue this objective.

Notes

1 *Political Quarterly*, July 1960.
2 Later Tony Benn. In 1971 he was an MP and Vice-Chairman of the Labour Party.
3 Later a Bennite MP.
4 Inigo Bing, 'New approaches to democracy' and Oliver Stutchbury, 'Reform of party organisation', in Inigo Bing (ed.), *The Labour Party: An Organisational Study* (Fabian Society, 1971), pp. 25, 46, 54.
5 Jim Daly, 'Let ALL the members vote!', *Socialist Commentary*, October 1976; Paul Tinnion, *New Statesman*, 21 October 1977; David Bean, *New Statesman*, 21 October 1977; Dianne Hayter, *The Labour Party: Crisis and Prospects* (Fabian Society, 1977); Dianne Hayter, 'NEC needs rank-and-file', *Labour Weekly*, 7 September 1979.
6 'Is it democracy?', *Labour Victory*, May 1977; CLV leaflet, 'Let's have some real democracy in the Labour Party', 1977.
7 Joseph Gray, *Labour Leader*, August 1978, p. 5.
8 Andy Harris, 'CLPD slams CLV "democracy" fraud', *London Labour Briefing*, June 1980.
9 CLV and Manifesto Group, 'Reform and democracy in the Labour Party', *Labour Victory*, October 1979.
10 Golding, *Hammer of the Left*, p. 109.
11 'Why the Labour Party structure must change' by Mike Thomas, George Robertson *et al.* (most of whom subsequently joined the SDP), *The Times*, 22 September 1980.
12 'Submission by the EETPU to the party Enquiry into organisation', 1980.
13 *The Times*, 6 November 1980; *Guardian*, 2 January 1981.
14 *Hansard*, 29 July 1998, col. 373.
15 Letter from Frank Field to Charles Clarke, August 1988 (with kind permission of the author).
16 *EETPU Political Bulletin*, August 1983, p. 4.
17 July 1984. The paper also noted how many of the left, having vigorously opposed reselection from a shortlist of one, then took advantage of this and faced no opponent.
18 *Guardian*, 11 February 1983.

19 Minutes of the CLPD AGM, February 1984.
20 *Guardian*, 29 June 1984.
21 *Guardian*, 24 July 1984.
22 Including by Heffer, despite his view the previous year, that 'I would have one person one vote both for election of leader and deputy leader and also for selection of candidates' (*A Week in Politics*, Channel Four, 13 February 1983).
23 Letter from NUM General Secretary to Labour Party General Secretary, 3 August 1984.
24 Letter from Tribune Group, 10 August 1984, signed by, amongst others, Tribune Secretary Chris Smith MP.
25 *Guardian*, 28 September 1984.
26 *Labour Solidarity*, November 1984.
27 *Ibid.*
28 NEC Organisation Sub-committee papers, February and March 1985.
29 *CLPD Newsletter*, March 1985.
30 Mike Craven, 'One person one vote', *The Journal*, Clause 4, Spring 1985.
31 The exception being the Independent Labour Party which, whilst highly critical of the right, nevertheless supported 'A democratic say for all the membership' in selections; John O'Brien *et al.*, *Who Rules: Annual Conference versus the Parliamentary Party* (Independent Labour Publications, 1979), p. 23.
32 CLPD Circular, 25 July 1985.
33 *Labour Solidarity*, January 1986.
34 John Evans (Chair), Betty Boothroyd, Gordon Colling, Roy Hattersley, Larry Whitty and Joyce Gould; Consultation Working Party, *Party Franchise* (Labour Party, 1987).
35 *CLPD Newsletter*, June 1987.
36 *Guardian*, 12 March 1987.
37 *Labour Solidarity*, February 1987.
38 John Evans MP, 'One member one vote democracy in the Labour Party', *Labour Club News*, April 1987.
39 Consultation Working Party, *Party Franchise*.
40 *Clause IV*, July 1987, p. 4.
41 *Clause IV*, July 1987, p. 6.
42 *CLPD Newsletter*, September 1987.
43 Jim Mortimer, 'Narrowing Labour's franchise', *Morning Star*, 15 July 1987.
44 CLPD Circular, 11 November 1988.
45 CLPD Circular, 20 December 1988.
46 CLPD Circular, October 1989.
47 *Report of the 1977 Annual Conference of the Labour Party*, p. 11.
48 *Ibid.*, p. 380.
49 *Ibid.*, p. 381.
50 *Ibid.*, pp. 379–82.
51 Owen favoured moving straight to OMOV. Other CLV members supported the principle but correctly sensed that the debate would focus on the proportions within an Electoral College.
52 *Report of the NEC to the 1981 Labour Party Conference*, p. 125. Option 4 of the agenda was a ballot of individual members, 'Report of the Conference Arrangements Committee', 24 January 1981, p. 2.
53 *Report of the NEC to the 1981 Labour Party Conference*, p. 127.
54 *Ibid.*, p. 145.
55 Chris Dunkley, 'The "Left" exposes itself', *Financial Times*, 28 January 1981.

56 Michael Meacher, 'Breaking the block vote', *New Statesman*, 13 November 1981.
57 For example, the *Financial Times*, 25 September 1981; 'How three top communists swung 200,000 votes to Benn', *Observer*, 28 June 1981.
58 David Cowling, 'One member, one vote: deputy leadership election 1981' (Briefing for Peter Shore).
59 NEC paper NAD/116/6/82, 23 June 1982.
60 Though some unions used other methods, such as the ISTC, whose General Secretary 'was determined that as the union was now to have some say as to who the next Labour leader would be then that decision ought to be made by as many people within the union as possible. We therefore asked all our 800 branches to let us know their views'; Sirs, *Hard Labour*, p. 130.
61 Peter Kellner, 'Widespread balloting gives Hattersley landslide', *New Statesman*, 7 October 1983.
62 *London Labour Party Report*, March 1984.
63 *Guardian*, 9 January 1988.
64 *The Times*, 21 January 1988.
65 'Leadership election', *EETPU Political Bulletin*, July 1988.
66 *EETPU Political Bulletin*, July 1989, Issue 27.
67 *Independent*, 7 March 1989.
68 Andy McSmith, *Faces of Labour: The Inside Story* (Verso, 1996), p. 323.

Part III
Groups

7

Manifesto Group of Labour MPs, 1974–83

This book makes the case that the Labour Party was, after many years of electoral failure, turned back towards electability by the activities of the traditional, loyalist right, particularly in the unions, which conspired to change the political balance on the NEC and thus deliver for a leader willing to change the party (Neil Kinnock) the necessary majority for his agenda. It is therefore mostly the story of the 'stayers' from the centre and right who remained after the 1981 SDP split and who redoubled their efforts to 'save' the party. The unions played a crucial role in this. However, other forces were also at work, in the constituencies and within the PLP. This chapter concentrates on the right-wing parliamentary grouping, the Manifesto Group of Labour MPs, set up in 1974 to counter the Tribune Group and to deliver the PLP's natural centre-right majority in internal elections. Although most of its activities pre-date the 1981 split, as there is no existing study of the Group, and few references to it in the literature, this chapter describes its history, reviews how successful it was and considers whether more could have been achieved within the prevailing culture in the party.

Divisions within the PLP were not new, the most seismic having been in 1971 when the cleavage was no longer between left and right but for or against the European Community. It heralded a longer-term split, which David Owen identified as the genesis of the SDP[1] and which followed the 1969 division over *In Place of Strife*,[2] when many of the traditional union right-wingers sided with the left.

Of perhaps more significance than divisions within the PLP was the fact that the majority of Labour MPs were increasingly out of sympathy with the party in the country. On Europe, on defence, on relations with the government and on constitutional change, the moderate majority in the PLP had little in common with the NEC or the conference. This minority position within the movement was the major cause of weakness for the Manifesto Group, forcing it to keep its membership secret and its presence apologetic, and making many MPs fight shy of it. Manifesto officers were intolerant of the 'humbugs' (in Dickson Mabon's words) or 'cowards in the middle' (John Horam), especially those whose public and private utterances were at variance. However, not all of them were themselves so brave. One trade unionist recalls that when he would make forthright contributions against 'the Trots' at his GC, John Cartwright (later to defect) would quietly murmur his support, but not actually speak. Reproached for this, he replied that, as the Council Leader, he had a responsibility not to be too provocative.[3]

Unpopularity within the party aside, other obstacles confronted the Manifesto Group. Firstly, they were provided with no protective shield by the leader, whether the left-wing Harold Wilson or, perhaps surprisingly, the more right-wing Callaghan, who saw his role as a balancing one, rather than as favouring either side. Secondly, they were effectively leaderless. Whilst there were strong and respected personalities on the right, none put him- or herself at the helm of the Manifesto members or provided a single icon behind which to rally supporters. When in government, membership of the Group had been confined to backbenchers. From 1979, when the Shadow Cabinet could join and when the right so needed a leader both to confront the NEC and to provide a sense of direction, the Group was unable to coalesce around any one candidate. Not until the 1981 deputy leadership election was the (then depleted) Manifesto Group wholly in favour of a single candidate – though they had come together for Healey in the final ballot in 1980 when he was 10 votes short of Foot's 139 votes.

A third weakness stemmed from Manifesto members' conflicting urges. One was loyalty to the leadership (a reflection of a deeply loyalist tradition). However, its members were initially those who had largely supported the defeated George Brown against Harold Wilson in 1963 and, in 1980, had favoured Healey in the final ballot against the victorious Foot. This was in stark contrast to the formative experience of many of them, who – in their younger personae – had been active in CDS. At that time, their loyalty to the leadership and their faith in Hugh Gaitskell came together in their shared position on defence. There was for them no conflict between loyalty and the incumbent Leader.

In the 1970s, an event within the PLP created the Manifesto Group: Tribune's surprise success in getting the veteran left-winger Ian Mikardo elected Chairman of the PLP after the February 1974 election.[4] The Tribune Group never had a majority of MPs (in 1977 it printed a list of 80 members) but the right had carelessly nominated 4 candidates (Arthur Bottomley, Fred Willey, Tom Urwin and Willie Hamilton). When the temporary Chair of the PLP meeting announced (contrary to normal practice although apparently without a shade of conspiracy or ill-intent) it was first-past-the-post, the right for once was too disorganised to react, leaving Mikardo home and dry. This was no sinister plot by the left but poor tactics by the right, who were then determined not to let that happen again. The centre-right majority had been organising votes for PLP positions, to counter the Tribune Group, with regular success. A no-name group had met informally in the tea-room to pass on intelligence and discuss tactics, voting slates and gossip. Jim Wellbeloved, Dickson Mabon, John Horam and others from this network formed the core of what became the Manifesto Group. So, after the Mikardo victory, when a first formal meeting was called, in the words of its first Chairman, Mabon, we just 'knew who to invite'.[5]

After the October 1974 election, the Manifesto Group – initially acting slightly informally – immediately regained the Chairmanship (with Cledwyn Hughes).

Then, in the November election for the backbench members of the joint government–backbench Liaison Committee, they also won the Vice-Chairmanship (Tam Dalyell) and took the next three positions (Willey, Mabon and Wellbeloved), leaving just two places for Tribune's defeated PLP Chairman, Mikardo, and Frank Allaun.

This was back to 'normality'. Part of the shock of Mikardo's March 1974 success had been its unusualness. For example, elections for the 1972 Shadow Cabinet (or the Parliamentary Committee as it appears in the rules) showed the right in firm control. *Tribune* described these results as 'obtained by a skilfully organised and determined campaign' by past members of the right-wing CDS; who made every effort to portray the contest as a final battle against the party falling into the hands of the left. An analysis of the MPs' voting patterns demonstrated how, by plumping for 7 of the 12 slots, together with judicious abstentions, the organised right ensured the election of the hard-line Marketeer, Harold Lever, as well as Shirley Williams, thus moving the centre-right Shadow Cabinet towards a more Euro-friendly position.[6]

The wake-up call from the first 1974 PLP chairmanship election, together with other trends in the party, consolidated the need for a more organised response from the right. Initially meeting with neither a name nor any officers, a group convened by Mabon and Wellbeloved decided that the Tribune Group could be contained only if the right marshalled its forces. Dickson Mabon recalled that 'however deep our heads were buried in the sands, we realised we had now lost control. So we said, all right, now let's do it.'[7] The main players were old hands at political organising, whether through student politics (Alan Lee Williams, Ian Wrigglesworth and Mike Thomas), in CDS (Denis Howell and Jim Wellbeloved) or within the Labour movement (John Cartwright and John Roper in the co-operative movement, Giles Radice in the unions). Mabon, the Group's first Chairman, had been left out of the 1974 ministerial appointments (no doubt reflecting his criticisms of Wilson) and was therefore available as a respected backbencher to attract widespread support.

It was not until after the October 1984 general election (and the Group's immediate success in regaining the PLP chairmanship) that named officers, a paper on the Group's purpose and its title emerged. Bill Rodgers claims authorship of the nomenclature, writing of the Group: 'My only contribution – as a minister I was excluded from formal membership – had been to suggest its name'.[8] However, the name reflected the members' defensiveness.[9] They could – despite the party's move to the left and its adoption of a more left-wing programme – live with the manifesto on which they had fought the 1974 election. But they wanted none of the further leftward shifts they felt around them. The importance of 'keeping to the manifesto' in Labour parlance did not identify them as right wing and, importantly, emphasised their loyalist nature, a leader's mandate being to implement the party's programme as contained in the manifesto. Hence support for that was a nod to the importance of conference decisions whilst expressing loyalty to the leadership – despite the then leader, Harold Wilson, having been the choice of few of the Group following Gaitskell's death in 1963.

To appreciate the defensiveness of these MPs – especially in relation to party activists and the NEC – it is important to remember the shift in party membership, to a younger, less deferential, more educated and articulate group, as a generation radicalised by the 1960s made their presence felt in small, sometimes moribund, local parties. Overlying this had been the frustration with the latter years of the 1966–70 Wilson government, damaged by in-fighting, the 1969 fall-out with the unions and the government's failure to criticise the US over Vietnam. It had not seemed like a government worth championing – even to some of the newer, centre-right MPs such as David Owen,[10] let alone the radical activists. The Manifesto Group, therefore, despite the majority it could deliver within the PLP, started life on the backfoot. Largely Euro-philes in a party of Euro-sceptics, Atlanticists in a party of unilateralists and about to challenge the moves to reselection of sitting MPs – they were not swimming with the tide.

Having selected its officers (Chairman Dickson Mabon, Secretary John Horam and Treasurer Neville Sandelson) and name, the Group was formally constituted at a well-attended meeting in Westminster Hall when its membership agreed to register as a group with the secretary of the PLP (depriving Tribune of its status as the only permanent organised PLP faction), its formation being recorded as 17 December 1974.[11] Its stated objectives (it could hardly say: 'to run slates') were:

> To work for the implementation of the policies . . . in the . . . manifesto and to support the Labour government in overcoming the country's acute economic difficulties;
> To act as a forum for constructive discussion designed to relate democratic social-ist philosophy to the needs of the present age;
> To endeavour to achieve a truly democratic socialist society through our represen-tative parliamentary system.

An early list identifies 72 members – though some subsequently resigned on becoming ministers. As it was (unlike Tribune) confined to backbenchers, its true list of supporters – or 'friends' as they are called in the papers and who received the agreed list of candidates for posts – was much higher with ministers included.[12]

Labour was in government during the Group's formative years, and facing that divisive issue: Europe. In opposition, following Roy Jenkins' and 68 other Labour MPs' vote with the Conservative government on 28 October 1971 to take the UK into the European Community, the party had, at Tony Benn's urging, decided in favour of a referendum on continued membership (causing Jenkins' resignation as Deputy Leader). Now in government, the party and Cabinet had to decide how to campaign in the 1975 referendum. A special party conference in April 1975 voted overwhelmingly against the government's renegotiated terms for remaining in Europe – despite opinion polls showing a 2:1 majority in favour of staying in, with Labour voters 5:3 in favour.[13] Tribune's 77 members (a quarter of the PLP, some-what swelled by the 1974 intakes) were delighted but it heralded a new round of disputes between MPs and their constituency parties.

One of the first to be affected was Reg Prentice. His was a cause close to the heart of many Manifesto members. The Group's Treasurer, Neville Sandelson (who would later experience similar problems before defecting to the SDP), asked the

Prime Minister to allow ministers to sign a statement in support of the beleaguered MP, who had fallen foul of his local party because of his right-wing views. Harold Wilson's response went wider and dealt with his role as a member of the NEC as well as his views on small local party membership. Hoping the NEC would not intervene, Wilson wrote that, should it do so, 'I propose to depart from a rule I have strictly followed since I became Leader . . . not . . . to intervene . . . in matters of party organisation, relations with constituency parties, the selection of candidates, proceedings in relation to candidates or Members of Parliament.' His rule would be broken because he felt himself duty bound to raise the question of actions by small, not necessarily representative, groups of members who had a degree of power within a constituency. He recalled his concern about small parties, especially in safe seats, being unrepresentative of the mass of Labour voters. His 1955 report had recommended that CLPs' membership should be at least one-twelfth of the Labour vote. In Reg Prentice's Newham CLP, 'this would mean a membership of 1,850, which would involve a greater degree of democratic control'. He stressed that the problem of small membership needed to be tackled urgently and went on to draw a distinction between the selection of a candidate and 'one who has received in a parliamentary election, the stamp of the electorate. Perverse action seeking to dismiss an M.P. can get very close indeed to constitutional interference in the rights and duty of an elected member.'[14] A strong statement of support for the rights of MPs in relation to local parties, and music to the ears of the Group.

Bill Rodgers, meanwhile, was making a distinction between the legitimate left and 'a relatively small number of activists, many of them new to the party but rich in experience of fringe politics . . . [who] do not share the democratic assumptions of the "legitimate" left . . . The clearest evidence of a new-style politics . . . has been the uncompromising attack on the position of a number of MPs.' Rodgers predicted that this new situation 'threatens the party of [Nye] Bevan as much as the party of Gaitskell', believing that 'the heirs of Bevan . . . should support the heirs of Gaitskell and help rally wider opinion'. The call went unheeded by the 'legitimate' left and would lie at the root of further divisions within the party. Rodgers called for new safeguards for MPs, with a joint NEC–PLP Conciliation Committee replacing rules which 'institutionalise conflict and treat human situations like a court of law'. What was most needed was to 'rally the party and to save it from enemies masquerading as friends. What is at stake is not a temporary phenomenon, characteristic of the ebb and flow of opinion within the Labour movement throughout its history, but a sustained attempt to destroy the movement from within.'[15] Writing long after the split, Rodgers reflected that 'this "legitimate left" failed to acknowledge that they had more in common with Shirley, myself and our friends than with the Trotskyites and other factions of the hard left'.[16]

Militant was high in the Manifesto Group's preoccupations. The NEC was to tolerate infiltration, despite protests from the Group, until the right began to change its political make-up in 1981/82. In 1976 the Manifesto Group protested helplessly at the NEC's decision to appoint the Militant Andy Bevan to its staff. Another concern was party policy. The Group submitted a Memorandum, drafted by Giles Radice, to Wilson in May 1975 which set out their view that a major economic initiative was needed. The Memorandum recommended a wages policy; bringing forward proposed public expenditure cuts; consideration of temporary and selective import controls; modernisation of industry; a larger role for the National Economic Development Council; and progress on industrial democracy.

Outside parliament, local parties were becoming more questioning of their MPs whilst the left-controlled NEC was giving the government headaches. Even before he became Leader, Callaghan, as Treasurer and hence on the NEC, was reprimanding it for 'leaping on every bandwagon that happens to be rolling by' instead of supporting the Labour government. He called on the NEC to be 'willing to defend the Government and explain the facts to the movement at large'.[17]

However, the purpose of the Manifesto Group was neither to get involved in CLPs, nor in the NEC, but – despite the lofty aims extolled for public consumption – to counter the Tribune Group and to marshal the moderate majority within the PLP for elections. 'Slates' were therefore its meat and drink. In general the Group was highly successful in this. In the Liaison Committee elections in November 1975, for example, Manifesto member Fred Willey topped the poll – thus becoming PLP Vice-Chairman – with the Group making a clean sweep of the remaining places, ousting the former PLP Chairman, Mikardo.

There were exceptions to this success. Two major obstacles faced them in the more significant PLP votes – for the leader and deputy leader of the party. One was the lack of a single leader. The other was the desire of some of the centre-right to support a left candidate to produce a more consensual leadership team.

Much has been written – most notably by Radice – about the rivalry between Roy Jenkins, Tony Crosland and Denis Healey.[18] Nowhere was this more obvious, or as damaging to the right-wing cause, than in the 1976 leadership election following Wilson's resignation. Ian Wrigglesworth, who had taken over as Manifesto Group Secretary, was Parliamentary Private Secretary (PPS) to Jenkins and played a key role in his campaign, as did Alan Lee Williams and John Horam. Other of their Manifesto colleagues worked equally assiduously for Healey, Crosland and for the eventual winner, Jim Callaghan (Jim Wellbeloved, John Smith, Roy Hattersley and Cledwyn Hughes).[19] Furthermore, some 19 centre and right MPs supported Foot on the first ballot – and as many as 30 in the run-off[20] – thus signalling a further split amongst the centre-right, with some registering 'none of the above' to Radice's trio of giants.

Callaghan's final 176:137 victory over Foot reflected the essential non-left majority in the PLP. Yet it took three ballots to reach and it saw the centre-right supporting four candidates in the first round to the left's two, and two (Callaghan and Healey) in the second round to the left's one. This was not an efficient marshalling of forces. The difference between this and internal PLP elections partly reflects the greater scrutiny by CLPs eager to know their MP's voting intention, with MPs from marginal seats keen to keep their activists happy – which they calculated a Foot victory would achieve. The result brought to a close conflicting electioneering by Manifesto members. However, it posed a question mark over the Group's existence, with the newly elected Prime Minister Callaghan calling for all such groups to wind themselves up.[21] Mabon immediately responded: 'We will dissolve the day after the Tribune Group dissolves.'[22] To which the new Prime Minister replied 'Quite right!'[23] Mabon's own ministerial career was secure but a number of MPs were concerned that, despite a number having campaigned for Callaghan, continued Manifesto Group activity might lead to a lack of preferment.[24] The Group also had difficulty in recruiting amongst the 1974 intakes – thus leaving it unattractive to both senior and newer MPs.

The second major vote, by MPs but with an impact beyond the PLP, was for deputy leader (which carried an NEC seat) following the resignation of Ted Short. This took place in December 1976. Despite the centre-right majority amongst MPs and her popularity in the country, Shirley Williams lost by 128:166 to the left-wing Michael Foot. It was reported that Callaghan favoured Foot, as conduit to the left and to union leaders, and to maintain some semblance of party unity by binding him closer to the leadership.[25] Despite the result, the Manifesto Group professed itself pleased with Williams' showing, which positioned her as a clear runner against any future left challenger such as Benn. However, with hindsight, the Group's inability to deliver for its own candidate presaged the leadership election which would follow four years later.

The Manifesto Group turned its attention to the next PLP elections, and to policy. It issued a statement in October 1976 on economic policy, *Keep on Course*, which called for curbs on inflation, reduction in borrowing and selective import controls plus an import deposit scheme. Success in internal elections continued, November 1976 seeing Cledwyn Hughes re-elected unopposed as Chairman of the PLP,[26] with fellow Manifesto Group member Fred Willey topping the Liaison Committee poll, and thus remaining Vice-Chairman. Manifesto members made a clean sweep of the remaining backbench places, with Tribune's entire slate defeated.

The Group was well established in the PLP's life, meeting weekly – at 6.30 pm on Wednesdays – to discuss 'Next Week's Business' (the standard agenda item for parliament, Shadow Cabinet and the PLP, covering the parliamentary timetable and voting arrangements), elections to PLP groups and the European Assembly and similar delegations, as well as policy. Their own elections also took place and, at the end of 1976, Sydney Irving became Chairman. A decision was taken to admit peers into membership, which was to see some 20 join by mid-1978, including (Dora) Gaitskell and former CDS member (Patrick) Gordon-Walker.

Increasingly, attention turned to party management and candidate selection (welcoming, if not endorsing, a call for all-member ballots for selections as early as October 1976). In December there was a lengthy discussion on Militant, and agreement on the need to field candidates in NEC elections. Recognising that unless the NEC took action Militant would not be tackled, 30 of the Group's number signed a resolution that noted 'with grave concern recent reports of infiltration into the party by extremist groups and calls upon the NEC in conjunction with the PLP to investigate the situation with a view to taking remedial action including a review of the rules governing the selection and reselection of parliamentary candidates'.[27]

Early in 1977 the Group made its most public appearance – and a break with its purpose of organising votes – with a pamphlet, *What We Must Do*. For academic audiences, this might be most noteworthy for its illustrious authorship: (later

Professor) David Marquand, (later Professor) Bryan Magee, John Roper, John Horam, (former Professor) John Mackintosh and Giles Radice. Politically, its significance lay in the recognition that the centre-right was ideologically barren after the IMF crisis; Keynesianism had been defeated and old-style Croslandism-in-one-country was in disarray. The left had all the good tunes – they had the Alternative Economic Strategy. The centre-right needed an ideological position. So it came out for a kind of marriage between Keynesianism and Monetarism. The publication was intended to take the social democratic case out to the wider move-ment where *Tribune* had been left a free hand. The pamphlet was well covered in the press.[25] It also reflected the impact made by John Wakefield, who had been appointed because of his 'intellectual spark' which the Group felt the right needed (over the favourite, Alec McGivan – later CLV Secretary), as a Rowntree-funded researcher/administrator to the Group.

The pamphlet was probably linked to the February 1977 establishment of the CLV, whose arrival was not greeted with universal delight within the Group. Some were upset at not having been informed in advance. Others were alarmed that attention on a non-Tribunite organisation would shine the spotlight on them within their CLPs, where their membership of the Group had been a well-kept secret. Nevertheless, given that the Manifesto Group was solely parliamentary, the majority view was that a constituency-based sister organisation should be wel-comed. Many of the key players were the same – especially CLV's two convenors, John Cartwright and Ian Wrigglesworth, Manifesto Vice-Chairman and Secretary respectively. From March onwards, a CLV report normally appeared on the Group's agendas so that members were updated on activities.

During 1977 the Manifesto Group discussed a wide range of issues at its weekly meetings, including industrial democracy, direct elections to the European Assem-bly, the Budget, the Lib–Lab Pact, pay policy, and internal party matters such as candidate selections, NEC elections and the Underhill report on Militant, which the Group urged should be published. More discreet matters were also raised. A cryptic, handwritten note on the Secretary's 11 May 1977 agenda reads: 'Peter Jay – tell D.O. [David Owen] privately'. It is hard not to infer some disapproval of the Foreign Secretary's appointment of Prime Minister Callaghan's son-in-law (Jay was married to Callaghan's daughter, Margaret) as the UK Ambassador in Washington. The Group also had guest speakers (such as Cabinet Ministers Eric Varley, David Owen and Denis Healey).

In November 1977, at the beginning of the parliamentary year, John Cartwright took over as Chairman from Sydney Irving. Cartwright was therefore a pivotal figure, being a member of the NEC (representing the Socialist Societies), PPS to Shirley Williams, active in CLV and the figurehead of the Manifesto Group. On becoming Chairman he outlined his priorities: to campaign in the country about the government; the manifesto for the next election; and reform of the party struc-ture. The latter had been a long interest of his, as he helped to produce *The Mechanics of Victory* in 1962.[29]

The Group's success continued with another clean sweep of the Liaison Com-mittee in 1977. A similar range of activities took place in 1978, with ministerial speakers Bill Rodgers and Roy Hattersley, together with discussions on European elections, immigration, industrial democracy and the party's Working Party on reselection. The Group was vehement in its protest about there being only three, rather than the requested seven, PLP representatives on this. Internal party matters had become the dividing line between the Group and the NEC. In July 1978, Secretary Wrigglesworth wrote to the party General Secretary protesting against Jimmy Reid's adoption as parliamentary candidate for Dundee East, as he lacked the required two years' party membership (having been in the Communist Party). Hayward's curt reply ('I acknowledge receipt of your letter of 20 July . . . I appreciate the propaganda motive in sending me this letter but I know you will also appreciate that I cannot recognise any group apart from our official group which is, of course, the Parliamentary Labour Party') was a deliberate put-down. Wrigglesworth's letter was ignored by the NEC, which endorsed the candidature by 12:6 votes.

The November 1978 AGM re-elected Cartwright as Chairman for what would prove a difficult year. 1979 started with a protest about the PLP's exclusion from the adoption process for the European Manifesto for the first direct elections – undermining the traditional NEC/PLP balance guaranteed by Clause V of the constitution. Major work took place on a March pre-election statement, 'Priorities for Labour', on economic and industrial policy. This stated starkly: 'We believe the Labour Party must be the party of permanent incomes policy'[30] and dealt with import controls, nationalisation and compulsory planning agreements (against all of them), favouring public spending, reform of the Common Agricultural Policy, tax reform and industrial democracy.

All was of no avail as the Labour government was swept away on 3 May 1979, following the Winter of Discontent and the failure of the government's incomes policy, by Thatcher's overall majority of 43 (71 seats more than Labour). Ministers lost their cars; Shirley Williams lost her seat; but Ian Wrigglesworth continued to organise. Within days, he was marking off a list of new MPs as: wet-centre, hard centre-left, OK (Tom McNally, a former Number 10 political advisor), soft-left, ambitious-left (Jack Straw), centre-left (Frank Dobson) and, delightfully, 'eccentric centre' (Dale Campbell-Savours). His list of the whole PLP, old and new, shows 149 from the right and centre, made up by 64 from the Manifesto Group and 85 from a broader centre-right. By contrast, his list of the left totalled 94, with 57 from Tribune and 37 others from the centre-left, leaving an unknown 25 from the depleted complement of 268. A comfortable centre-right majority.

Despite Wrigglesworth's prediction, McNally claims never to have joined the Manifesto Group (though he attended an early meeting). Partly McNally attributes this to not being a joining type, and to his distaste for some of its members such as Sandelson. But mostly it was because he was under intense pressure from his new GC (having been too close to the last government) and could not risk being linked to a centre-right group.[31] In fact every new MP declined to join[32] although Roger Thomas wrote that on crucial occasions, such as voting the Shadow Cabinet, he would support their slate. It was not simply new members who held back. Former ministers could now join, but Healey held aloof. Seeing factions at work on the

NEC, when a party employee decades earlier, had made him very anti all such groups. He also slightly mistrusted those running it – claiming to have been correct because John Horam and Reg Prentice later joined the Conservatives (and many more the SDP). Like McNally, he too found Sandelson very odd – demonstrating that the Group's Treasurer was not the most effective recruiting sergeant. Even so, by 13 June 1979 the Group had 59 members and 81 supporters.

The first post-election meeting in May 1979, chaired by Wrigglesworth, had 40 in attendance, including a good number of former ministers (such as Peter Archer, David Ennals, John Golding, Roy Hattersley, David Owen, Bill Rodgers and Sam Silkin), although there was a lack of new members. Discussion turned to the forthcoming Shadow Cabinet elections as well as to the Group's role. On the former, there was a lengthy debate about whether to run a slate, and if so whether to have a full slate of 12, or just 9 so as to allow some non-aligned members to be elected. Pat Duffy was against any slate for this first round as this would offend non-members (especially amongst the trade union group). In contrast, Jack Ashley strongly favoured a slate, if only of 9 names, whilst Fred Willey thought a slate of 12 was needed as that was what Tribune would have. Most others supported a slate for this popularity contest, including Bruce Douglas-Mann, who wanted a list of 9 to leave space for people like Peter Shore and John Silkin – who were anti-European but attracted broad support.

Regarding the Group's purpose, John Golding argued it should give voice to the silent majority as well as fight elections whilst Mabon stressed the need to make speeches to outdo the left. Mike Thomas wanted the Group to become a broader church as well as a source of ideas. Denis Howell was already looking outside of parliament and warned of the parlous state of the party and, in particular, of union leaders having opted out of the struggle. Bryan Magee reminded them of the need to oppose the Conservative government as well as Tribune, whilst Peter Archer stressed they should get rid of the idea of the Group being less socialist as it was in main tradition. David Ennals wanted the Group to do some policy thinking because Transport House wouldn't, whilst others wanted links with unions. David Owen correctly predicted that the EEC would be the great issue but pleaded that it not be allowed to divide the Group. Despite being temperamentally opposed to groups, Roy Hattersley conceded that they needed them to organise. That evening after the meeting, Wrigglesworth wrote to supporters asking for support for Fred Willey (as Chairman of the PLP) and Michael Cocks (as Chief Whip). Both were elected comfortably – Willey by 151 to Tribunite Norman Buchan's 87; Cocks by 188 to Martin Flannery's 44.

The next meeting, on 21 May, had 32 present including, for the first time, John Smith (as a minister he had not been eligible to join). It voted by 23:3 that members could not be ordered to refrain from standing for the Shadow Cabinet, and decided on a slate of just 9, despite Wellbeloved's support for the maximum of 12. Those selected to be 'recommended to members and friends' were former ministers Hattersley, Healey, Mabon, Mason, Owen, Rees, Rodgers, Smith and Varley. There was some discussion about the remaining places and the need to ensure that three Tribunites did not top the poll. The meeting also agreed that the Shadow

Cabinet could be full members, though whether they could hold office was left open.

The slate was circulated by Wrigglesworth on 24 May, adding that in choosing nine the Group recognised that members might wish to support individual personal preferences in addition to the slate. All but Mabon were elected, the remaining places going to John Silkin and Peter Shore (in second and third place to Healey's first, suggesting strong Manifesto support though also a strong anti-European sentiment in the PLP as both were known sceptics). Only Stan Orme and Albert Booth from Tribune were elected. John Silkin later boasted that during this period he was the only MP elected who was not on a slate.[33] He was not as generous with his own votes: 'A scrutineer at a Shadow Cabinet election noticed a ballot paper with a single cross for Silkin and was assured . . . that this was his habitual practice'.[34]

The June AGM re-elected Cartwright as Chairman, with George Robertson replacing Wrigglesworth as Secretary, the latter having stood down after three years. Robertson, a former official with the GMWU, was a formidable organiser. There was a distinct northern flavour to the Group, reflecting its traditional moderate stance. Horam (who was TGWU sponsored), Radice (GMWU sponsored) and Wrigglesworth represented the North East, supported by strong regions of the TGWU and GMWU. Such solid back-up would be needed in the months ahead.

A new political landscape confronted the Group. Firstly, there was the shock of electoral defeat with the recognition that the party needed to re-engage with voters if it was to win in 1983/84. Secondly, an increasing number of members were under pressure from their local parties. Thirdly, an enormous debate was taking place on democratising the party – demands for mandatory reselection, NEC control over the manifesto and a wider franchise for the election of the leader. The Group concentrated on influencing the PLP discussions on these, but also collaborated with CLV in producing a joint statement, 'Reform and democracy in the Labour Party'. Its opening words were: 'The Labour Party in 1979 is at the crossroads'. It hinted that a lengthy period of opposition might be in prospect, pointing to declining membership, poor organisation and weak finances, and asserted: 'We cannot accept the allegation that Labour Governments have consistently betrayed the platforms on which they were elected'.[35]

This marked clear water between the Group and the predominant Bennite position. The paper recognised the failure to find a solution to problems of low growth and slowly rising living standards, but went on to concentrate on internal party matters, pointing to the 1979 general and European election results as being the worst since the 1930s, and to a party £1 million in debt. The system of electing the NEC was criticised for failing to provide a proper balance of opinions. The left-wing majority on the NEC was taken to task for failing to face up to the party's multifarious problems – financial and Militant (the report on which the NEC had refused to publish) – as well as acting as if it were in permanent opposition to the Labour government. The paper rebutted the proposals for constitutional change and proposed its own 'Agenda for reform'. This encompassed increasing membership (so that CLPs were representative of Labour voters), restructuring the NEC to make it representative of party opinion (creating PLP and local government sections) and improving policy-making to enable proposals to be discussed with the PLP and TUC before adoption.

Meanwhile, debate raged within the PLP. On 19 June, Benn and Heffer called for the full PLP to have final authority over the day-to-day work of the party in the Commons; the right to discuss all proposed appointments; shadow ministers to be elected by *open* ballot; portfolios to be agreed by the PLP; and subject groups to recommend frontbench speakers for debates and to nominate for positions on committees. In addition, no names should be proposed for peerages, there should be regular NEC/Shadow Cabinet meetings, and Shadow Cabinet staff (then employed by the individual MPs) should become party staff. Their paper envisaged these changes continuing when the party was in office.[36] Perhaps the most far-reaching proposal would have been the open ballots. The comfortable centre-right majority in the PLP produced through confidential voting would hardly survive scrutiny from left-wing CLPs. The centre-right controlled the Shadow Cabinet, and the Benn–Heffer paper envisaged it losing virtually all its powers, as well as its staff.

While the Bennite/CLPD proposals had been debated in the press and at party conferences, this paper now put the PLP itself on the agenda. It spurred the right into action. A flurry of meetings and papers swirled around the House, with MPs Mike Thomas, Phillip Whitehead and Giles Radice submitting a four-page memorandum on 'The working of the PLP' in July. This was no defence of the *status quo*, as it recognised the lack of democracy within the parliamentary party. Neither was it about MPs' relationships with other parts of the movement (the unions, CLPs or conference) although it deplored the suggestion that Labour MPs should be intimidated by the removal of secret ballots in PLP elections. The authors' proposals were hardly far reaching. They called for a formal agenda for PLP meetings, more consultation of the PLP by government, increased backbench input into policy, and an extension of Clause V to give a greater role to the whole of the PLP (not just the Shadow or actual Cabinet) in the manifesto process. The paper went some way towards the Benn proposals, with backbench groups nominating to parliamentary committees and wider consultation before portfolios were allocated. It also suggested an increase of the Shadow Cabinet to 15 elected members, with up to 3 additional spokesmen appointed by the leader, and agreed that funds for the opposition from parliament should be deployed for that purpose and an annual budget approved by the PLP, with consideration given to a new, elected post of PLP Treasurer. So the paper, overall, was a pale shadow of the Benn–Heffer document, with no radical alternatives on offer.

Consideration of these matters was something of a sideshow as the debate on the three major constitutional reforms was taking hold within the wider party. The centre-right felt particularly unsupported by the PLP leadership. On 25 July 1979, a strongly worded letter, signed by 107 MPs, was sent to Callaghan. This expressed their deep concern about the changes in the constitutional position of Labour MPs and of the PLP being advocated, and went on:

we believe the time has come for you and the Parliamentary Committee to make it clear to the NEC that to make changes of the kind proposed – on the PLP's rights over the party Manifesto, on reselection of MPs and on the election of the party leader – would be to reduce the [PLP] to the role of poodle of the Party Conference and to move dangerously close to making individual MPs mandated delegates on pain of losing their jobs.

The letter called on the leadership to take these views to the wider party and concluded that as the NEC proposals were designed to upset the careful balance between the different roles of the components of the party, 'They comprise a major threat to the unity of the party. The time has come to say to this group on the NEC that "enough is enough". Over 100 MPs – for once unafraid to be named – represented a significant expression of opinion (which would have been even larger had the Shadow Cabinet been able to sign – by convention they never signed round-robins) and effectively positioned the Manifesto Group as the majority voice in the PLP. But it had little impact. The House rose for the summer and the party conference, where the left's agenda would be in the ascendancy.

Rodgers described the 1979 Brighton Conference as

a disaster . . . Although the proposal on the election of the leader was [temporarily] lost, resolutions on mandatory reselection and the manifesto were carried. Conference also established a Commission of Enquiry on organisation and finance . . . [however] the NEC minimised the role of parliamentarians on it and ensured that it had a built-in majority of the left. Apart from the Leader and Deputy Leader, none of the 19 MPs on the NEC sufficiently command the support of their own parliamentary colleagues to get elected to the Shadow Cabinet, and 14 were unequivocally on the left.[37]

There seemed little impact the PLP could make within the wider party. But in the Commons, the Manifesto Group's work continued, with Robertson circulating a list of candidates for the chairmanships of PLP Subject Groups to sympathisers at the end of the recess, and a call for a full attendance at a vital PLP meeting at the end of October, with a special plea to stay until the end and vote. He similarly wrote urging votes for Radice, Thomas, Urwin and Whitehead for the five backbench places on the internal enquiry (leaving a fifth place for others).

As matters deteriorated, with the NEC and PLP moving further apart, the Group discussed its response. In November members worked on their evidence to the Commission of Enquiry set up at the 1979 conference and sought a meeting with the Party Leader, Callaghan, about the state of the party. At the time, Giles Radice, the Vice-Chairman, thought that their main task might simply be to get all the Manifesto Group members reselected.

It was at this time, as the NEC–CLPD proposals gained ground, that the first warnings appear of what was later to happen. First there was the 22 November 1979 Dimbleby Lecture when Jenkins first floated the idea of a breakaway party. Earlier that day, John Horam, a Manifesto Group Vice-Chairman, told Rodgers 'that the Labour Party was finished'.[38] A key staging-post can be seen in Rodgers' speech in Abertillery. In the very town that some see as the home of Labour in Wales,[39] the former CDS organiser, Cabinet minister and political-fixer predicted that the party had 'a year . . . in which to save itself . . . A year to start winning friends amongst the ... 30 million ... who did not vote Labour last time'. He warned that 'A party of the far left – in which Tribune members would be the moderates – would have little electoral appeal . . . If the hard-line leaders of the left want a fight to the finish, they can have it. But if as a result they should split the party, they should not suppose that the inheritance will be theirs.'[40]

If not before, it was clear from this date that senior Manifesto members could envisage a split within the party. In private there were more signs. The day after his Abertillery speech, in a meeting with Roy Jenkins and Shirley Williams, Rodgers found himself discussing the prospects for a new party which could survive without trade union money.[41] From then on, it is hard to believe the Manifesto Group could have succeeded in holding the social democrats within the party, given the views of their leading lights. Furthermore, the chance of it attracting any more supporters ended with such open talk of a split. Behind the scenes, even more planning was taking place, with a group meeting in West London around former MPs Michael Barnes and Colin Phipps, the former having circulated to a select group a paper on 'A new centre party' which was discussed on 6 January 1980.

Before the year-end, Rodgers – stalwart of the parliamentary right and of the constituency-focused CLV – was to have another public fall-out with the party. On 12 December 1979, one of Labour's election broadcasts carried a strong anti-European message. The Shadow Cabinet Member wrote angrily to Callaghan the next day condemning the broadcast as appalling and irrelevant to a by-election. More fundamental was his charge that it seemed deliberately designed to divide the party. Whilst recognising that the Common Market was unpopular, and seeing no objection in exploiting that, Rodgers distinguished that from the party positioning itself as against membership on principle and being ready to consider pulling out.

If 1979 appeared stressful, it was only a gentle preparation for 1980. Nowhere were the issues as clearly contested as in the Manifesto Group, which brought together the pro-Europe right, aghast at the NEC and conference decisions, but faced with two emerging alternatives: to stay and continue the fight to bring the party back to where it had a chance of being elected, or to take the risk of creating a new party, without union affiliates but able to capitalise on the electorate's emerging anti-Thatcher feelings. The arguments were strongest within the Manifesto Group, as these were the key MPs whose defection, or continuation, would 'make or break' any new party.

In early 1980 Manifesto meetings exhibited uncertainty, worry and overwhelming isolation. Recognising that the left had made all the running in party debates, members also acknowledged that they lacked the backing of union leaders and were failing to attract non-left PLP members, evidenced by the creation of an alternative centre grouping (the 'soggy middle' in Phillip Whitehead's words), Labour First. The Group's right-wing image put off many MPs and helped split the non-left. The formation of Labour First led to difficulties in agreeing the November slate for the Shadow Cabinet – a serious weakness just when the moderates needed to be at their strongest. The PLP was preparing its submission to the Commission of Enquiry, and thus the centre-right needed a concerted voice.

The NEC meanwhile sought to formalise groups within the PLP and wrote seeking details of staffing, funding and objectives. The Group's May 1980 response set out the original three aims, confirmed that membership was open to MPs and peers who took the Labour Whip, listed the officers' names and, somewhat sadly, recorded no finances other than membership subscriptions and a tiny amount from sales of publications, the Rowntree funding for a research assistant having ended after the 1979 general election.

The less-remembered first Wembley conference, in May 1980, unsettled Manifesto members. Summoned to endorse the party's 'Peace, Jobs, Freedom' policy statement, it represented the adoption of a further left policy agenda but, more significantly, reflected the tone of debate then current in the party.[42] 'The new brutishness was very much on show.'[43] At one point, Militant delegate Terry Fields (speaking immediately before the present author who herself was well barracked) shouted to the right to 'Get out of our Movement. There is no place in it for you. Cross the House of Commons, join Prentice'.[44] The treatment meted out to David Owen was a significant factor in his move from the Labour Party.[45]

In June, Rodgers opened and Owen wound up a Group discussion on 'The present position within the party'. Later meetings reflected the Group's mounting concerns. Neville Sandelson, openly admitting to panicking, confessed he couldn't decide between cutting his throat or taking an overdose but nevertheless urged colleagues to stand and fight. The MP told the press that the NEC was dividing the Labour movement and sickening Labour supporters. He called the party's ruling body 'malevolent', having 'diseased the party with its support for Communists, Trots and psychotic anti-social elements who have flooded in and [with] its espousal of ideologies which will destroy us at the polls' and warned that unless the composition of the NEC changed in the autumn, 'the Labour Party will break up. There is no chance of winning the next election with this poisonous bunch dictating our policies.'[46] His colleagues might not have argued with his analysis, but it was exactly such intemperate language which put some MPs off the Manifesto Group. His six-year spell as Treasurer of the Group ended at this time; he was replaced in July by the more emollient Ken Weetch.

The PLP and the Electoral College

However, the major preoccupation for the centre-right was what was happening in the wider party and on the Commission of Enquiry where, to their dismay, Callaghan (and subsequently the Shadow Cabinet) had accepted the concept of an Electoral College to choose the leader. David Basnett, GMWU General Secretary, had already swung behind a College giving 50 per cent to the PLP with 25 per cent each to CLPs and unions, leaving the Manifesto wing of the PLP increasingly isolated over this issue. As rumours of the Commission accepting an Electoral College circulated, the Group condemned the outcome as profoundly unsatisfactory with grave implications for the relationship of the different parts of the party. It feared it could undermine the party's commitment to parliamentary democracy. Furthermore, it felt the Commission was at variance with the view of the PLP, which had overwhelmingly rejected the proposal of an Electoral College. The Group, in vain, called on the Commission to produce proposals which would win support across the whole party.[47]

During the summer recess members were busy, with two major newspaper initiatives. The first was the 'Open letter to their fellow members of the Labour Party' from Williams, Rodgers and Owen in the *Guardian*,[48] which labelled them the 'Gang of Three'. The second, in *The Times*, led to what became known as the 'Dirty Dozen' statement.[49] This article on 'Why the Labour party structure must change' not only appeared to accept the possibility of a new centre party, but it downplayed the likelihood of the centre-right making gains in the forthcoming NEC elections and also questioned the union role in financing the party and casting block votes at conference. Pointing to the historically low level of membership, it queried whether the party could claim to represent Labour voters. The article proposed six changes to the party's structure, including OMOV for the selection of candidates, restructuring the NEC (to represent ordinary members, MPs and local government) and the creation of a directly elected party chairman. All 12 of 'the Dozen' were senior Manifesto Group figures, including its Chairman Cartwright, Secretary Robertson, Vice-Chairman Horam and former Secretary Wrigglesworth.

Despite such centre-right initiatives, the October 1980 conference was a triumph for the left. Although they lost the vote on control of the manifesto, they won the principle of the Electoral College. Late in the day, the Manifesto Group had begun to consider an all-member OMOV to choose the leader, as an alternative to a College. However, as this would have completely removed the choice of leader from the PLP (and thus undermined their main argument), it didn't receive much support until it was far too late to be championed successfully. Owen and Rodgers called for choice of leader to be by complete OMOV (using the alternative vote system), for any candidate nominated by at least one-fifth of the PLP. Hattersley meanwhile accepted the wider franchise, with 55 per cent for the PLP and 45 per cent spread between other parts of the movement (the largest part to CLPs, with OMOV and split preferences used).[50] Tribunites John Silkin, Albert Booth and Stan Orme supported 40:30:30 (the PLP having the 40 per cent), leaving each GC to decide whether to ballot its own members. (Apparently forgetting his support for a minority for the PLP, Silkin later resented this outcome, complaining – when standing for the deputy leadership – of the time he had to spend touring CLPs and union conferences.[51]) As the PLP vote approached – on the Shadow Cabinet's motion for at least 50 per cent of the College to be for the PLP – 18 Manifesto members tabled an amendment that if OMOV were not assured, then the PLP declined to accept a wider franchise. In the PLP meeting, Willie Hamilton sought to have the in-principle decision for a College rerun, but Jack Straw urged support for the conference decision. The left tabled an amendment to reduce the PLP's proportion to a third but the PLP adopted the Shadow Cabinet's motion in November, when the Group was simultaneously busy ensuring the re-election of Fred Willey as Chairman of the PLP.

The last outing of the old rules to elect the party leader

In October it was, however, the leadership campaign which took precedence, following a disastrous conference for the right, and Callaghan's resignation on 15 October. The following day, Robertson wrote round to ensure a good turn-out for the coming PLP meetings (to halt attempts to elect an interim leader until an Electoral College be put into place). The officers confirmed the Group's position of not endorsing any one candidate (though Radice was known to be helping Healey's campaign[52]), but agreed to seek a meeting with each candidate to discuss the problem issues facing the party. Such meetings were surely meant to help Denis Healey, who largely shared their views. The Group agreed to draw up a list of questions to put to the candidates. Thomas wrote the first draft, opening, 'This election is being held at a time of crisis for the party and the nation' and stressing two major issues: firstly, parliamentary democracy and the constitution and democratic functioning of the Labour Party; and secondly, the credibility of the policies to be put to the electorate. He was emphatic about any leader's willingness to defend the independence of the PLP and individual MPs, and about the need to reform the NEC and policy-making – as well as some of the policies (such as renationalisation without compensation, unilateralism and exit from NATO).[53] On 20 October, a meeting turned Thomas' draft into a list of 16 questions – including on secret ballots, union block votes, rights of MPs, NEC restructuring, the PLP's rights, the EEC, unilateralism and incomes policy. The final two questions must have been aimed at Foot: 'Do you see yourself as a caretaker?' (a reference to a rumour that, if elected, Foot would stand aside for Benn); and 'Are there any personal factors – age, health – that you feel might inhibit your performance as leader?'

Whilst the questions were put to all four candidates, the greatest impact of the meetings was to alienate Healey's own supporters. The delegation, which included John Horam and Mike Thomas, got 'decidedly short shrift. Healey was trying hardest to get the votes of the centre, of people scared of their constituency parties, above all of party loyalists unhappy at the new snarling developments, but prejudiced against splitters. He thought and said to their faces that they had nowhere else to go'.[54] This might have cost him votes. Whilst Barry Jones from Healey's campaign team was asked by David Owen and Bill Rodgers to inspect their ballot papers to see they had voted for Healey, at least three MPs (Tom Ellis, Neville Sandelson and Jeffrey Thomas) who later left Labour, first voted against Healey.[55] Even for some who did vote for him, Healey's behaviour helped push them to show there was an alternative, by establishing the SDP (indeed, Mike Thomas nearly sent Healey a postcard the day the SDP was formed saying 'Have found somewhere else to go'). Healey's mishandling of his natural supporters, together with his refusal to pen an article for the *Guardian* or to issue a manifesto, was sufficient to make one of his own lieutenants, Phillip Whitehead, vote for Shore in the first ballot before supporting him in the decider.[56]

Foot's election on 10 November 1980 was the trigger for some members' subsequent defection.[57] For the entire Group, however, Healey's defeat was a body blow.

Nevertheless, the work of the members continued, Radice and Robertson touring the Commons to maintain the nerve and resolve of despairing members.[58]

In November, the Group met with Frank Chapple, one of its few supporters within the senior ranks of the unions. The December AGM opened with an obituary tribute to Lord Gordon-Walker, one of the Group's links to the predecessor CDS. Radice took over as Chairman from Cartwright (who was to leave the party within months), with Weetch elected Treasurer. An issue which pushed some beyond the pale was also aired. Rodgers had thought to join Owen in not standing for the Shadow Cabinet but was persuaded by John Roper and others to run. He did well, coming joint eighth – only to be offered what he considered low status or inappropriate portfolios (such as Northern Ireland) by the new Leader, Michael Foot. It was not just personally insulting; it sent a signal to his allies that they were not valued or even wanted within the party. For Roper, it was his psychological moment of departure.[59] A year earlier Ian Wrigglesworth had been criticising the number of left-wingers given frontbench positions by the centre-right Leader, Jim Callaghan; now a left-wing Leader was failing to bring the right on board. The AGM also discussed the NEC's attempts to side-step conference's rejection of its demand for sole responsibility for the manifesto (the Clause V issue), which was seen as further undermining the PLP.

Immediately after Christmas, the most dramatic and personally difficult of all the Manifesto meetings took place as the schism between stayers and leavers became clear. Beforehand Chairman Radice had written in the *Guardian* on 'Why the Labour Party must not split'[60] and circulated a 'Note on the Manifesto Group's future'. His note described the Group's achievements, pointing to the PLP elections, where they had won 9 out of the 12 Shadow Cabinet places, along with the PLP chairman and most of the Subject Group chairmen. The Group had been most successful in articulating a centre-right viewpoint in parliament, and had sustained a centre-right coalition in the PLP, much wider than its actual membership. Furthermore, it had helped keep the last Labour government in office. However, Radice did not flinch about the Manifesto Group's weaknesses: it had never had a constituency presence and its trade union links were weak. He listed the current risks: the formation of Labour First (which damaged its recruitment prospects); the swing to the left on the NEC, at conference and in the CLPs; reselection; and what he termed 'divisions within our own ranks' – in other words, an acknowledgement that some had decided there was no room for a centre-right viewpoint within the party. However, as most Manifesto Group members believed that the situation was retrievable and that the fight should continue inside the party, its Chairman recommended concentrating on: winning PLP elections; articulating centre-right views; holding speaker meetings; helping members with reselection problems; and establishing trade union links. This articulated the stayers' response to the potential defectors.

The 14 January 1981 meeting witnessed an outflow of emotions. Its Chairman recalls it as the infamous meeting, where there was the big row between Hattersley and David Owen, Mike Thomas and Ian Wrigglesworth about them leaving. The memorable contributions were the statements of intent, albeit scarcely legible in

Robertson's fast-deteriorating handwriting. Owen thought it was understandable that people would take different views as few had imagined the party would degenerate so quickly, but he asked members to be tolerant if people go in different directions. Thomas felt that the fighting within the Labour Party had been tried but failed. Wrigglesworth worried about the voters who were deserting the party and was not prepared to see that vote further decline. He recalled that he had tried really hard, including by setting up CLV to work in constituencies. But the stayers held their ground. Though some (Wayland Young) said they were hanging on by an eyelash, John Golding refused to abandon the inheritance to what he described as a bunch of lefties. Bob Mitchell similarly recalled that the left stayed in and fought when they were in the minority, so now urged members to do the same, whilst admitting this might be a different ballgame if some of the MPS were deselected. When David Owen hinted that there might be a coming together again at a later date, Phillip Whitehead thought it would be unlikely as the circumstances of a split would mean bad blood for a generation. Instead, he urged the Group to persuade people not to leave. Hattersley, the most senior non-defector to speak, recalled how their section of the party had grown up being in the majority and were unaccustomed to being a minority. However, so long as they retained control of the Shadow Cabinet, they would be able to control the manifesto, as he was determined not to fight an election on an anti-EEC or unilateralist manifesto. He warned that the chances of fighting back were weakened if people threatened to leave.[61] After the meeting (which endorsed the Chairman's paper), the two factions each gave separate press conferences. No doubt Radice was upbeat at his but, asked in 2002 to assess the Manifesto Group, he judged: 'It was a failed group – not entirely. But failed – because some of our members left and set up another party.'[62]

A separate meeting with the Leader prior to Wembley, with 28 MPs and 5 peers present, urged him to do more to preserve the PLP's position. Foot protested he had done everything in his power to win acceptance for the 50:25:25 formula for the Electoral College, but without the AUEW it was not possible. He stressed he wanted to keep people in the party, and offered to do anything he could to help MPs under pressure from reselection. The Manifesto Group members pushed him on Militant, the proposed referendum on the EEC and on what Dickson Mabon called 'death by a thousand cuts', whereby the left repeatedly pressed things defeated at conference. Whitehead feared that the party was on the brink and called on Foot to speak out in the interest of coalition or it would fall apart. Mason sadly recalled that he had never seen such nastiness and intolerance in CLPs and begged Foot to appeal for more tolerance or the party would split. The Group would stay and fight from within but to do so it needed his support. The Leader's response, to the despair of many – and shortly to be proved wrong – was that he did not think the party was 'on the brink'. This further disheartened this wing of the party, their Chairman judging Foot's performance as awful.

Events worsened when, on 24 January 1981, the special conference decided on the precise composition of the Electoral College agreed in principle in October. The result was the worst of all possible outcomes for the PLP: just 30 per cent of the total compared with 40 per cent for the unions and 30 per cent for the CLPs.[63]

It provided the defectors with a popular cause on which to split (unions being unpopular after the 1978–79 Winter of Discontent) rather than the European issue, which united the defectors but scored negatively in opinion polls. The Gang of Four exploited the unsatisfactory outcome to the full in the Limehouse Declaration the following day, as a dozen Labour MPs lined up to join what was clearly going to be a new party.

The Manifesto troops were traumatised. Meeting days later, 29 of them shared their despair. The first resignation (of Lady Burton of Coventry, after 36 years in the party) was reported but a number who were later to defect were there. Many still hoped the inevitable would not happen, Willie Hamilton talking of 'if' not 'when' and Bruce Douglas-Mann (who would be one of the very last to leave) seeing Limehouse as a catalyst, a warning to people including Tribune. Bryan Magee thought the Limehouse supporters might one day wish to come back and urged colleagues not to push them. Ken Weetch similarly urged that the door be kept open, even whilst admitting the time for any conciliation was very short, provoking Bob Cant to retorted that Owen 'the ambitious' and Rodgers 'the conspirator' had so weakened the Group that if they were welcomed back then he would resign. A major concern was the very future of the Group. Bob Mitchell acknowledged that their association with Reg Prentice had harmed them. Reg Underhill warned that any suspicion that the Manifesto Group was connected with the Limehouse group would further damage them. However, he foresaw that if the unions did not split then the Group would not. John Parker concurred that there was no future for a socialist party without roots in unions. These predictions were to prove accurate, the unions' complete solidarity helping Labour to triumph over the SDP. Summing up, Radice announced that the public statement would be: 'we stay and fight'.

Later, on the eve of the Council for Social Democracy's metamorphosis into the Social Democratic Party, Radice and Robertson, as Manifesto Chairman and Secretary, issued a statement predicting that the SDP was bound to become more right wing and anti-union; furthermore it could stop Labour candidates winning and so assist another Conservative election victory. They claimed that running away from the struggle for a broad based, tolerant Labour Party in favour of an illusory middle ground was both defeatist and a betrayal of party supporters.[64] There were no personal attacks and the authors kept their sadness to themselves. Given that those leaving included their former Secretary (Wrigglesworth), Chairman (Cartwright), Secretary and Chairman (Horam) and Treasurer (Sandelson), together with name-giver Rodgers and a host of their close political friends, this showed remarkable constraint. To Ian Wrigglesworth, his predecessor as Secretary, George Robertson wrote on 16 March, 'You did much for the Group, and within the party. Maybe that is why your departure is so sad'.

And so a chapter ended. The Group continued to exist, bereft of a swathe of its members, until after the 1983 election. It had to contend with distaste arising from its former association with those who had defected, as well as suspicion that others might yet leave (as many indeed did). Furthermore, it was now fighting on two fronts: against the left in the PLP and against its former members in the SDP.

Despite this, activity did not wane. Circulars went out urging attendance at PLP meetings, which had been surprisingly poorly attended, to make the voice of the centre-right heard. The Group held meetings with Healey (Deputy Leader) and Hattersley, and an important one with the Leader on Militant, when members spelt out the effects Militant was having in constituencies. At this, John Palmer related how Militant had wiped out the total executive committee of one Bristol CLP and led to many TGWU members no longer paying the political levy. (It was similar pressure elsewhere, particularly in Liverpool, which was finally to force the unions to press for action on Militant.) Magee described hordes of them arriving from the neighbouring Newham CLP into his Leyton constituency and how Militant had plenty of money, whereas the party did not have the resources to fight them. He called for the reintroduction of the Proscribed List, while predicting that would not happen with the current NEC. He foresaw Militant destroying the party. Bob Mitchell, facing two full-time Militant organisers in Southampton, described how the TGWU was experiencing widespread political levy withdrawal. Betty Boothroyd recalled there was already a Proscribed List of one – the Social Democratic Alliance (the NEC had ruled SDA members ineligible for party membership, in the light of the SDA's threat to run candidates against the party).[65] She thought this Proscribed List could be widened to include Militant (Robertson's notes musing that there was no word about witch-hunts when the SDA was proscribed). Ben Ford recounted how Edward Lyons was spending all his time in Bradford West fighting Militant, the older members having been pushed out in the sick atmosphere which prevailed. John Golding, mocking their characteristic 'Nazi-salute-with-arthritis', pointed out that Militant had more organisers than the party, and that they kept meetings going until 3 in the morning, so no-one could compete. He pleaded that they be stopped from destroying the party. Whitehead's experience was similar; it was hard to get people to go to meetings and in Derby there were disaffiliations from the Associated Society of Locomotive Engineers and Firemen (ASLEF) and the TGWU. Underhill added to his earlier report, describing how Militant had branches in CLPs and full-time organisers. They were getting money which should be going to the party.

Responding to this catalogue, Foot pledged to take what they said seriously whilst reiterating that he did not believe Militant was going to take over the party and that it could be counteracted effectively by defeating it in debate, the Proscribed List not being the answer. He did acknowledge the problem of violence and intimidation, and the difficulties some MPs were having in reselection, but thought the priority was to engage in the argument rather than act organisationally. Even as he said this, he correctly surmised that his response might be seen as inadequate. After Foot left the meeting, the Group – whilst expressing their disappointment – agreed to gather further documentation, despite fearing that others were likely to leave after conference so there was no time to waste.[66]

In the Group's internal discussions, John Smith warned of the possible consequences of the forthcoming political fund ballots, but mostly members contemplated the potential effects of reselection whilst re-affirming their role in defending the leadership and in countering the well-organised hard-left. They were also still busy on policy, setting up working parties on industrial policy and defence.

However, as soon as the Group settled down to its new existence, it was confronted by the first ever deputy leadership election not to be decided by MPs alone. At the beginning of April, Benn announced he would challenge Healey, using the new Electoral College. Ever loyalist, the members agreed they had to rally around Michael Foot – to protect him from those who voted for him – whilst also ensuring a 'thumping' vote in the PLP for Healey. They agreed to campaign around support for the existing leadership and – unlike Solidarity – they openly took sides, urging all their members, and as many MPs as possible, personally to nominate Foot/Healey for the joint leadership and to get CLPs to support this ticket. There was a third candidate, John Silkin, but given he favoured nuclear disarmament and withdrawal from the EEC,[67] he would never find support in the Manifesto Group. By the hair of one of his famous eyebrows, Healey retained the deputy leadership. In October, the Group backed Jack Dormand for PLP Chairman, who polled 102 votes on the first ballot. The runner-up, Ian Mikardo, with 65, then withdrew, removing the need for a second ballot.[68] A full slate of 15 for the newly enlarged Shadow Cabinet was circulated, the Group having helped ensure Cocks' re-election as Chief Whip by 156 to left-winger Martin Flannery's 51. It had lost the battles over reselection and the Electoral College, but was not going to admit defeat over Militant, appealing (unsuccessfully) to the NEC not to endorse Militant supporter Pat Wall as a prospective parliamentary candidate, and to declare the activities and organisation of Militant as incompatible with the party's constitution.[69]

An end-of-year letter from the Chairman and Secretary recorded: 'This has been a traumatic year for the party, and for the Manifesto Group. However, we must not be disconsolate.' It took comfort from the NEC gains and from their efforts on Militant having sparked off a process which led to the Hayward/Hughes enquiry. The officers urged members to get resolutions in to the NEC supporting the Leader and the Militant enquiry, as opponents were already organising.[70] This represents the first documented attempt by the Manifesto Group to influence the NEC, perhaps reflecting the increased number of Manifesto friends now on it.

The Group continued to meet throughout 1982, agreeing a full slate of 15 for the Shadow Cabinet and maintaining pressure over Militant. The NEC had finally voted to set up a Register but George Robertson predicted that the debate at the autumn conference would be violent and rigorous, as Militant was mobilising its forces and would mount a fierce propaganda campaign. It had a Fighting Fund of £103,000 and a well-drilled organisation with enormous energy fighting for its very existence. An added problem was that resistance to a Register was being well orchestrated, often by non-Militant people, so in July 1982 the Secretary urged members to write to the press, and to get resolutions from local parties and unions to the NEC. Opposition to Militant now extended beyond Manifesto and Solidarity members (for example, to Jack Straw[71]) but it was far from universal. 'Labour against the Witch-hunt' (with many Tribune MPs in support) was flooding the NEC with resolutions.

One of the first organisations to apply to go on the new Register was the Manifesto Group, setting out its officers, purposes and finances in a letter of 19 July 1982 to the new General Secretary, Jim Mortimer. So the Group had achieved one of its long-standing aims – action against Militant – but only after the SDP split and when its own membership was at its smallest: just 27 MPs and 7 peers. Within the PLP, the Group continued to meet for another year, when it merged into Parliamentary Solidarity, where its members continued to organise Shadow Cabinet slates.

The Manifesto Group was set up to marshal the centre-right majority for PLP elections. In this, it was – with one major exception – overwhelmingly successful. It dominated the PLP, holding the chairmanship and vice-chairmanship continuously from late 1974, making a clean sweep of the Liaison Committee from 1976 to 1979 and winning most of the Shadow Cabinet places after 1979. Whether it was wise to 'take no hostages' and to enforce such hegemony is open to question, as it delayed any rapprochement with the centre-left and gave an impression of authoritarianism. That was not how its members saw things. Excluded from the NEC, beleaguered within their own CLPs, Manifesto members with some hundreds of years of membership between them, who had loyally supported first the Labour government and then the opposition leadership, now found themselves first perplexed and then angered by their alienation from the new left within the party to which they had given their lives. They saw their success in internal elections as a fair representation of the views of the PLP. Some of the older MPs, influenced by their 1952 'Keep Calm' Group attempts to co-operate with the left, vowed not to make the same mistake again.[72]

In the single most important PLP election, however, that between Foot and Healey in October 1980 – they failed to deliver, and thereby contributed to the creation of the SDP. Some of the failure can be laid at Healey's door, and some to the short-sightedness or cowardliness of the centre. Nevertheless, the Manifesto Group failed because of its inability to build a coalition for Healey's candidature.

Before looking at its wider success and failures, it is worth outlining the Group's strength and weaknesses. Its major handicap was its isolation from prevailing opinion on the NEC, on GCs and at party conference. Some of its members were not sufficiently linked into the party; they were perhaps intellectual socialists rather than embedded in the party's grassroots. Shirley Williams and John Cartwright aside, they had little contact with members of the NEC.

Others of the Group's members added to its problems, with both 'that ass'[73] Neville Sandelson and Reg Prentice putting off potential recruits. Its hard-right image made it unattractive and it failed to recruit the non-Tribune centre who were key to achieving its objectives. However, it was not just the Group's image that hampered recruitment, but the fear – even terror – of pending reselections which dominated MPs' waking hours. Even Tom McNally, who distrusted Sandelson, admitted that the real reason for not joining the Manifesto Group was his fight with his own GMC, where he felt real hatred. His experience was not unique. Party membership had declined so much that it could no longer be said to represent Labour voters, to whom MPs feel a strong affinity. The party – all of it, not just the

PLP – had failed to respond to this and to the arrival of the 1960s generation amongst party activists. This was a party-wide problem but it particularly weakened the Manifesto Group. The PLP was out of tune with the wider party, and this was reflected in – rather than caused by – the Manifesto Group. Furthermore, although loyal to the leadership, the Group got little in return by way of support, whether from Wilson, Callaghan or Foot. Its members had voted for neither the first nor last of these, yet they were committed – in their aims and by temperament – to supporting the leadership: an unrequited loyalty. The Labour Government's unpopularity was also a problem, as the Group was committed to its defence before a party troubled by its record.

A major drawback was that the Manifesto Group was effectively leaderless. Its hard-working officers had neither the stature nor status to offer an alternative to the scene-stealing Tony Benn. Healey was outside the Group, whilst the Cabinet (and later Shadow Cabinet) was debarred from holding office. Shirley Williams, a possible contender, was outside the House from May 1979. So a surfeit of talent failed to be translated into effective leadership. Finally, the Group had within it the seeds of its own destruction. The SDP split came entirely from within it, and on the very issues that had united its members against party conference: Europe, unilateralism and the Electoral College.

Ranged against these manifold weaknesses was the Group's single strength: its size. Whether measured by Callaghan's 1976 majority over Foot (176:137), Wrigglesworth's 1979 estimate of 149:94 or by the 107 MPs willing to sign a letter to Callaghan protesting at the party's constitutional changes, the views represented by the Manifesto Group were those of the majority of the PLP. Thus whilst MPs might have been out of step with the party, the Group was not out of step with them.

Given all its weaknesses, and its one single strength, did the Group achieve its aims of supporting the government in implementing manifesto promises, acting as a forum for constructive discussion, and working to achieve a democratic socialist society through parliamentary means? In truth, such aims were beyond the means of an underfunded gathering of MPs, without staff for most of its existence. Had the Manifesto Group not been created, however, it is difficult to imagine where the centre-right, loyalist, pro-leadership view would have been articulated. The NEC and Tribune attacked the government; the NEC and the party became preoccupied with internal party reform. There was no other machine championing Labour values against an increasingly radical Tory government, and no-one else arguing against EEC withdrawal, unilateralism and renationalisation without compensation. Had this flag not been kept flying, it might have taken Neil Kinnock much longer to begin his rewriting of policy into an electorally attractive package. Finally, on internal matters, only the Manifesto Group (and CLV) supported OMOV prior to the SDP split, and only the Manifesto Group (and later the St Ermins Group and Solidarity) kept up the pressure on Militant which was eventually to lead, timidly under Foot, wholeheartedly under Kinnock, to action against it.

The Group failed in its desire to restructure the NEC to include representatives of ordinary party members, local government and (crucially for them) the PLP.

These changes had to await Blair's premiership. The Group also failed to promote any alternative modernisation agenda to reselection and the Electoral College. It was late to champion OMOV (largely because this would have excluded trade unions from candidate selection and removed the PLP's monopoly in leadership elections). It thus had no positive agenda to offer. However, its stated aims never included party reform so it might be unfair to rank this as a failure to meet objectives. The most valuable success of the Group – despite Radice's view that it failed because the party split – was to prevent a greater haemorrhaging by offering solidarity to MPs under pressure, reassuring them they were not alone and proving, after 1981, that centre-right, social democrats could be at home within the Labour Party.

Notes

1 'The true story of the formation of the SDP begins here in early 1971'; David Owen, *Time to Declare* (Penguin Books, 1992), p. 172.
2 The 1969 White Paper on union reform which was withdrawn in the face of opposition from the PLP, NEC and unions.
3 Arthur Bonner interview.
4 Rodgers, *Fourth Among Equals*, p. 167.
5 Dickson Mabon interview.
6 *Tribune*, 17 November 1972.
7 Dickson Mabon interview.
8 Rodgers, *Fourth Among Equals*, p. 167.
9 The Group originally considered calling itself the 'Social Democratic Group'; Bradley, *Breaking the Mould?*, p. 60.
10 Owen, *Time to Declare*, p. 91.
11 Bradley, *Breaking the Mould?*, p. xii.
12 Tribune Group membership: *Economist*, 26 April 1975. The Manifesto Group also had the 'tacit encouragement of the Cabinet's moderates'; *Financial Times*, 9 March 1977.
13 *Economist*, 26 April 1975.
14 Letter of 21 July 1975 from Prime Minister Wilson to Neville Sandelson.
15 Rodgers Press Release, 28 August 1975.
16 Rodgers, *Fourth Among Equals*, p. 168.
17 *Report of the 1975 Annual Conference of the Labour Party*.
18 Radice, *Friends and Rivals*.
19 *Ibid.*, pp. 235–6.
20 Peter Kellner, 'Anatomy of the vote', *New Statesman*, 9 April 1976.
21 *Sunday Mirror*, 2 May 1976; *The Times*, 22 April 1976. Callaghan disliked factionalism. When Chapple complained about the lack of organisation of the moderates on the NEC, the then Chancellor retorted: 'We don't want a return to the squabbles of the Bevanite period' (Chapple, *Sparks Fly!*, p. 105). As Prime Minister, he changed his mind, appreciating John Golding's efforts to co-ordinate support for the government in 1978/79.
22 *The Times*, 22 April 1976.
23 Dickson Mabon interview.
24 *The Times*, 22 April 1976.
25 *Financial Times*, 22 October 1976.

26 *Report of the 1977 Annual Conference of the Labour Party*, p. 83.
27 Letter from Ian Wrigglesworth and others to Cledwyn Hughes, Chairman of the PLP, 7 December 1976.
28 *Telegraph* and *Financial Times*, 9 March 1977; *The Times*, 11 March 1977; *Spectator*, 19 March 1977.
29 Young Fabian Group, *The Mechanics of Victory* (Fabian Society, 1962).
30 Letter from Ron Hayward, General Secretary of the Labour Party, to Ian Wrigglesworth, 27 July 1978.
31 Although McNally told this author he never joined (interview, 27 November 2002), a February 1980 ballot paper in his name (voting against disclosure of the list of members) is in the archives; in June 1981 he is listed as a member of a Manifesto working party.
32 Brian L. Brivati, 'The Campaign for Democratic Socialism 1960–1964' (PhD thesis, University of London, 1992), p. 285.
33 Silkin, *Changing Battlefields*, p. 80.
34 Pearce, *Denis Healey*, pp. 538–9.
35 CLV and Manifesto Group, 'Reform and democracy in the Labour Party', *Labour Victory*, October 1979.
36 Tony Benn and Eric Heffer, 'The future work of the Parliamentary Labour Party: an agenda for discussion', 19 June 1979.
37 Rodgers, *Fourth Among Equals*, p. 190.
38 *Ibid.*, p. 198.
39 Eddie May, 'The mosaic of Labour politics, 1900–1918', in Duncan Tanner *et al.* (eds), *The Labour Party in Wales, 1900–2000* (University of Wales Press, 2001), p. 77.
40 Bill Rodgers Press Release, 30 November 1979.
41 Rodgers, *Fourth Among Equals*, p. 200.
42 *Sunday Times*, 1 June 1980.
43 Pearce, *Denis Healey*, p. 532.
44 *Report of the Annual Conference and Special Conference of the Labour Party, 1980*, p. 251.
45 Bradley, *Breaking the Mould?*, pp. 74–5.
46 Press Release from Neville Sandelson MP, 26 June 1980.
47 Manifesto Group Statement, 18 June 1980.
48 *Guardian*, 1 August 1980.
49 *The Times*, 22 September 1980. Thomas undertook much of the publicity around this and took delight in the 'Dirty Dozen' attribution.
50 *Guardian*, 24 November 1980.
51 Silkin, *Changing Battlefields*, pp. 33–4.
52 Pearce, *Denis Healey*, p. 537.
53 Mike Thomas Paper, 16 October 1980.
54 Pearce, *Denis Healey*, pp. 542–3.
55 *Ibid.*, p. 543.
56 Phillip Whitehead interview.
57 Tom McNally interview.
58 Giles Radice interview.
59 Personal communication at the time.
60 12 January 1981.
61 George Robertson's handwritten notes of 14 January 1981.
62 Giles Radice interview, 7 October 2002.
63 *NEC Report to 1981 Labour Party Conference*, pp. 155–6.

64 Manifesto Group Press Release, 25 March 1981.
65 *NEC Report to 1981 Labour Party Conference*, p. 8.
66 From Robertson's handwritten notes, 18 March 1981.
67 June 1981 letter from John Silkin to all CLPs.
68 PLP Circular, 5 November 1981.
69 Letter from Radice, Robertson and Weetch to Ron Hayward, General Secretary of the NEC, 2 November 1981.
70 Letter from Radice and Robertson to Manifesto Group members, December 1981.
71 Jack Straw, 'Militant: the party's constitution must be upheld', *Tribune*, 9 July 1982.
72 Michael Stewart, *Life & Labour: An Autobiography* (Sidgwick & Jackson, 1980), pp. 85, 268.
73 Letter from George Cunningham to the author, 11 May 2003.

8
Labour First

For a section of MPs, the Manifesto Group was a bridge too far. Tainted by being so right wing, and concentrating on organisation rather than discussion, it held little attraction for MPs who disliked the two established sects but recognised the need to meet together for support and debate. Labour First's inaugural meeting took place on 25 March 1980.[1] At the time, the PLP felt marginalised by the left, particularly by their demands for mandatory reselection, taking the choice of leader out of MPs' hands, and for removing MPs from decisions on the manifesto. Labour First was set up amidst numerous PLP meetings agreeing a joint submission to the Committee of Enquiry, and when cataclysmic warnings about whether the party could ever form a government were in the papers daily.

The MPs who formed the Group (Brynmor John, David Clark, Terry Davis, John Grant and Edmund Marshall) were not just concerned about winning the argument within Westminster. The choice of name reflected the founders' desire to put Labour, as opposed to any particular faction, first. They thought the other two groups (Manifesto and Tribune) were undermining the unity and cohesiveness of the party, both in parliament and in the country, and wanted to counter such divisions. However, this was seen by others on the right (such as Phillip Whitehead) as the 'soggy middle' – at best naïve, at worst cowardice – leading to the soubriquet, 'Safety First'. Nevertheless, the some 30 MPs joined, although the atmosphere dictated that the list be kept secret.

The Group embarked on an active programme of debates, largely organised by its hard-working Secretary, Edmund Marshall. Within 2 years, Labour First organised 16 meetings outside the House, in which panels of MPs answered questions and participated in discussion with party activists. Five of these were conference fringe events, but 11 others were held around the country.[2] In the House, 32 meetings were held, virtually all with speakers, including Michael Foot, Denis Healey, Roy Hattersley, Tony Benn, former Prime Minister Harold Wilson, former Chief of the Defence Staff Lord Carver, Director General of Fair Trading Gordon Borrie, and trade unionists Alan Fisher, Clive Jenkins and Len Murray.

The Group also produced one paper, on internal party organisation.[3] At the end of 1980, when the conference had decided in principle to amend the system for electing the leader, but had failed to agree a method, the PLP sought to coalesce around one position. Labour First's submission called for an OMOV ballot of all party members, instead of an Electoral College. This was supported by many of the MPs who subsequently defected but not by the Shadow Cabinet or the PLP (which went along with an Electoral College, with half the votes for MPs). In this one collective position, therefore, Labour First firmly placed itself on the right. Yet, by holding aloof from the Manifesto Group, it was seen by the Chairman of the latter as damaging his Group's recruitment prospects and weakening the centre-right in the PLP.[4]

What was the purpose of this non-aligned Group, and what did it achieve? Its instigators wanted a forum for discussion outside the polarised choice which then existed in the PLP. Benn described it as being 'set up by people who are dissatisfied with the Manifesto Group which is right-wing and pro-common market, and with the Tribune Group which they think of as dangerously left-wing'.[5] However, Golding wrote that 'the moderate members of Labour First were far from being dissatisfied with the Manifesto Group and helped create Labour First as a meeting point with those in the Tribune Group who opposed the excesses of Wedgie and Eric Heffer'.[6] John Grant, one of the original Vice-Chairmen, defined it as a Group which was deeply unhappy with the faction fighting which bedevilled the party.[7] One Manifesto Group stalwart was less charitable: Jim Wellbeloved called them 'soft-left and decent but who could not bring themselves to call themselves right'.[8] Perhaps 'soft-right' would have been more appropriate.

Brynmor John (the Chairman throughout Labour's First's existence), Grant, Marshall, Clark and Davis had sounded out other like-minded MPs to set up something to counter the polarisation and foster a spirit of tolerance in the party. They resented the effectiveness of the other two slates, and – according to Grant – in 1981 put up their own list, representing 'the middle', which helped see Brynmor John, Gwyneth Dunwoody and Peter Archer elected to the Shadow Cabinet. The Secretary of the Group, Edmund Marshall, remembers it differently, claiming that Labour First did not run any slate although recognising that members of Labour First would have supported any of its members who were candidates.

The Manifesto Group sensed there was a separate slate and resented the consequent dilution of its own effectiveness. Despite such hiccups, members from Manifesto were welcomed into Labour First, and there were a number active in both (such as Archer) as well as some who were later prominent in Solidarity (Woolmer, Jack Cunningham, Clark, Mitchell and O'Neill) and others subsequently to defect to the SDP – Grant, McNally, Douglas-Mann and, much later, Marshall when no longer an MP. Perhaps the most significant role the Group played was the provision of mutual support. The pressure on MPs was intense, and the bitterness in the party palpable. For example, although Clark had no Militancy within his own CLP, his experience in another seat which he visited as a Labour First speaker remains live in his memory:

> I remember speaking at one in Haltwhistle, with Arthur Davidson (who was himself close to Tribune) in the Miners' Hall. The feeling was intense. My wife was there – and

had a box of leaflets under her chair. One woman at the meeting – a long-standing councillor – said to my wife: 'I hope that's a bomb.' Such was the atmosphere. Then they slagged off Arthur. Said he and others were 'milking the Labour Party; lining their pockets'. Arthur Davidson – a QC – said he could make far more as a barrister.[9]

For Clark and his friends, Labour First provided a handrail on the route back to a more collegial party and a source of support and encouragement. Labour First continued to meet until Easter 1983, when attention turned to the forthcoming general election. By the year end, the Group had been subsumed (along with the Manifesto Group) into Parliamentary Solidarity, with Brynmor John becoming Chairman of the new grouping and Clark a Vice-Chairman. The size of the election defeat (leaving only 209 MPs) was the trigger, together with the shock of the response on the doorstep. 'Two per cent fewer votes and we'd have been finished. After that, the soft-Tribunites were talking very differently' said David Clark.[10] That the left was split, between those (like Benn) who considered the 1983 election a victory for a good socialist manifesto and the bulk who acknowledged the scale of the crisis, was evidenced by the likes of Tony Blair and Gordon Brown who, as new MPs, joined the Tribune Group. The presence of such typically centre and centre-right members in Tribune altered its colours and nearly shot the right's fox. The Common Market had also dimmed as a marker, not least as events in eastern Europe (such as Solidarity in Poland) were shifting the European debate. It was time for a new focus in the PLP; Labour First found it quite comfortable to make the move into Labour's Solidarity.

Looking at the Group's achievements, its former Secretary concluded:

> it is difficult to measure any specific legacy left by Labour First. Clearly we did not dissuade the formation of the SDP, nor did we have any marked effect on restoring Labour Party fortunes. One indirect result of our existence may have been the failure of Denis Healey to become leader of the Labour Party, which election came only shortly after he had baldly declined an invitation to come to speak at one of our meetings! Michael Foot did accept such an invitation.[11]

However, the fault for this clearly lies with Healey, who similarly upset the Manifesto Group. Marshall does not mention what might have been Labour First's greatest strength – to bring some of the soft-left into debate with the centre-right. To a degree, this was a characteristic of the Group from the start, drawing on a wider spectrum within the PLP than the Manifesto or Solidarity groupings could. A number of Tribunite and non-Tribunite left were found in its midst, the more sceptical views on Europe of some Labour First members perhaps making this easier. Thus Labour First maintained a dialogue which even Solidarity found difficult to sustain. This was to pay off at least once when, after the 1983 election, two vacancies occurred in the North East when MPs announced their retirements. Labour First was able to do a deal with the Tribune members in the region, whereby one Group would run a candidate in each seat, with both Groups then working to support each other's nominees – vital in CLPs where Militant was strong. Labour First, given Gateshead East, ran Joyce Quin; Tribune chose Albert Booth for Sunderland North. In the first case, Quin won by the slenderest of majorities against Militant (though she queries how much real help was supplied by Labour First). In Sunderland, despite considerable work by Labour First, the ex-MP and older Booth was unable to fight off Bob Clay. However, it showed the potential of the Groups co-operating against the far-left.

The full centre and soft-left alignment, which only really occurred after the 1987 election, was helped by these earlier activities, but might perhaps have been brought forward had this grouping been more strategic and concentrated on that objective. At the time, it was instead seen by the right as being coy about declaring its anti-Benn sentiments. By failing to take an early stand against the hard-left, it could be said to have provided the breathing space that allowed this left to continue to damage the party and its electoral prospects. Nevertheless, for its members it gave support and solidarity – attributes sorely lacking but essential for the day-to-day political battles.

The Group had one more contribution to make. After the 1987 election, Solidarity was wound up. But neither the individuals concerned, nor the need for organisation, disappeared. On behalf of the phoenix which arose, Spellar wrote to Brynmor John on 6 November 1987 seeking permission to take on the name. In response, John gathered the remaining members together to wind up the original Labour First formally, and then bequeathed the name to the emergent body which still exists today.

Notes

1 It was initially called the 'Non-Group' meeting (letter from David Watkins to the author, 19 April 2004).
2 Edmund Marshall (Secretary, Labour First), 'Report on the year's activities', 31 March 1981 and 20 April 1982.
3 'Proposed amendments to the Labour Party Constitution to implement a new system for electing the Leader of the Labour Party', Labour First, 11 November 1980.
4 Note to the Manifesto Group from Giles Radice, January 1981.
5 Benn, *Diaries 1980–90*, p. 12.
6 John Golding, 'The fixers: the rise and fall of Benn and Heffer' (unpublished manuscript, 1988), chapter 14, p. 7.
7 John Grant, *Blood Brothers* (Weidenfeld & Nicolson, 1992), p. 102.
8 Jim Wellbeloved interview.
9 David Clark interview.
10 *Ibid.*
11 Edmund Marshall, letter to the author, 12 November 2003.

9
Background to the St Ermins Group

The St Ermins Group of moderate trade union leaders was born on 10 February 1981. However, a number of overlapping developments preceded this. One was a 'Loyalist Group' on the NEC; one was a 'chewing the fat' coterie of moderate general secretaries, often over dinner at the St Ermins Hotel; a third was a pro-incomes policy grouping; a fourth was of union political officers; and yet another was a subset of unions which supported the constituency-based CLV. Thus, prior to the St Ermins Group, the key players met in a variety of gatherings as well as at the TUC General Council.

Another dimension linked many of the people who were to play key roles in the party's fortunes. By 1981, a significant group of Midlands men found themselves occupying national positions in London: Denis Howell (MP for Birmingham Small Heath, former CDS union organiser,[1] President of APEX); Roy Grantham (former Midlands Organiser, General Secretary of APEX); Jim Cattermole (former East Midlands Labour Party Organiser); Terry Duffy (Black Country AUEW President); John Golding MP (brought up in Birmingham Sparkbrook) and Bryan Stanley (General Secretary of the POEU, a close colleague of the party's National Agent, Reg Underhill, from the latter's days in the Midlands). Later activists included the West Midlands AUEW's Ken Cure, together with two staffers who had first collaborated in South Lewisham Young Socialists in the 1960s: Roger Godsiff and John Spellar (both later West Midlands MPs). Other alliances were important, such as the 'Triple Alliance' of coal, steel and rail, which saw the ISTC's Bill Sirs in close contact with the NUR's Sidney Weighell.

The dramatis personae of the St Ermins Group

The background of these men helps explain their politics. They comprised, in the main, general secretaries of manual unions, men who had left school at 14, with little formal education, and who made their way up through their unions – a demonstration of intelligence, leadership, determination and sheer hard work. Sandy Feather, one of their number (though not a general secretary – albeit the son of a TUC general secretary), attributes a further quality to the coterie: the ability to 'fix it', though not usually employed for their own self-interests.

Sidney (Sid) Weighell's grandfather, father and brother worked on the railways,[2] although he alone made a union career which saw him become NUR General Secretary as well as a Labour Party agent in the 1950s and on the NEC in the 1970s.[3] It was here he saw the left caucusing and began his passion to 'save the party from the left'.[4] He wanted Labour to be a broader-based party whose conference would accurately reflect the views of ordinary rank-and-file and Labour voters and with an NEC comprising a powerful and balanced representation of trade unions, constituency parties and MPs.[5] He believed passionately in the party. At the height of the Winter of Discontent, he let it be known that he was 'in the business of saving the Labour government'.[6] Despite his role in St Ermins – and his personal sacrifice – Weighell received little thanks, being offered no peerage and being beaten by a young Anthony Blair for the Sedgefield nomination in 1983.[7]

Terry Duffy, the straight-talking President of the AUEW, was endlessly underestimated – even mocked – by Labour's intellectuals. Yet he was to prove the fulcrum on which the party's fortunes turned. He had beaten left-winger Bob Wright for the Presidency – a feat which was seriously bad news for the left both in his union, and in the Labour Party.[8] Under Duffy, Neil Kinnock knew he could count on the AUEW's block vote.[9] However, many others failed to recognise the brain behind the face. Following the 1981 Wembley conference (when the AUEW was locked into a previous decision to support nothing less than 50 per cent of the College for the PLP and thus unable to vote to prevent a worse outcome), the middle-class, university-educated John Silkin (unfamiliar with union procedures) disparagingly suggested that the working-class Duffy supported a 40 per cent, 40 per cent, 40 per cent formula.[10] Duffy's union collaborators saw him differently. Roger Godsiff called him superb, always delivering on what needed to be done. POEU General Secretary Bryan Stanley said he was like a breath of fresh air, prepared to work to make things better because he saw that the union and Labour movement were being held back with things as they were. Outsiders recognised his effectiveness, seeing both Duffy as President and John Boyd as General Secretary, two classically anti-communist leaders,[11] as particularly important for the success of the counter-insurgency against the left.[12] Dick Clements, who worked for Foot and Kinnock, described Duffy as helpful: 'he would say "tell me what you want me to do and I'll do it" – and then did'.[13] However, many of the 'chatterers' were dismissive of Duffy and underestimated him and the vital role he played in initiating the St Ermins Group. Amongst all the Group papers, almost the only reference to anyone by name occurs when Duffy's death was noted with sadness in October 1985, not only for the Group but because of the loss of a powerful vote within the General Council. 'More than any other union leader, he was the one who halted the TUC's leftward drift.'[14]

Bryan Stanley helped convene the first meeting of the Group. A self-styled middle-of-the-roader, he was an unlikely ally: opposed to the Common Market and a unilateralist. But his similarities were greater than any policy differences. A Post Office employee from the age of 14, Stanley's strengths lay in the characteristics of his union and in his personality. The POEU was neither very big nor in a mainstream industry, so was not seen as trying to poach members. It was twentieth in size so other unions were not afraid of it. Stanley's personality also helped. His ability to get on with everyone enabled him to encompass the ego-driven David Basnett and keep an eclectic group, from the staunchest right-wingers to the left-leaning, together. Outside the meetings, he was able to get Basnett, Chapple and Duffy round the same table over lunch – but he knew he had to be there. They argued all the time and he had to stop them dealing with subjects where they would fly apart. In Kinnock's words, politically, Stanley 'was terrific! This guy had never been a phone engineer – but his phone-engineering, in terms of thinking through circuits and finding answers, was terrific. He saw politics as serious business. This wasn't for sectarian or sectional purpose within the Labour Party. It was for the party'.[15]

Stanley had been on the NEC and was in contact with other general secretaries who shared his distaste about what was happening in the party. He decided to do something. As did Roy Grantham. The APEX General Secretary was midwife to the Group, not just ensuring it was delivered but producing its nurse-maid, Roger Godsiff, without whom St Ermins might have been born a poor wee thing. Grantham's union was central to the right – in the European movement, CLV and later Solidarity.

John Golding learnt his fixing as the POEU education officer. At that time, it was unusual for working people to have access to telephones at work. Post Office engineers were the exception. So early on Golding became accustomed to 'ringing round' to ensure people turned up or supported particular candidates. He helped run BLOC (the moderates within the union), which was a miniature St Ermins, controlling elections to the executive; the skills thus learnt remained with him. He became an MP (thanks to his colleague Stanley)[16] and a minister, though his heart remained with the union and he later resigned his seat to return as General Secretary. But it was on the NEC that he forged his lasting reputation. In 1978, when the left had apparently been strengthened by the election of Dennis Skinner and Neil Kinnock to the NEC, the little-noted election of Golding, a right-wing machine politician determined not to compromise in the counter-insurgency against the new left, was equally significant. 'He was to play the leading role in challenging and eventually defeating Benn's and Heffer's leadership of the NEC.'[17] Golding was the Group's link with the leader's office and head office. Early on, Kinnock realised that 'the very effective organiser of this combined action and the main political stimulant was John Golding. And that he was putting into literal effect the maxim "the victory of political ideals must be organised"'.[18] No matter how intense the politics, Golding's 'hinterland' was never far away. He fished enthusiastically and would have a TV at meetings to watch the racing. Bill Sirs wrote: 'The man who was a fount of information and most active was John Golding. None of the politicians could hold a candle to him'.[19]

In time, Charlie Turnock took over Golding's role as the moderates' whip on the NEC. Self-taught and an alumnus of the National Council of Labour Colleges, Turnock has an extensive library, ranging from Lenin and Trotsky through virtually the whole of Labour history. Gordon Colling recalled how, at meetings, Turnock would have a big leather case, bursting full of files, into which he would delve to find the requisite paper.[20] His nose for detail was to prove devastating for Militant, particularly in Liverpool, when he chaired the Enquiry. His life was not always led out of a briefcase. He followed his father on to the railways at 14, before going into the Commandos. After the war he rose from a passenger guard to become an NUR Organiser. Beaten by Weighell to the general secretaryship, he remained a staunch ally of his new boss and collaborated with him in furthering the St Ermins Group. Together with Duffy, he is the only other member named in the minutes, on his retirement in September 1987, being thanked for his unstinting efforts and outstanding contribution. Another NUR man was Russell Tuck who, recalled Kinnock, was 'nobody's idea of a right-winger but frustrated by the weakness of the party. And as a classic NUR man, he wanted to do something about it. Absolutely classic role of the National Union of Railwaymen over the first 80 odd years of its history'.[21]

Gordon Colling, who became one of Kinnock's closest confidants, recalled the cloak-and-dagger mode of invitation. 'Somebody sidled up to me and said: "A group of us meet now and again. Exchange information and views. Would you like to come along? Interested in discussing NEC positions"'.[22] He shared their objective of returning the party to sanity and electability and, according to Sandy Feather, was the Group's 'rock'.

EETPU General Secretary Frank Chapple attended only the first St Ermins meeting (and then sporting a dinner jacket, being en route to some other function) as he then left the business to his lieutenant, John Spellar. But he was a powerful figure behind the Group's success. As with Grantham, part of his contribution was to bequeath the services of his political officer, Spellar, to its work. Chapple was an experienced organiser who had taken on and beaten the Communist Party within his own union. He had served on the NEC – where he had remonstrated with Jim Callaghan, the then Chancellor of the Exchequer in 1965, that the moderates were not putting up any sort of fight.[23] Much later, during the 1978/79 Winter of Discontent, he tried to rescue Prime Minister Callaghan: 'I don't actually support any fucking incomes policy, but I will support one now if it will help this fucking Government'.[24] The determination he had shown against the communists reappeared against the Bennites and Militants in the Labour Party. He kept Healey briefed about the Group, who later admitted: 'I didn't encourage them. They encouraged me'.[25]

There was one empty chair. Despite the GMWU's traditional centre-right politics, its 'weak and vain boss',[26] David Basnett, was never to grace the meetings. His colleagues put this down to personality. The kinder attribute it to a role he sought for himself: 'Basnett wanted to keep close to the TGWU and to Clive Jenkins. He didn't bother with the St Ermins group people'.[27] 'He saw his role as the mediator between left and right, even though he was basically a moderate. Also, he didn't get on with Frank Chapple – because of the Isle of Grain inter-union dispute. I still have a message sent by Basnett to Callaghan which reads: "The Isle of Grain is keeping us all apart"'.[28] Others are less charitable. Callaghan's aide-de-camp, Tom

McNally attributed his absence to Basnett's vanity, remarking that he was the first GMWU leader to take pride in being thought of as part of the left rather than taking pride in being a good old right-wing union boss who looked after the leader; he got flattered by the left into re-positioning the GMWU in ways which made life difficult.[29] Foot's aide-de-camp, Clements, similarly found him a chore, describing how he had to go through the whole palaver over and over again. With other leaders, matters were easily settled, as with Duffy who'd say, 'Tell me what you want me to do and I'll do it' – and then did. Clements reports how Basnett needed many lunches, many explanations to assist the leader.[30] This indecision – or need of flattery to make him feel in charge – is echoed by Godsiff, who judged that Basnett would not go to the St Ermins Group because he couldn't run it,[31] and by Feather: 'Some of our people would approach Basnett. He was usually reliable but would never deliver 100 per cent – because he wanted some say himself. Of course he would always need to support the TGWU. But he would chop and change his votes for the smaller unions'.[32] Godsiff developed a *modus operandi*: 'Once it was agreed what would be done, I had to phone Basnett to tell him – but in a certain style. For example, when they wanted to support Sam McCluskie, I said "How would you feel about Sam as treasurer?" He said "Quite happy". I'd then say "*You'd* be quite happy". That was how it had to be done. Basnett had a veto'.[33]

Only one commentator attributes Basnett's stand to any political belief. Shaw incorrectly assumes that the whole union kept its distance from St Ermins. He suggests that Basnett swung the traditionally solidly right-wing union on to a more centrist course, his footnote adding: 'Thus the GMWU never participated actively in the St Ermine's [*sic.*] Group of right-wing unions.'[34] In fact, GMWU NEC members Tom Burlison, Neville Hough and Alan Hadden did attend and, from the first meeting until he was elected to the Shadow Cabinet in 1983, the former Head of the GMWU Research Department, Giles Radice, represented the union, acting as a 'go between' with Basnett.[35]

Stanley was the other conduit. He saw some rationale behind Basnett's caution. Radice's replacement as Head of Research, Larry Whitty, was very close to the communist trade unionist Ken Gill's wife, Tess Gill, and Basnett perhaps knew there would be few secrets between them. It led to some cloak-and-dagger meetings, as Stanley recalled:

> in his heart, he knew the extreme left in the Labour Party and the extreme left in the TUC had to be defeated. But he would not stick his head above the parapet. Automaticity[36] was where Basnett was true. He'd never show it but he was true to this Group. But I had to meet David Basnett in his secret GMWU office in Duke Street or where he was having lunch – or sometimes, at conference, I had to go to his bedroom.[37]

There were other senior trade unionists, some on the TUC's General Council, some on the NEC (overlapping membership being banned), who were active in the Group, such as Tony Clarke of the UCW; Alan Tuffin (UCW General Secretary); Tuffin's predecessor, Tom Jackson; Sandy Feather, Roy Evans and Keith Brookman of the ISTC; the GMWU's Neville Hough and Tom Burlison; Tom Breakell (EETPU); Alex Smith (National Union of Tailors and Garment Workers); David

Williams (COHSE); Bill Whatley (USDAW); Richard Rosser (Transport Salaried Staffs' Association (TSSA)); John Weakley (AUEW); and David Ward (National Communications Union). No names were included in the Group minutes and no list ever circulated.

The power behind the St Ermins Group was the initial core (Chapple, Duffy, Grantham and Stanley) together with Golding and Turnock. But there were two other 'special ingredients' to whom all pay tribute and without whom the venture would have had little success: Roger Godsiff and John Spellar. 'They were the mechanics.'[38]. Neil Kinnock described them as

> ultra-diligent – they left no stone unturned. They were figures men. They worked the columns. They used the phone. They got in touch. Nothing was too hot or too heavy. They did play a hell of a big part. Ensuring first that their people have voted. Secondly that they have all voted in a consistent, organised way because they explained the purpose of following it through. And why elections to regional executives mattered. And why who was on the political committees of the national union mattered. And worked it through in a systematic, organised way – without which politics is pleasant, but it's only poetry.[39]

Now MP for Denis Howell's old West Midlands seat, Godsiff's contribution was his masterminding of voting figures. He was

> one of the small circle of union officials who, when every one else in the Labour Party appeared to retreat before the advancing Bennites, set about counting where the block votes lay and brokering secret deals to turn them over . . . [He] was the man with the pocket calculator, who worked out exactly how many block votes were pledged to each candidate in . . . NEC elections.[40]

John Golding described him as the master of calculation and the formulation of deals, thinking arithmetic all the time, always working out what deal to make; his key understanding was that winning seats was more important than the size of the majority, except to individual egos.[41] Neil Stewart from Kinnock's office confirmed that Godsiff's figures were always reliable.[42] Even when there was bad news to impart, 'Roger would put deals in an absolutely honest way – you will get more votes but you won't get on'.[43] A number-cruncher extraordinaire, he was also trusted. He got on well with Golding from the start and managed to persuade some unlikely figures to follow his road-map. He did not simply use a calculator. If not actual strong-arm tactics, there were smoke-and-mirror methods in his armoury: 'the best wheeler-dealer ever – even with Clive Jenkins' admired Sandy Feather.[44] Approval came from the top: at a conference reception when the Godsiff formula had been pulled off with just 40,000 votes to spare, Kinnock made a point of crossing a crowded room to thank its architect in person.

Spellar's Midlands connections started through his wife (who hailed from his original Birmingham seat) but grew through St Ermins and the Labour movement. His Warley West seat now places him firmly amongst the Midlands Labour right. However, from his south London origins he hardly crossed the Thames (parliament aside), spending his working life at the Bromley-based EETPU, as Political Secretary to Chapple, Hammond and Jackson, successive General Secretaries of an ever amalgamating and name-changing union. It is hard to overemphasise Spellar's impact on the Group, whose members – being elected national officers (mostly general secretaries) – were senior to him and Godsiff. Alan Hadden, a former party Chairman, judges that 'Spellar was the real political push' behind the Group.[45] He was not afraid to take on the left. At one London party conference, 'Arthur Latham, in the Chair, asked "if anyone wanted to vote or speak in favour of good socialist comrades being thrown out of the party". One voice "Yes!" It was John Spellar. He was heartily booed. However, Ken Livingstone later remarked: "But two years later they were out; and four years later his side had won"'.[46] Spellar was trusted by his various bosses, and was their surrogate at St Ermins meetings. Golding described Spellar as the Group's long-term thinker and short-term progress chaser, an energetic driving force, continually pushing hard and persuading the hard right to agree to deals from which they got little immediate benefit.[47]

Earlier groupings

Those are the *dramatis personae* of the St Ermins Group. The Group's birth followed a gestation period when some were already beginning to conspire to change the party. A 'Loyalist Group' on the NEC had been instigated by Stanley in 1978. He asked Golding to form an alliance with Tuck, the left-wing Sam McCluskie (who was responsive largely as a result of being defeated by Heffer for the chairmanship of the Organisation Committee) and others to organise a defensive group for the Prime Minister, Jim Callaghan, following the NEC's constant attacks on his government. Not all were right wing, but all were from the unions, motivated by the need to unify to win the election. It was a minority, but it offered some resistance to the unremitting attacks on the government. It also accustomed an inner group to working together, reaching agreements and keeping to them. This Loyalist Group, chaired by Tuck, first met at the North Western Hotel in Euston when Golding was made the convenor (despite being a minister, he was reckoned to have the time!). The Group worked by agreeing voting arrangements – taking account of each person's personal and union sticking points – often arriving at what Golding called 'a shoddy compromise'. The convenor's job, to maximise the support for the Prime Minister and the government, involved pre-planning but also ensuring that loyalists stayed for vital votes on the NEC and voted as they had agreed. If there was no hope of winning a vote, Golding's job was to prevent a decision being made. There were major obstacles, not least that the left held all the chairmanships and controlled the staff.[48]

Despite the Kogans' assertion that the union group had no pre-meetings,[49] meetings were held but kept secret – a pattern later followed by the St Ermins Group. But one man did know: Callaghan approved of what was going on and took comfort from their few successes. How rare these were is shown by the loyalists' delight on winning a resolution supporting the Labour government – on 28 March 1979, the day of the Vote of No Confidence in the Commons.[50] Their influence was more critical over the manifesto when, in coalition with the Cabinet at the Clause V meeting, they helped ensure that the election was fought on a realistic manifesto.[51] However, where they wanted to differ from Callaghan (such as over abolition of the House of Lords, where they would have sided with the left), they were unable to extract any concession from the Prime Minister.

In addition to the Loyalist Group, the problems in the party led a number of unions to support the activist-based CLV. APEX, the POEU, NUR, GMWU, UCW, AUEW and even a section of the NUM took advertisements in its publication, *Labour Victory*.[52] When, in due course, CLV's leading lights largely defected to the SDP, the union members stayed loyal to the party.

A further dozen general secretaries were brought together over dinners at the Great Northern Hotel in King's Cross by junior minister, John Grant, who persuaded them to sign a pamphlet on pay policy.[53] The signatories included Chapple, Duffy, Grantham, Jackson, Sirs and Weighell, who would comprise the core of the St Ermins Group two years later. Yet another group had been meeting in David Owen's office in Old Scotland Yard well before Wembley. Although mostly MPs, it included Chapple, Weighell, Sirs and Grantham, as well as political officers Spellar and Feather. The staffers were already members of the Trade Union and Political Officers Group (TUPO) which met at the Commons. This was a selective grouping of trusties, who came with their general secretaries' blessings. It was rather clandestine and too junior to achieve much. However, it spread useful intelligence and began co-operating on number-crunching for TUC and NEC votes.

At a senior level, Grantham and friends (especially Duffy) had been meeting before 1979. This (no name) group met over dinner at the St Ermins Hotel to discuss TUC General Council business – and to talk politics. At one point, a party official wrote complaining about the meetings. Grantham's reply, to the effect that 'general secretaries have to look after the other interests of their members – so do have meetings. The unions were the creators of the party, and have to decide what to do as unions about certain things', appears to have forestalled any further enquiry. This group wanted to change the make-up of the NEC, with an attempt in 1978 to remove Joan Maynard and Renee Short from their seats.[54]

The NEC and the government fall out

It was the continuous undermining of the Labour government and the breakdown in government–NEC relations which formed the backdrop to St Ermins and led to the determination of these general secretaries to change the composition of the NEC. The unions were vital to the party. They had set it up and trade unionists formed the backbone of the membership. In the 1950s, three-quarters of trade unionists were affiliated members but by the mid-1980s this had shrunk to little more than half.[55] From early on, constituency membership was to the left of the unions and the PLP. In 1952, for example, Bevanites won six out of the seven constituency places on the NEC, whilst Gaitskell was leader of the moderate factor inside the parliamentary party and the favourite of the big unions, which voted him into the party treasurership in 1954 and saw him as their candidate for the post-Attlee leadership.[56] CLP seats on the NEC were thenceforth filled by the left, with their candidates winning all seven places from 1967 to 1969. Denis Healey successfully challenged this monopoly between 1970 and 1974, the complete left-wing monopoly being re-established in 1975 for a decade with the sole exception of Jack Ashley in 1977.[57]

It was not simply that the unions were on the right. They had an ingrained loyalty to the leadership. 'During the Attlee governments the right-wing trade union leaders that dominated the movement had often shared the sentiments of resolutions criticising government economic policy, but had always successfully instructed their delegations to vote against them.'[58] The unions were not uncritically leadership led, crucially refusing Gaitskell's attempt to change Clause IV. As Radice foresaw, 'If there was ever to be a real chance of changing the clause, then the leader had to have both the big unions and potentially hostile rivals like Bevan and Wilson on his side'.[59] The unions did, nevertheless, at the second asking, support Gaitskell on defence. They had earlier chosen him as Treasurer and, in 1967, repeated their prediction for leader by electing Callaghan Treasurer over Foot.[60] At this stage, the NEC supplied comfort to the leader. Jack Jones recalls how, in 1964, he was unimpressed with his first meetings of the NEC, when the ministers loyally supported Prime Minister Harold Wilson. Being told that 'the trade union section always vote together . . . we hope you will follow the same pattern', Jones responded that if that meant he was expected to vote with the top of the table, it was not on. His reaction surprised them.[61]

Jones marked a leftward shift in the unions. As early as 1965, Ian Mikardo sensed a new political radicalism amongst the union delegations at party conferences and appreciated what this might mean for the party: 'Watch the unions: that's my tip', he told readers in *Tribune*.[62] Union hesitancy on some policies was evident, with conference votes against the war in Vietnam, economic policy and incomes policy. It was not only the government's policies that were being challenged. Loyalty to the government also brought into question the authoritarian manipulation of the unions' block votes by their own leaders and helped see the election of left-wing union leaders in the late 1960s in four of the six largest unions. By the mid-1970s, the changes had produced a left-wing majority on the NEC, with the right-wing trade union block vote no longer dominant at the party conference.[63]

A left-dominated NEC was bound to be on a collision course with a more right-wing PLP and government. Joe Haines has described the party pressures upon Harold Wilson which arose from continuous tension. Whereas in 1974–76, the party in the country remained his source of strength, relationships with party headquarters, Transport House and with the NEC were bad and worsening. Even in opposition he had to fight against the party being committed to some breathlessly hare-brained schemes, with a continuous struggle about the supremacy of the parliamentary leadership versus domination by the party outside parliament. There was a temporary reconciliation with the left-wing NEC after the first 1974 election victory but then the Leader–NEC relationship further deteriorated.[64] Wilson's tactic for dealing with the NEC was simply not to turn up and to ignore its decisions but this was only to lead in time to demands for more formal powers for the NEC. The NEC had become unrepresentative of the movement and by the end of Wilson's premiership in 1976, the situation was little short of open hostility. Callaghan had little better luck. At a tense Cabinet–NEC meeting in February 1977, for example, he upbraided the NEC for being too negative and urged that they tell the country more about the government's achievements.[65] The NEC members did not heed his request, casting 23 successive votes critical of the Labour government over 14 successive meetings.[66]

Under Wilson, the NEC refused to do anything to prevent MPs being sacked by their CLPs.[67] Under Callaghan, the NEC attacked the government, went public, refused to take action in 1975 on the Underhill report on Militant and endorsed left-wing parliamentary candidates whilst upholding the deselection of right-wing MPs.[68] Furthermore, the polling evidence showed the policies supported by the NEC were deeply unpopular with the electorate.[69] Yet it was the union block vote which kept an unrepresentative minority in control of the NEC throughout the 1970s, despite most union leaders being from the right and centre-right.[70]

At the 1976 conference, Callaghan used his first address as Prime Minister to voice his goal of re-establishing the dominance of the parliamentary leadership over the NEC.[71] In 1979 he appointed David Owen to the TUC–Labour Party Liaison Committee, which he hoped would become as important as the NEC.[72] He succeeded in neither ambition. The 1969 *In Place of Strife* episode had lined up many centre-right MPs against the government and seen Labour's left-wing collaborating with union leaders who had hitherto resided in a different camp. By tradition, a silent self-denying ordinance by the unions not to use their voting strength to dominate the party on political matters[73] meant that even left-wing union leaders were cautious of pre-empting the autonomy of the parliamentary party, and did not see themselves as rivals for political leadership of the party.[74] However, the 1969 experience gave rise to the left's belief that the unions were the principal base for socialist advance, and led to the left's successful attempt to capture power on the NEC. The alignment of the unions with the Tribunite position in the early 1970s produced an unprecedented degree of influence by the left on party policy.[75] The estrangement of the unions from the party leadership and the desire for revenge after the Winter of Discontent, together with a demoralised and divided right, were crucial in the success of the left.[76]

The unions' reaction to *In Place of Strife* and the Winter of Discontent fuelled a union/left-wing alliance which helped cement a left-dominated NEC. This gave them the chairmanships of the major committees (from 1978 all three were chaired by the left: Benn, Lestor and Heffer) as well as control of staff appointments – something which an earlier Leader, Gaitskell, never allowed to happen. He had ensured that Transport House was packed with his placemen – an advantage which Wilson lost through neglect.[77] Tony Page was the last non-Bennite to join the party staff for a decade, the subsequent recruit being the Militant Andy Bevan. Bevan's appointment fuelled Stanley's determination to end the left-wing majority on the NEC which was helping to destroy the party. He had been astounded to find the party General Secretary voting for the Militant Bevan and the NEC rubber-stamping the decision, appointing the very person who was the greatest danger to the Young Socialists as their Organiser. Whilst new staff were henceforth Bennites, the majority of existing employees – especially in the regions – remained on the centre. The resulting fissure between the left-led NEC and its employees, and the NEC's constant attacks on the government, led to staff demoralisation. The overturning by the NEC of recommendations from regional officials was particularly resented because it undermined their political standing. By suggesting they did not enjoy the full confidence of their masters, it diminished their authority.[78]

It was not just on the NEC that the moderates were losing. Godsiff describes how the left won again and again because they were organised; the right had the numbers but failed to use their majority. There was nobody to pull it together. NUPE and its Organiser Reg Race were running rings round them. Nowhere was this more clear than in the left's agenda for constitutional change. Their three demands were for mandatory reselection of MPs, a wider franchise for the election of the leader, and the NEC having sole control over the manifesto. These became the battleground. Between 1979 and 1982, the issue of democracy and power in the party became dominant, virtually making the substantive issues secondary.[79] Even before any change in rule had been passed, the NEC used its majority to determine the manifesto for the 1979 European Parliament elections without involving the PLP.[80] These were the first direct elections so there was no precedent for agreeing a manifesto. However, for general elections, Clause V of the constitution was clear: a joint NEC–Cabinet (or, in opposition, Shadow Cabinet) meeting made the decision. The Euro-manifesto episode reflected the changing balance between the parliamentary leadership and the NEC.

The unions never pressed for the changes promoted by the left which threatened the balance of the coalition groups inside the party by entrenching activist and NEC power to establish a left-wing hegemony.[81] Indeed, as Minkin has demonstrated, in 1979 not one single resolution or amendment was submitted by the unions on the three constitutional issues; indeed, the union majority actually voted against the amendments.[82] Before the 1979 conference, a high level delegation of Trade Unions for a Labour Victory (TULV) to the NEC gave the unanimous view that all constitutional matters be put off until a Commission of Enquiry into the organisation of the party had been established and reported. Nevertheless, the NEC stood up to this plea from their unions and, whilst agreeing to an enquiry, refused to take the issues off the 1979 agenda.[83]

The Commission of Enquiry immediately caused upset. It was established with a 2:1 majority for the left[84] and with no PLP representation (other than the leader and deputy). The PLP attacked the way the NEC had rigged the Commission, by appointing seven left-wingers to represent itself, whilst the unions chose a balanced team of five, picked from all the main currents of opinion. MPs were allowed only two representatives (Jim Callaghan and Michael Foot), thus giving the NEC an in-built left-wing majority. The PLP appointed Healey to put its case to the NEC: 'They simply ignored my arguments.'[85]

The Electoral College is born

The Commission, started in January 1980, led to the *casus belli* of the SDP split. Its final meeting at Bishop's Stortford on 15 June agreed, by seven votes to six, to recommend an Electoral College (with 50 per cent for the PLP, 25 per cent for the CLPs, 20 per cent for trade unions and 5 per cent for the socialist societies) to choose the leader. Commission secretariat member Jenny Pardington recalls Callaghan remonstrating with its proponents: 'you only want it because it would elect Benn'.[86] Nevertheless, he gave way. For the right, Callaghan's capitulation remains inexplicable. Grantham reflected: 'Good men don't always do the right thing'. He thought that the Prime Minister did not talk enough to friends, who rarely went to Number 10, yet the critical issues were party, not government, ones.[87] Could the decision have been overturned? Healey judged that:

> A battle against the Bishop's Stortford agreement would have meant a break, not only with Jim, but with the majority of trade union leaders who had supported it, believing that it would at least protect the party from a takeover by the left. The fight I was being asked to lead . . . had no prospect of victory. It would have meant splitting the party.[88]

Frank Chapple's view was different; he blamed Callaghan for going along tamely with those who sought to remove from MPs the exclusive right to choose the party leader.[89] A crisis was developing. By tradition, the unions were expected to stabilise the party. However, with the NEC under the control of the left and deeply hostile to the interventions of union leaders, there was also no consensus on the right as to how to move forward.[90] There was a lack of both leadership and organisation. Minkin maintains that reform of the election of the leader could have been averted had the right been able to get some agreement on what it wanted, communicate this to its union allies and organise a united strategy.[91]

The proposal for the manifesto to come under total NEC control was defeated in 1980 but two of the left's changes were passed. Mandatory reselection was adopted by 3,798,000 to 3,341,000, probably without a union majority in favour.[92] More significantly, delegates voted by only 98,000 to support an Electoral College. As one of the founders of the St Ermins Group later wrote: 'The moderate unions were completely outmanoeuvred by the Bennite forces.'[93] There was probably a union majority against this and it would have failed without NUPE's increased affiliation (from 150,000 in 1974 to 600,000 in 1980).[94] Furthermore, had each union respected its mandate, the proposal would have been lost. The boiler-makers' union had decided, at its pre-meeting, to vote against the Electoral College. However, when the two senior members, Chalmers and Hadden, were called away, the delegation was left in the hands of Len Hancock. When the leaders got back, they found Hancock had voted contrary to that decision.[95] Without the boilermakers' 75,000 votes, the motion would have been defeated by 3,586,000 to 3,534,000 – a majority against of 52,000.

The unions had, by accident or design, created the Electoral College and cemented mandatory reselection – both seen as undermining the PLP. The left majority on the NEC – provided in part by the unions – put itself at the service of those demanding change.[96] The out-numbered centre-right ploughed a lonely furrow. Even in Chapple's time, when there was a right-wing majority on the NEC, Wilson seldom used his authority as Prime Minister, simply ruling himself out of disciplinary matters, saying he did not want to be an unfair influence, and on other issues the organising was not done. On one crucial vote, for example, when Labour was in disarray over entry into the Common Market and Chapple had been persuaded to attend an all-day NEC as heads had been counted and his vote was vital, Shirley Williams, who was supposed to be against a special conference, voted for one. 'Once again the moderates had miscalculated'.[97]

Later, when there was no chance of having the numbers, the moderates paid the price of having lost control over the bureaucracy. The Bennite research staff would try and swamp the committee with so much paper that things would slide through. NEC members John Cartwright, Shirley Williams and Tom Bradley therefore 'devised a system where we would each take chunks of the agenda and see what was going on, so we could alert the others. And there were some other trade unionists who worked with us. Not very organised on their part. But we three were more organised.'[98] Cartwright found the new Prime Minister no different from Wilson:

> Callaghan was a great disappointment to me. Given his reputation for being an apparatchik, and product of the organisation, I assumed when he took over as leader he'd take greater interest but he didn't. He was trying to keep the government, the policy and the PLP on an even course. The battle with the left therefore never really took place on the NEC. There was no organised attempt to fight it. He was never interested in head-on battle.'[99]

NEC meetings had become bear-fights. After the 1979 election, Williams was out of parliament but remained on the NEC, which she found increasingly unpleasant and unrewarding.[100] 'The main battlefield in the war for the Labour Party's survival was its National Executive Committee, which in 1979 was solidly dominated by the left.'[101] Healey – a beachmaster in the war and never afraid to take on the enemy – had lost his NEC seat in 1975 so there was no political leadership for the moderates. In addition to Bevan's appointment, the other decision which convinced Bryan Stanley that that left majority had to go was the Underhill report: in spite of its clear evidence, the left-wing majority on the NEC described any attempt to criticise or to investigate Militant as a witch-hunt; they used every excuse to take no action and to cover up the damage that was being done to the party and to its prospects of forming a Labour government.

Whilst moderate union leaders grew exasperated at the party, elsewhere things were moving apace. Despite Shirley Williams' 1979 view that there had been a shift of power in the unions, which were moving back to the centre with only a small handful remaining on the far-left,[102] she and her fellow Social Democrats despaired of progress and the Gang of Three published an appeal in the *Guardian* on 1 August 1980. Trade unionists had been slipping away electorally, with Labour winning only half of their vote in 1979 whilst the Tories won nearly a third.[103] As the unions felt the impact of a Conservative government (unemployment, tax concessions to the wealthy, public expenditure cuts, privatisation, erosion of union rights), their leaders became increasingly anxious to restore unity and prepare the party for office.[104]

The Social Democrats prepare to leave

The 1980 conference was the final straw for many Social Democrats, though the failure to agree a formula for the Electoral College delayed the inevitable until after Wembley. Whilst the Gang of Four (with Roy Jenkins now added) planned their move, many sought to dissuade them. Healey spent several hours in a private discussion with Owen, Williams and Rodgers in September, telling them that the moderates had a good chance of winning a majority on the NEC and transforming the situation – although 'this was bound to take several years'.[105]

Union leaders tried: the NUR's Sid Weighell and Charlie Turnock had a long meeting with Shirley Williams at the Charing Cross Hotel over lunch, about a month before Wembley, trying to persuade her of 'the error of her ways' but 'there was no going back with her. She listened to the arguments. But she was too deeply committed with the other three'.[106] Her own union, APEX, also tried, with Denis Howell and Roy Grantham working hard on her. The persuasion was not all one way. The postal workers' Alan Tuffin was in their sights: 'I was being canvassed quite heavily by Shirley about leaving the Labour Party. They were desperate for a big union. It never happened. Just wasn't going to happen. Even today, with the party, it's not so much national, it's local. There are thousands of trade unionists who are local Labour councillors. Their union – the break would destroy that. Never, never a reality'.[107]

At the January Wembley conference, the arguments continued. Stanley recalled:

> Shirley Williams approached me in my seat at the end row of POEU delegates. Since I held the union's voting card, I was reluctant to move far away from my seat so we had to sit on the stairs. Shirley's message was clear. Owing to the left-wing control of the NEC and Trotskyite infiltration, the Labour Party was unelectable and it was time to look at a new party based on social democratic beliefs. Shirley was saying to me: 'Look, I don't agree with you on everything but you are prepared to fight Militant and the extreme left. That is what we want to do, but in a new Social Democratic grouping. Will you join us?' I said 'Now look, Shirley, I do respect you and I do like you personally, but I will never leave the Labour Party. I've been a member for 30 years, and I want to be a member until the day I die. I agree with you that things are wrong, but what we've got to do is work together to put them right; and if that means organising to defeat the well-organised machine that the left operate, then we've got to do that from inside the party. If you go, you will come to grief because there's an innate loyalty of Labour Party members and trade unionists to the party. There is no way the majority of us are ever going to leave'. I tried to persuade her not to go.[108]

Before the final vote, there were pleadings from defectors and stayers. At a packed Fabian lunchtime meeting chaired by the author and fortified by sandwiches from the near-empty CLV meeting next door, Hattersley made a vigorous case for staying. For the Fabian audience, it was an effective rallying cry. But organisationally, it was a disaster. Radice realised, too late: 'the left were going round switching to the USDAW formula. It was such a cock-up. We had been out-manoeuvred by the left'.[109] Over the lunch break, CLPD decided to support USDAW's 40:30:30 amendment and, as Stanley also acknowledged, 'In the absence of effective organisation on the moderate side, it was a foregone conclusion that the better organised left would dominate the conference'.[110] The result was due to disarray of the right.[111] It was all unnecessary: the unions could have outvoted the constituencies but they were disorganised and uncertain.[112] The AUEW, forced to abstain by a prior decision of its executive, bequeathed USDAW's formula to the party, the largest share going to the unions (unpopular with the electorate) and handing this issue – rather than unpopular Europe – to the Gang of Four as the rationale for their defection. It was, said Weighell, 'A disastrous Saturday's work'.[113] The Limehouse Declaration followed the next day, Sunday 25 January 1981, foreshadowing the SDP.

The lesson of Wembley

For Giles Radice, 'That was the background to St Ermins – lack of organisation; how incompetent we'd been'.[114] Alan Tuffin watched from the balcony:

> Ken Livingstone was there and said: 'the unions will always win these arguments'. I thought: that's not right. It was the beginning of a lot of us realising we were not paying enough attention. We all had our own industries to run and we were not paying enough attention to what was going on. Typical situation, like NEC meetings, London EC[115] meetings, they would sit there patiently to the late hours, provided they always had a quorum. And people like myself, who'd been working all day in the office, and a case full of work to take home. So 10 o'clock – I'm going home. This was their work. It wasn't our work.[116]

Post-Wembley, things were going to be different for the unions. Sandy Feather admits it was the SDP split which 'forced the party to recognise the reality, that if the good guys didn't get together, the left would always win. The split made Sirs, Grantham and the others say: "we've got to do something about this"'.[117]

Frank Chapple, who had been close to CLV and those who were to form the SDP, contended that 'if a Labour split was inevitable then it should be the left, not those who truly represented millions of working people, who should be forced to quit . . . The best prospect for halting the leftward drift lay within the unions and not in the confusion of a new fourth party', noting that Roy Jenkins had 'declared that a trade union based rescue of Labour was unacceptable'. He now decided: 'I wanted to help mobilise trade union moderates to oust the unrepresentative left-wing majority on Labour's NEC'.[118] Stanley was similarly determined. 'I made up my mind that I would do my utmost to bring together leaders of the Labour movement to combat the organisation and manoeuvring of the left-wing factions.'[119]

Notes

1 Denis Howell, *Made in Birmingham: The Memoirs of Denis Howell* (Queen Anne Press, 1990), p. 103.
2 Sidney Weighell, *On the Rails* (Orbis Publishing, 1983); Terry Pattinson, 'Obituary of Sidney Weighell', *Independent*, 15 February 2002; John Lloyd, *Financial Times*, 18 February 2002.
3 Weighell, *On the Rails*, p. 23.
4 John Lloyd, *Financial Times*, 18 February 2002.

5 Weighell, *On the Rails*, pp. 135–6.

6 Donoughue, *Heat of the Kitchen*, p. 266.

7 *Independent*, 15 February 2002.

8 McSmith, *Faces of Labour*, p. 135.

9 *Ibid.*, p. 136.

10 Silkin, *Changing Battlefields*, p. 38. (He would perhaps rue such comments when the AUEW helped defeat his bid for the deputy leadership.)

11 Sir John Boyd was not just anti-communist. He could not tolerate Trotskyites and wanted to 'cleanse' the party, describing Militant as 'a sewer with all sorts of rubbish floating in it' (*Guardian*, 24 April 1982); Eric Shaw, *Discipline and Discord in the Labour Party* (Manchester University Press, 1988), p. 234.

12 Panitch and Leys, *End of Parliamentary Socialism*, p. 150.

13 Dick Clements interview.

14 McSmith, *Faces of Labour*, p. 137.

15 Neil Kinnock interview.

16 The Newcastle-under-Lyme party invited Stanley to be their MP. He 'declined but recommended the young John Golding. The Potters [Ceramics] union conveniently called a meeting half an hour before the start of the selection conference, though expenses for attending would be handed out after the selection. The 90 or so who went, and stayed throughout the party meeting, ensured Golding was selected' (Bryan Stanley interview). Golding admitted the selection had been fixed – not as a confession but to expose the injustices of the old selection system (*Guardian*, 14 July 1983).

17 Panitch and Leys, *End of Parliamentary Socialism*, p. 151.

18 Neil Kinnock interview.

19 William Sirs, letter to the author, 21 October 2002.

20 Gordon Colling interview.

21 Neil Kinnock interview.

22 Gordon Colling iinterview.

23 Chapple, *Sparks Fly!*, p. 105.

24 Donoughue, *Heat of the Kitchen*, p. 267.

25 Denis Healey interview.

26 Donoughue, *Heat of the Kitchen*, p. 266.

27 Roy Grantham interview.

28 Giles Radice interview, 7 October 2002.

29 Tom McNally interview.

30 Dick Clements interview.

31 Roger Godsiff interview.

32 Sandy Feather interview.

33 Roger Godsiff interview, 4 December 2001.

34 Shaw, *Discipline and Discord in the Labour Party*, pp. 359–60.

35 Roger Godsiff interview.

36 The system for electing the TUC's General Council; see pp. 105–7.

37 Bryan Stanley interview.

38 Gordon Colling interview.

39 Neil Kinnock interview.

40 McSmith, *Faces of Labour*, p. 219.

41 Golding, 'The fixers', chapter 13, p. 8.

42 Neil Stewart interview.

43 Golding, *Hammer of the Left*, p. 182, quoting Doug Hoyle.

44 Sandy Feather interview.
45 Alan Hadden telephone interview.
46 John Lloyd interview.
47 Golding, *Hammer of the Left*, pp. 181–2.
48 *Ibid.*, chapter 4.
49 David Kogan and Maurice Kogan, *The Battle for the Labour Party* (Fontana, 1982), p. 74.
50 Golding, *Hammer of the Left*, pp. 77, 79.
51 Golding, 'The fixers', chapter 4, p. 6.
52 Gerald J. Daly, 'The crisis in the Labour Party 1974–81 and the origins of the 1981 schism' (PhD Thesis, University of London, 1992), p. 267.
53 *A Better Way*, published by the Signatories (which did not include its un-named author, Grant), January 1979. It also 'shows a new preparedness to organise on the Labour right' (*New Statesman*, 2 February 1979). The pamphlet sold 8,000 copies. A slight surplus (£395.57) was later sent to charity. See also Chapple, *Sparks Fly!*, pp. 148–9.
54 Patrick Wintour, 'Can the left win this time round?', *New Statesman*, 20 July 1979, p. 87.
55 Silkin, *Changing Battlefields*, p. 7.
56 Radice, *Friends and Rivals*, p. 98.
57 Patrick Seyd, *The Rise and Fall of the Labour Left* (Macmillan Education, 1987), p. 207.
58 Panitch and Leys, *End of Parliamentary Socialism*, p. 21.
59 Radice, *Friends and Rivals*, p. 114. Tony Blair had Gordon Brown and John Prescott, as well as the unions, on his side when he achieved this over 30 years later.
60 Chapple, *Sparks Fly!*, p. 109; Owen, *Time to Declare*, p. 153.
61 Jack Jones, *Union Man: An Autobiography* (Collins, 1986), p. 167.
62 Panitch and Leys, *End of Parliamentary Socialism*, p. 21.
63 Seyd, *Rise and Fall of the Labour Left*, p. 47; Shaw, *Discipline and Discord in the Labour Party*, p. viii; Daly, 'The crisis in the Labour Party 1974–81', p. 63; Panitch and Leys, *End of Parliamentary Socialism*, p. 22.
64 Haines, *The Politics of Power*, p. 13.
65 Golding, 'The fixers', chapter 2, p. 1.
66 Tom McNally interview and Daly, 'The crisis in the Labour Party 1974–81', p. 113. To some, this was 'just rewards' for Callaghan's 1969 vote on the NEC when, although a Cabinet member, he voted against *In Place of Strife*; Owen, *Time to Declare*, p. 154.
67 Haines, *The Politics of Power*, p. 14.
68 Daly, 'The crisis in the Labour Party 1974–81', p. 113.
69 Lord (Bernard) Donoughue interview with Gerald Daly, 5 April 1989 (*Ibid.*, p. 121); Owen, *Time to Declare*, p. 430.
70 Panitch and Leys, *End of Parliamentary Socialism*, p. 148; Lewis Minkin, *The Labour Party Conference* (Manchester University Press, 1980), pp. 358–61.
71 Panitch and Leys, *End of Parliamentary Socialism*, p. 176.
72 Owen, *Time to Declare*, p. 421.
73 Allan Flanders, *Trade Unions and Politics; London Trades Council 1860–1960 Centenary Lecture* (London Trades Council, 1961).
74 Panitch and Leys, *End of Parliamentary Socialism*, p. 25.
75 Alan Warde, *Consensus and Beyond: The Development of Labour Party Strategy since the Second World War* (Manchester University Press, 1982), pp. 163, 171.
76 Daly, 'The crisis in the Labour Party 1974–81', p. 164; Keith Middlemas, *Power, Competition and the State* (Macmillan, 1990), p. 245.
77 Haines, *The Politics of Power*, p. 13.

78 Shaw, *Discipline and Discord in the Labour Party*, p. 216.
79 Minkin, *The Contentious Alliance*, p. 192.
80 Owen, *Time to Declare*, p. 149.
81 Daly, 'The crisis in the Labour Party 1974–81', p. 17.
82 Lewis Minkin, *Exits and Entrances: Political Research as a Creative Art* (Sheffield Hallam University Press, 1997), pp. 127, 277.
83 Panitch and Leys, *End of Parliamentary Socialism*, p. 179; and Minkin, *The Contentious Alliance*, p. 197.
84 Sked and Cook, *Post-War Britain*, p. 423.
85 Denis Healey, *The Time of My Life* (Michael Joseph, 1989), p. 474.
86 Jenny Pardington interview.
87 Roy Grantham interview.
88 Healey, *The Time of My Life*, p. 475.
89 Chapple, *Sparks Fly!*, pp. 161–2.
90 Minkin, *The Contentious Alliance*, p. 201.
91 *Ibid.*, p. 200.
92 *Ibid.*, p. 195.
93 Weighell, *On the Rails*, p. 137. The figures were 3,609,000 to 3,511,000; *Report of 1980 Labour Party Conference*, p. 152.
94 Minkin, *The Contentious Alliance*, p. 199; Panitch and Leys, *End of Parliamentary Socialism*, p. 152.
95 Alan Hadden interview; Robert Taylor, *Observer*, 5 October 1980.
96 Minkin, *The Contentious Alliance*, p. 196.
97 Chapple, *Sparks Fly!*, pp. 129–30.
98 John Cartwright interview.
99 *Ibid.*
100 Rodgers, *Fourth Among Equals*, p. 192.
101 Healey, *The Time of My Life*, p. 471.
102 Panitch and Leys, *End of Parliamentary Socialism*, p. 151.
103 Healey, *The Time of My Life*, p. 466.
104 Minkin, *The Contentious Alliance*, p. 194.
105 Healey, *The Time of My Life*, p. 477. In 2002, his memory was slightly different: 'In my meeting with Shirley and others, I told them just to wait 6 months. The NEC would change. I knew from Roy Grantham that things were happening. I knew who the candidates were, and who would win'; Denis Healey interview.
106 Charles Turnock interview.
107 Alan Tuffin interview.
108 Bryan Stanley interview.
109 Giles Radice interview, 7 October 2002.
110 Bryan Stanley interview.
111 Daly, 'The crisis in the Labour Party 1974–81', p. 198.
112 Phillip Whitehead, *The Writing on the Wall: Britain in the Seventies* (Michael Joseph, 1985), p. 361.
113 Weighell, *On the Rails*, p. 139.
114 Giles Radice interview, 7 October 2002.
115 London Labour Party Executive Committee.
116 Alan Tuffin interview.
117 Sandy Feather interview.
118 Chapple, *Sparks Fly!*, pp. 164–5.
119 Bryan Stanley interview.

10

The St Ermins Group

> Both in 1931 and afterwards the influence of the trade unions had steadied the Labour Party: in 1931, when there was a danger that MacDonald might carry a greater number with him; afterwards, when the reaction threatened to swing the Party over to the Left.[1]

The union leaders, outflanked at Wembley, had worse to contend with the following day, as some of their erstwhile friends lined up behind the Limehouse Declaration. All their gentle persuasion had come to nothing. A stark choice faced them. They would not leave, but would they do more and steady the Labour Party as their predecessors had done 50 years earlier? Their response drew on the groupings that already existed, but suddenly it was serious. This chapter sets out what they did, and how.

Grantham talked urgently to fellow general secretaries. Together with Stanley and with the wholehearted support of Duffy, he quickly convened a meeting for 10 February 1981. It was to turn into the inaugural meeting of a very significant grouping. Bryan Stanley recalls the event:

> There was no letter. We were approaching people on the phone. We approached the general secretaries or their equivalents in all the unions where we felt we could trust people. We decided the best place would be a central London hotel. We asked all to keep confidence. We invited Denis Healey because he seemed the person in the top levels of the party who could help us greatly if we were going to be effective. We met in the Charing Cross Hotel and we immediately realised that we were all on the same wavelength. Whilst Denis said 'I cannot be party to any grouping that you have, you are doing the right thing which is so badly needed. But I can't be part of it: I wish you well.' He left. The meeting went on and we appointed people to do various jobs. The most significant of the appointments was to take up Roger Godsiff's offer to be Secretary/Organiser. John Golding was going to be the contact in PLP. I was going to be the link with all the different groups that we had to consult, bring together, notify of what we were going to do.[2]

MP and APEX President Denis Howell chaired this first 'Meeting of General Secretaries' at which 17 were present. Beginning a practice that continued throughout the Group's life, no list of attendees appears in the minutes, but participants included: Roy Grantham, Bryan Stanley, Frank Chapple, Terry Duffy, Denis

Healey, Sid Weighell, Tom Jackson, Charlie Turnock,[3] Bill Sirs, Giles Radice, Bill Whatley, John Golding, Sandy Feather, John Spellar and Roger Godsiff.[4]

Godsiff had already demonstrated the value of careful number-crunching. Immediately prior to the Wembley conference, he had prepared a paper for APEX on the Electoral College. This detailed each union's size and voting intention, and concluded that a consensus position giving the PLP 50 per cent could be won, provided it had some CLP support, although the attitude of USDAW would be crucial in determining the final result. He was right. The Group knew they had lost at Wembley through lack of planning, organisation and discipline. Now, in front of this intimidating array of general secretaries and three former ministers, the young research officer ventured: '"With respect, if you look at the figures, you can achieve things if you put it together." They more or less said "OK; get on with it". So I did a paper with the figures for NEC seats for the next meeting.'[5] Godsiff was to be proved right again: before, the right had the vote but did not organise; once they did, they won.

The rationale behind the Group was clear. The unions wanted a Labour government and believed it would only come with a move to the right.[6] 'The aim of the Group was to retrieve the party from the mess it was in and ensure the TUC General Council was reformed to become a better representative of the unions' said Roy Grantham,[7] Bryan Stanley agreeing: 'St Ermins came together for the purpose of removing the artificial dominance of the left over the NEC and General Council.'[8] The Group never dealt in policy, only in positions together with the structure of the TUC. The absence of policies made co-operation easier, as some of them came from left-wing unions where they had difficult situations to control. So the agreement was that they would talk about mechanisms, the means by which they could, in their words, 'return sanity to the party'. Tony Clarke commented: 'The cement that brought us all together was not only self-preservation of the unions but our dream – all we wanted to achieve needed a Labour government. That was the common denomination. Survival and social progress. We had to be electable for our aims to be attainable.'[9] Turnock knew that the Group had to change the NEC but also what was going on in the TUC and the structure of its General Council, which he saw as intertwined with the NEC.

There was a degree of self-interest for some unions which were denied a seat at the table by the existing political carve-up. So the Group offered mutual protection, with everyone gaining something; the leadership got a supportive NEC whilst the members simultaneously pursued their own unions' objectives. For the ISTC, for example, getting Roy Evans elected to NEC was an important objective, which it achieved through the Group. Similarly for the National Graphical Association (NGA later to become part of the Graphical Paper and Media Union), an entrée into the political councils was central to its industrial interests. APEX's Roy Grantham had been kept off the TUC because of his pro-Europeanism but the St Ermins Group was to rectify that.

The February meeting established their way of working. Monthly meetings would henceforth take place (up to 1995). Detailed papers were prepared by Godsiff. Spellar liaised with union political officers and Golding with the PLP. Bryan Stanley recalled:

[I] realised that if anything was going to succeed, someone had to link up with all the prominent players who wouldn't link up themselves. And therefore I was the go-between. I would personally arrange a meeting with each of the principal unions who shared our view. And they, if the general secretary or president, they would arrange a lunch and we'd deal with it, or more frequently, they would nominate a representative. I had to go to every union to clear the way forward, to determine the names of candidates and then, after the meetings where it was finalised, to convey to them what was going to happen and to be sure we'd got their support. There was absolutely no point in putting forward candidates which were going to be shot down because there was no unity. So I had to go and clear all the candidates.[10]

This is referred to in the minutes as 'Further discussions', or code for work that had to be done behind the scenes.

Meetings were to be kept completely confidential, though not without an initial hiccup, as Stanley vividly described:

Just before we left that first meeting, everyone expressed the view that the meeting *must* be behind closed doors otherwise it wasn't going to succeed. Everyone present said 'no publicity'. I had a drink in the hotel bar with one or two before we left. There were newspaper sellers outside the Charing Cross Hotel, a placard which bore the heading 'The march of the Labour Party moderates'. It was the *Evening Standard*. It was reporting the proceedings of the meeting I'd just left. It must have been printed while the meeting was going on! Fortunately, we had anticipated that the Charing Cross was too prominent a place and so we'd agreed to arrange the next meeting in St Ermins – more off the track. They let hotel rooms set up for conferences; we just gave out the hotel room number. So from then on, although the left found out we were meeting at St Ermins, there was no leak and no publicity but we became known as the St Ermins Group.[11]

St Ermins Hotel, near Scotland Yard, had long been a venue for Labour movement machinations. Used for the bondage scene in the 1985 film 'Mona Lisa', this former monastery played host to innumerable business meetings and surreptitious liaisons (including diplomatic and political), as well as to the Prime Minister's team in the 1979 election. Used as offices during the war, it was considered as party headquarters afterwards but reverted to a hotel. It remained a favourite – for meetings between union leaders and the General Secretary (Morgan Phillips) and Treasurer (Hugh Gaitskell) in 1955,[12] for a 'tactics' meeting between Bill Rodgers and the party's conference-fixer, Derek Gladwin, before the 1970 special conference on Europe,[13] and for the meetings which led to the formation of CLV.[14] Union leaders frequented it – often linked to negotiations with employers. On such occasions, after the hard bargaining was over, talk would turn to union and party matters. Sometimes union leaders would have a lunch together after the NEC or General Council, as they both used to meet on the same day on a Wednesday morning,[15] so everyone was in London and hungry, making it convenient to organise lunch there.

The Group, with only two minor exceptions, henceforth kept the proceedings almost completely secret.[16] Part of this success lay in the virtual absence of written material and the bland minutes produced. Members were highly cautious about what they said and wrote. Sandy Feather only ever wrote 'Group' in his diary. Gordon Colling, who joined a little later, was intrigued:

> The letter inviting you just said: 'There will be a meeting at this place at this time'. They made it clear to me, that I'd been well vetted and that the meeting was secret. If a story broke which had come from the Group, there would be a 'Court of Enquiry'. How could anyone know that? It must be someone here. And in some way, the one who was suspected wouldn't come any more! Someone would say 'the only person there who hadn't been before was so-and-so'. Ones who'd been before were trusted.[17]

There were only one or two leaks throughout the Group's existence – and both when outsiders had joined it for a specific item. It is surprising that journalists found out so little as, by the end of 1981, the Group had moved to Swinton House (the ISTC's headquarters) in Gray's Inn Road, where it then remained. This was chosen, according to Grantham, because it was cheaper, very discreet with no journalists around and away from the limelight. However, his description was not entirely accurate as Swinton House is

> virtually next door to Acorn House, the journalists' union. And we drank afterward in the Lucas Arms – the NUJ pub. Some of St Ermins people were not that well known but even so . . .! It was extraordinary it wasn't rumbled. It helped that Mrs Thatcher was distancing herself from the union movement. Therefore unions were less important, less courted and less covered and less followed by the press.[18]

As a result of the self-discipline, the literature revealed little of the Group until 2003. Maintaining their oaths of confidentiality, neither Weighell, Chapple nor Howell ever mentioned the Group in their autobiographies.[19] Even like-minded politicians knew nothing about it. Academics fare little better. Seyd makes no reference to it, despite claiming that 'Only one . . . group, the Campaign for Democratic Socialism [in the 1960s], on the Labour right, compares for organisational ability [with CLPD] in the history of Labour factionalism'.[20] Shaw does not include St Ermins in his index, though it appears twice in footnotes, both times mis-spelt as St Ermine's.[21] Pearce also misnames it St Ermine's and completes his description in five lines.[22] Kogan and Kogan make no mention at all.[23] The main chronicler of the unions, Lewis Minkin, makes passing references to the Group and, by inference, mis-dates its creation. He suggests that, in 1981: 'An extension of the "St Ermin's" [sic.] alliance took place. The leaders of the AUEW, . . . APEX, EETPU, ISTC, NUR, POEU and USDAW (the core of the St Ermin's [sic.] Group) were now joined by the GMWU and the UCW, which had in recent times kept aloof from the rightwing grouping'.[24] The UCW was in fact involved from the start, whereas the GMWU leader held aloof. Panitch and Leys completely misunderstood the modus operandi: 'The right-wing St Ermin's [sic.] group of unions similarly began to take the initiative for the counter-insurgency from the TULV, flexing their muscles with well-publicised plans to reverse the Wembley decision and to secure right-wing control of the NEC.'[25] Well publicised they were not! Whilst 2003 saw John Golding's brilliantly atmospheric descriptions of many of these events published posthumously,[18] he too maintained silence in his lifetime.

The St Ermins Group was not the only response to Wembley and the SDP. At the 4 March Group meeting, Denis Howell

> gave a report on the Labour Solidarity Campaign which had been set up with the support of 120 MPs. He referred to the work to secure office accommodation, issue a regular bulletin, obtain finance and donations and to set up regional organisations. He also advised the meeting that a letter would be sent to trade union general secretaries, explaining why the Solidarity Campaign had been set up. It was agreed that wherever possible the Campaign should be supported by the placing of advertisements in their bulletin.[27]

The Group's initial objective was to win NEC seats. Godsiff produced a paper for the March meeting, the first of four held at the St Ermins Hotel, concentrating on the five women's places. Although theoretically elected by the whole conference, the unions' near-90 per cent share of the vote gave them control. Godsiff's paper set out the 1980 results, emphasising that the top three runners-up (Betty Boothroyd, Shirley Summerskill and the Fabian Dianne Hayter) were all 'sensible', whilst the left-wing Margaret Beckett,[28] lying fifth, was a prime target. Carefully detailing every union's size and voting intention, he indicated which votes needed to be harnessed, and concluded: 'If there is a will on the part of moderate trade unions to make really big changes in the composition of the NEC then it can be done in both the trade union and women's sections but it requires a belief, commitment and voting discipline which has been lacking in the past'. Golding, meanwhile, had begun discussing a slate. 'Betty Boothroyd, Shirley Summerskill, Dianne Hayter and Gwyneth Dunwoody had "picked themselves" for the women's section' and by April the Group had 12 names for the union seats, including McCluskie and Kitson – supposedly on the left.[21] The minutes record that 'Attention was drawn to the need to ensure that "uncommitted" unions were contacted' to get their support for the list. For this initial round, no deals were made. The aim was to harness the moderate unions to support the slate. It was the first time it had happened, and it proved that the NEC could be changed by co-ordinated organisation.

The first organised contests

Discussions with the swing votes were about to begin. However, on 2 April, plans were thrown into disarray by Benn's challenge to Healey. Suddenly there were more important stakes; item one of the April agenda was the deputy leadership, the NEC elections taking second place. Much of 1981 was taken up with this contest, which many saw as a struggle for the survival of the party. The 24 June meeting, for example, discussed a paper on the deputy leadership which identified which unions needed to be contacted, and members undertook to make various approaches. The Political Officers' Group (TUPO) continued to meet, convened by Spellar and Golding, and fed in other intelligence – such as changes in affiliation (and hence voting numbers).

Three other items appeared on that summer's agenda. One was the Group's (half-hearted) attempts to revise the Wembley formula (to 50:25:25), which got nowhere. The second concerned the seats on the TUC's General Council. A meeting was held as soon as the list of nominees appeared, to deal with these elections. The Group had difficulty finalising its slate, so Grantham asked them to phone him in Blackpool on the eve of voting to be given the final recommendation. The third was the election of the party treasurer. At its April meeting, the Group agreed to support Eric Varley. NUM-sponsored, a former minister and, importantly, former Chairman of the PLP Trade Union Group, he would start with the advantage of NUM support, despite his centre-right and their left-of-centre politics.

These moves had not been kept completely secret, although the Group's name never appeared. The *Daily Mirror* reported that 'A hit list of left-wingers has been drawn up by Labour's increasingly active right' and said the Group 'hopes to dent – or even overturn – the left's dominance of the ruling National Executive . . . Top of the hit list is party treasurer Norman Atkinson . . . Other prime targets are left-wingers Joan Maynard and Renee Short'.[30] *The Times* added that 'With the minor scandal of the right wing slate for the TUC General Council elections unburied, it came to light that the anti-left liaison group[31] wants a clean-up of the militant-dominated Labour Party leadership. The list circulated to unions proposes that four left-wingers should be ousted'.[32] The *Mirror* repeated its story[33] whilst political journalist David Gow discounted the chances of success.[34]

The tally and rallying of votes for the treasurership and other NEC seats were critical to the September results. Just two days after Healey's wafer-thin victory over Benn, five seats fell to the moderates. Varley beat the left-wing incumbent and AUEW member, Norman Atkinson, but only by Duffy persuading his delegation to withdraw support from one of their own members. Margaret Beckett and three other left-wingers lost their seats. The right was strengthened enormously. Boothroyd kept the seat she had inherited on Shirley Williams' resignation, and was joined by Dunwoody and Summerskill.[35] At the result, Renee Short shouted: 'This is all your fault, Terry Duffy'; 'Guilty' Duffy cheerfully retorted.[36] However, it was not Duffy's handiwork alone. The results were no surprise to those close to Godsiff. A comparison between his prediction and the actual results shows a mere 4.4 per cent error. Golding won a wager with Callaghan over this result but – perhaps because he had used insider information with Godsiff's predictions – he never cashed the cheque.

'Moderates sweep to victory on the NEC' claimed the *Financial Times*;

> The changes mean that there has been a fundamental change in the balance of power within the Labour Party. They indicate, far more convincingly than Mr Denis Healey's narrow victory . . . that the tide has now turned against Mr Tony Benn and the far left and that at last the attempts of right-wing union leaders to organise against the left have paid off. They mean that Mr Foot should now be able to command a majority on the executive, . . . on most issues Mr Benn will now be in a minority.[37]

A little premature, but its analysis that the left's 19:10 dominance had been replaced by a committee with the balance in favour of the moderates and centre-left by 15:14 was about right. Boothroyd recalled the moderates (without mentioning the St Ermins Group) doing 'spectacularly well in the NEC . . . We broke the hard left's grip by making five gains. I held my seat with strong trade union support and Gwyneth Dunwoody swelled the anti-Militant ranks ... The terminal dangers facing the party were far from over, but we had edged away from the abyss'.[38]

Panitch and Leys acknowledge the significance of the result:

> The Labour new left's defeat ... was not restricted to the deputy leadership ... far more important ... was another set of votes for the National Executive ... The right-wing leadership of the Engineering Union finally fulfilled its promise ... to produce a right-wing delegation ... (t)hat went so far as to vote to remove Norman Atkinson, himself a member of the union, from the post of party treasurer ... It was, however, only a small part of a much larger targeting and purge of those members of the NEC who supported the new left.[39]

The *Mail*, hailing Duffy as the mastermind, claimed the new group of moderates had 'served notice that their next targets would be the Trotskyist Militant Tendency'.[40] The moderates chalked up one other success – defeating the NEC's proposal to have sole responsibility for the manifesto – their case being articulated in the debate by Radice and Stanley.[41]

The right did not, however, have a majority on the NEC as Foot refused to support them, voting to leave the existing sub-committee chairmen in place – Benn retained the home policy and Heffer the organisation chairmanships.[42] The PLP responded badly to Foot's action.[43] It had voted Benn off the Shadow Cabinet in 1980 and against him for deputy leader. His re-election to this NEC position accentuated the PLP/NEC divide. Furthermore, Benn got the Organisation Sub-committee to reject an enquiry into Militant. It was a year to the day that Foot had been elected Leader, since when the SDP had defected, Healey had nearly lost the deputy position and PLP/NEC relations had hardly improved. The left continued to exert their strength, replacing Tuck as Chairman of the NEC Finance Committee with Kitson,[44] further incensing the Group. Despite their five gains, they knew they must redouble their efforts for 1982.

The 1981 successes assisted negotiations for the coming year. However, the Group recognised that even sympathetic general secretaries needed to keep their delegations on side. The slate therefore embraced as many unions as possible, with general secretaries given latitude to vote for a left-winger, favoured by their union, who was bound to get on, so that they could then support a marginal name on the list. This attention to marginal candidates was in part the secret of Godsiff's success. As Gordon Colling described it,

> Sometimes, right-wing unions might have to vote for a leftie – it was part of a deal. Naturally I would question that: 'are you *sure* you want me to do that?' 'Absolutely, then we can get someone else to vote for you'. We were relying on the skills of the organisers. The list they sought support for was maximising the support they could get for the Group as a whole. When they were working on the list I had to get the OK from my union political people that I could trade votes. And others could trade votes. And you didn't do it yourself. Everything done through Spellar and Godsiff. We would try and get as far down the St Ermins list as possible. Some of the people on the list squeezed in by the narrowest of margins. Only way it could be done was to leave Spellar and Godsiff to do it. If we'd all tried, we'd get chopped up and would fail.[45]

Twenty years later, one union official, the NGA's Arthur Bonner, still recalls the horror of being asked to vote for Scargill (for the TUC). It hurt, but by following orders it got another union to support a marginal candidate the Group wanted elected. At times, Godsiff managed some unlikely deals. He recounted one:

> The EETPU could never get their person on – but nevertheless ran Tom Breakell. But GMWU wouldn't support him – so for a couple of years this became a bit difficult. I told Eric Hammond that the EETPU must vote Hoyle, so as to get ASTMS to vote for the rest of the St Ermins slate, and told him – a general secretary! – that he had to show the ballot paper at 2.30 pm. There was Clive Jenkins and Doug Hoyle, plus Eric Hammond and John Spellar plus the ballot papers. ASTMS had indeed voted the St Ermins slate other than for the EETPU. After this, Hoyle asked me 'Will I win?' To which I replied 'no'. And he didn't that year.[46]

Godsiff recognised that union loyalty and institutional ties (such as between the GMWU and NUPE) had to be respected, particularly the Triple Alliance of mining (NUM), rail (NUR) and steel (ISTC). Other factors helped: it was easier to get Tony Clarke elected because 'everyone loves a postman'.[47] The marshalling of votes to prevent some of the left getting elected continued on the conference floor right up to the time that the ballot papers went into the ballot box.[48] According to Godsiff, in the year Colling was elected, Stanley had persuaded his leftish POEU delegation that the NGA was on the left. After the meeting, Alan Meale, the organiser of the left's slate, visited the POEU delegation and said 'Hang on!' and explained the real politics. So the union had a second delegation meeting and swapped – but although they dropped Colling they supported another St Ermins candidate.[49]

The TUC General Council and Automaticity

The Group meanwhile turned its attention to the composition of the TUC General Council, where a restructuring was the objective. At the time, the whole TUC voted for the seats in every section – such as engineering, transport, electricity. This gave the big unions – particularly the TGWU – considerable power, as they effectively determined the composition of the whole Council. The big unions were politically insensitive in their use of these votes, preferring communists from smallish unions (such as Ken Gill) to the mainstream, pro-European Grantham – who was out of line with the left-wing TGWU.[50] In the 1960s, this strength had been used to keep the EETPU's Les Cannon off, in favour of a small union (which later became part of the TGWU). The main electricians' union – and the only one with the muscle to close the country down – was therefore not represented at the unions' top table. This weakened the TUC as it did not reflect industrial reality. The TUC also did not represent the politics of its true paymasters – the rank-and-file of affiliated unions. In the 1970s, the Communist Party 'probably played a larger part on the national scene . . . than ever'.[51] With the support of Jones and Scanlon, the TUC left, largely marshalled by Bert Ramelson (the Communist Party's industrial organiser) and Ken Gill, co-ordinated the unions' fight against the two Wilson governments.[52] Chapple had wrested his union from communist control, only to see it denied a place at the TUC by that same Communist Party. Although by 1981 the electricians had won their seat, the sheer outrage felt by the EETPU fuelled its motivation to change the system.[53]

By picking people who were so unrepresentative of the unions in any particular group, the TGWU ensured that eventually there would be a response. Stanley was the mastermind:

> We saw the key to breaking the stranglehold. If we could persuade the unions in all the sections that they were going to benefit by changing the voting methods – whether lefties or not – their union interest was to make the change. I had a brilliant young research officer, Chris Bulford. I talked to him in total confidence. 'This is the problem and this is the objective: to free General Council from these extreme left-wingers (even communists). We can't whilst the TGWU votes in every section. But we won't get change without getting it through the Congress probably for two years running because there'll be a fightback. The scheme has got to hold water and has got to pull the votes of the middle range of unions'. He said 'I'll come back with some ideas'. That was how the two of us formulated the POEU motion for Congress.[54]

Their answer was 'Automaticity', whereby all the larger unions were represented on the General Council, with 11 seats reserved for unions with under 100,000 members.

The effect was enormous, not just on the TUC but on the Labour Party because the myriad of deals done for the NEC and General Council had been intertwined. Once the TUC places were released from TGWU control, unions could cast their NEC votes without jeopardising their own Council seat. Even behaviour at the TUC changed, as smaller unions no longer needed TGWU patronage and so did not have to 'kow-tow'; they could say what they believed. Stanley was right that it took two years to achieve, as there was stiff resistance. 'There were people in the TGWU – Walter Greendale – terrifically opposed to anything which smacked of democracy.'[55]

Stanley and Bulford devised the strategy but St Ermins produced the votes. The 1979 TUC Congress had asked the General Council to consider Automaticity but no progress had been made. It had been raised in 1980 but no action was taken.[56] The POEU's first attempt in 1981 saw the motion adopted, but left-wing unions quickly launched a campaign to overthrow the proposals just approved. An invitation-only meeting, chaired by Kitson, was called 'to assess the strength of opposition to the proposals which were comfortably approved by congress'.[57] Meanwhile, St Ermins discussed the issue in May, June and July 1982, when it finally, after much behind-the-scenes work, seemed likely that the General Council would support the decision of the 1981 Congress to give automatic representation to unions with 100,000 or more members. A number of unions which had originally opposed the change were by then prepared to support the decision. In August they were discussing an attempt to defer the decision for a year. The period had witnessed intensive persuasion, as the Group gradually brought all but the TGWU on board. These talks were kept very quiet, Bulford having advised keeping everything confidential so that the TGWU would never realise how many votes were coming over. Any leak – especially about the Group's confidence they could win – would have produced a heavyweight counter-response. The TGWU was so convinced they would retain the system they had run for so long – one official laughing at the idea of defeat – that they were surprised when it went through. Bulford attributes some of their success to the TGWU being in crisis, as Moss Evans was ill, leaving Kitson in charge (whose interest was the NEC rather than the TUC) and the union less focused than under Jack Jones.

However, it took until 1983 for Congress to implement the new system.[58] This was a difficult year for its architect. Stanley was in hospital with cancer of the hip. His doctors advised him to put his affairs in order but his response was that he had to go to Congress. He left hospital, went home and learnt to walk on crutches. At Blackpool, when called to speak, he was jeered as he hobbled up, delegates trying to block his way and one threatening: 'we'll break the other leg'. They had misunderstood both his strength and the determination of the St Ermins Group.

Automaticity did not relieve the Group of any effort, as unions with fewer than 100,000 members still competed for 11 seats. However, hard and persistent work would ensure that the St Ermins Group slate had won all 11 seats by 1986.

1982: the crunch year for the NEC and for Sid Weighell

The NEC seats were, nonetheless, the Group's focus and where they made the biggest impact, especially in 1982, when there was, however, one big downside: Sid Weighell put his neck on the block. He broke his union mandate and did not vote for the Triple Alliance (miners; steel; rail – they always voted for each other). Godsiff had the figures and showed them to Weighell, saying 'we can't quite do it'. Weighell's response was 'Unless I don't vote for the miners'. 'I said "I know I can't ask you not to do that". He said no more. And then he didn't vote for the miners. It was done *not* for the NUR man but the wider Group. The NUR man was in anyway – he was on both slates, left and right. So it was done for the wider Group'.[59]

The vote for a St Ermins Group candidate (Breakell) rather than for the NUM's Eric Clarke was immediately obvious – not least to an NUR scrutineer. Weighell faced the wrath of his executive and offered his resignation. Within weeks, a special delegate conference voted to accept it – 'a sorry day for the NUR'.[60] Weighell's conscience was clear because he thought Labour had little chance of winning the next election if it was run by the far left and he believed his actions were in accordance with the wishes of the majority of party supporters.[61] At least one other general secretary (Bill Sirs, according to Richard Faulkner who worked with him) did the same as Weighell with his union's votes in 1982 but was not found out. Sirs and Weighell both believed the party was finished unless it moved back to the centre.

Weighell's fellow union leaders had not asked him to break his mandate and, according to Stanley, did not want one person to take the responsibility on his own shoulders. They wanted to persuade the delegates who to vote for or to give the mandate to the general secretary. They did not want people to *defy* their instructions as it would bring their efforts into disrepute. Furthermore, Weighell's control of the NUR was already tenuous – and Grantham thought that should not be jeopardised. St Ermins had lost a stalwart founder member but the 1982 results gave them the majority they desperately sought on the NEC. Howell (who had chaired the first St Ermins meeting) beat Eric Clarke and Anne Davis defeated hard-left Joan Maynard. Furthermore, friends within the National Union of Labour and Socialist Clubs (Labour's drinking clubs) enabled MP John Evans to oust Les Huckfield from the Socialist Societies' seat, whilst Varley beat off Meacher's challenge for the treasurership.[62]

The results caused considerable interest on the Tuesday morning of conference. The NUR vote and Davis' unexpected victory were followed at 10.55, just as Chief Scrutineer Dorothy Lovett finished, by a bomb scare which evacuated the building.[63] Standing outside, Stanley heard party staff debating 'How did Anne Davis come from nowhere, an unknown, and get elected?'[64] The conspirators – who kept their support for Davis secret to prevent any counter-measures – had done their job well.

The Group did not win everything. The NUR and APEX tried unsuccessfully to change the structure of the NEC, so as to create a PLP section, confine the CLP section to non-MPs and add two local government seats. This was similar to what Blair introduced 15 years later but it had little support in 1982. The NEC election results were also offset by the carrying of a pure unilateralist motion by the very same votes which had just decimated the left on the NEC, passed moreover by a two-thirds majority.[65]

Nevertheless, the moderates had obtained their majority on the NEC, a victory celebrated with a cake baked by Patsy Feather – iced with the words 'St Ermins'. The NEC's Register of Non-affiliated Organisations – the first step in dealing with Militant – was overwhelmingly endorsed by conference.[66] The moderates took control of the NEC committees in November, when they used their voting strength single-mindedly, taking no prisoners. 'We moderates were exhilarated and the left utterly demoralised as we walked out of Walworth Road that day. What we had done . . . was to end the dominance of extreme left wing socialists . . . and bring about the fall of the Benn–Heffer axis which would never carry credibility again'.[67] Benn, Heffer, Richardson and Allaun were culled from the key chairmanships, and the moderates then set about their objectives. The NEC proscribed Militant at the end of 1982, and went on to expel the five members of its editorial board.[68]

Dining and plotting

The injection of numbers also changed the dynamics of the NEC. Healey, as Deputy Leader, had found his role difficult as Foot never involved him, so he was unable to organise. With the extra votes, Healey provided more leadership. His political advisor, Richard Heller, started writing briefing notes for the NEC and sub-committees, working alongside Golding, and advising Healey which sub-committees to attend. They were assisted by the triumvirate of women: Boothroyd, Dunwoody and Summerskill. Golding ascribes successes at the NEC more to his plotting and the Group's cohesion than to Healey's politics. Planning tactics for the NEC was as important as winning seats. Before 1982, this had been arranged by Golding's ring-rounds. Following the increase in numbers, a more formal approach was taken and one dinner held at Locketts restaurant. It was hardly an auspicious start: by chance Foot was there and must have noticed the troupe of moderate NEC members. The dinner did sort out the arrangements for the take-over of sub-committees, but its location would not guarantee confidentiality.[69] A subsequent dinner was therefore held at Boothroyd's flat, and a couple at Howell's before they settled on the Tufton Court home of Helen de Freitas (the widow of Boothroyd's former boss, MP Geoffrey de Freitas). From then on, immediately after the St Ermins Group (which met on the evening before the NEC at Swinton House), those who were on the NEC would bundle themselves into Tony Clarke's or Ken Cure's car and make off for Tufton Court. Here they would meet up with their NEC allies, the MPs plus the trade unionists not in the Group.

Boothroyd's autobiography revealed all. At the time, however, neither Healey, Radice nor even Stanley knew of these secret suppers. 'We called ourselves the Beaujolais Group because we planned our strategy over food and a glass of wine. I kept the accounts. It was hardly high living; we ended 1984 with a deficit of £24.05, which was cleared by everybody paying a modest sum'.[70] The group in time included Hattersley, Dunwoody, Colling, Renee Short (once she had joined the moderate cause), Howell, Turnock, Tony Clarke, Hough, Cure, McCluskie, Golding, Ambler,[71] Davis, Tierney, David Williams and Tuck (but never Healey or Varley). They met to discuss tactics on the eve of every meeting of the full NEC. Sam McCluskie usually sat in Helen de Freitas' spacious rocking chair, although he tended not to go when there was something on the agenda on which he could not deliver. The suppers always finished by the 10 pm vote 'so that nobody would notice our absence . . . It was an effective alliance, masterminded by John [Golding] . . . He reported the results of our deliberations immediately after every meeting to Neil'.[72] Turnock, who later took over as 'whip' of the moderates, described how they used these suppers to decide 'Who'd move resolutions; whether we took a particular line'. When he was elected in 1983 'The moderate group on the NEC consisted of 14 members. Three did not attend the meetings but accepted the decisions. Some others attended irregularly'.[73] Out of an NEC of 29, it was a useful dinner party. Nevertheless, decisions were not sufficient. Delivering the Beaujolais vote was also challenging: 'I had to place myself at NEC meetings not only so that I could always catch the Chairman's eye but also so that none of the mods could leave without passing me. I had constantly to keep a majority – or if that was not possible, to ensure there was no quorum'.[74] The group increased the NEC quorum from 10 to 15 'to make it impossible for the left ever to regain a working majority'.[75]

Many of the St Ermins Group hailed from the Midlands. Another group (Clarke, Colling, Stanley and Turnock) lived in St Albans, Bedford, Borehamwood and Radlett, so discussions continued in the journeys home as one of them acted as chauffeur. They then took to the telephone. Golding, whilst whip, would spend hours on the phone on Sunday evenings as did Colling later: 'I would ring them every Sunday – especially Sunday before NEC but actually *every* Sunday. 2 pm to about 7 pm every Sunday.'[76] If an issue proved difficult, he would get Kinnock to make the necessary call.

Successes and failures

This intelligence, planning and confidentiality were vital because of the issues facing the NEC, press interest, party hostility and their lack of a comfortable majority. Militant was the major challenge but there were other decisions, including the appointment of a new general secretary, preparation for the election, Europe, party management and OMOV. The St Ermins Group held 59 monthly meetings (with an average attendance of 10.5) between 1981 and 1987 to work on a range of issues.

The first challenge – which they lost – was the replacement in December 1981 of Ron Hayward as General Secretary, where Foot's support for the former Chairman of the Advisory, Conciliation and Arbitraton Service and London Transport Board Member, Jim Mortimer, saw him beat the unions' Alex Ferry by one vote. The left never subsequently claimed much success for Mortimer's tenure. As Dick Clements – former editor of *Tribune* and a close ally of Foot, albeit a candidate for the post – admitted: 'Everyone thought he was a good organiser but no-one questioned his politics!' Asked when it became obvious that Mortimer was not the best choice, he replied 'Pretty early on. He was a sad mistake.'[77] The right's opposition was vindicated by Mortimer's hopeless performance in the 1983 election but at the time his appointment was a reverse for the moderates and this defeat strengthened their desire to get control of the NEC.[78]

One crucial vote – and an important thank-you – the moderates did win, despite a vehement campaign from the left, was when the NEC endorsed Godsiff as the prospective candidate for Birmingham Yardley.[79] The Group similarly took pleasure in Spellar's election in the Birmingham Northfield by-election in October 1982. The NEC also dealt with appeals from sitting councillors deselected by their local parties. St Ermins Group allies on the London Regional Executive (Spellar, Tuffin, Hayter, Bonner and Helen Eadie) had done their best to prevent the destabilisation of Southwark, where council leader John O'Grady and others had been ejected by the left. Some were reinstated, but not all, and the row was growing. The NEC asked Heffer and David Hughes to seek a solution. This failed and, in due course, led to the ill-fated Bermondsey by-election (when Labour's left-wing and gay campaigner Peter Tatchell lost a supposedly safe Labour seat) – caused as much by Foot's ineptitude as by the St Ermins Group's weakness on the NEC.

Another individual who was to cause trouble was Tariq Ali. He had stood (whilst in the International Marxist Group (IMG)) against Syd Bidwell, the MP for Southall, in 1979 (winning 77 votes). Bidwell described him as a 'rich playboy' – in contrast to Benn's description: 'civilised and charming'.[80] He now applied to (re)join the party.[81] Golding and Healey moved 'that Tariq Ali be not accepted into membership' (Benn and Maynard pressing acceptance). The former duo won 11:6. However, the local party (Hornsey) voted to admit him and had to be brought into line by the National Agent. In August 1982, his exclusion was re-confirmed by the NEC although it had to be endorsed at the 1983 conference. He was finally expelled at the 26 October 1983 NEC.[82] In these long and twisting sagas, Golding recalled, 'I would need to seek advice on how to play it from my brothers at the Swinton

House meeting.'[83] These meetings – chaired by Stanley or sometimes by Grantham or Howell – settled into a regular pattern, sustained by fruit and coffee. Golding would report on what was happening on the NEC, and especially on a number of pet projects near to the moderates' hearts, such as the introduction of OMOV. More often than not, however, in the early days he had to impart bad news – that it was Michael Foot and not the moderates that had control of the NEC.

This was often the case when dealing with the other perennial problem – of MPs under threat of deselection. Sometimes, as in Brent, the NEC could help, and one major victory concerned rules for new parliamentary boundaries where the 1981 conference had sought to make MPs go through a second reselection if their boundaries changed. This was causing considerable alarm to an already jumpy PLP. Delays (helped by the Chief Whip) led to the NEC agreeing a new system whereby MPs in constituencies with no major changes could retain their seats without a further reselection. Even this did not assist every case. In Tower Hamlets, where Peter Shore represented Stepney and Poplar, with Ian Mikardo in Bethnal Green and Bow, the Boundary Commission rotated the divide, making the seats 'Bethnal Green and Stepney' plus 'Bow and Poplar'. The left were happy with Mikardo but not with Shore. The NEC had agreed that any MP who, after boundary changes, still represented a majority of the new constituency, would be automatically reselected. If it was less than 50 per cent, there would be an open selection. Shore fell just below 50 per cent. The left was entitled to a full selection. Friends came to his aid; David Bean (now the high court judge, Sir David Bean, then a mere Solidarity activist) drafted a let-out clause:

> Where the boundaries of two or more constituencies adjacent to each other with endorsed candidates are altered, but where the number of seats remains the same and no other constituency is involved, then each of the endorsed candidates shall be treated as having a majority claim in any of the new constituencies which includes a part of his or her old constituency.

This went (from the National Agent's Department) to the NEC.[84] The moderate majority adopted it with Benn, Shore's old family friend, muttering 'I know what you're doing!'

Dealing with Militant was a continual challenge for the NEC members, who reported back to the Group on progress and setbacks, including how CLPs facing legal challenges from Militant were faring and proposals to rid the Young Socialists of Militant. They also dealt with organisational issues, from the 1986 launch of *Labour Party News*, rules for Socialist Societies and regional conferences to staffing matters. Staff appointments were very important in changing the party, and recommendations were often made. The Group's later Whip, Colling, ended up chairing the Staffing Committee, working with General Secretary Larry Whitty on clearing out the staff situation. This had been highly organised by Militant, Andy Bevan having become the leader of the staff group.

The Group's Whips

The St Ermins Group's achievements owed much to planning, discipline and single-mindedness, as well as to effective whipping. Golding had originally been the task-master. On his departure in 1983 he was replaced by the newly elected Turnock.[85] It was an inspired choice. Well read, hard-working and committed to the party's re-election, he tackled the task with gusto. He was also a smart political operator, understanding the need to anticipate press attention. One example relates to an incident when there was a vacancy for chair of the Home Policy Committee. Hattersley was anxious to take this on, so he could table more appropriate papers than those produced by party staff.[86] The Group was in favour but Tom Sawyer was also standing – and could attract soft- and hard-left support. Turnock warned his colleagues that they must leave it to him to count the votes at the meeting, as the absence of any one of them could mean defeat and a major embarrassment for the Deputy Leader. Turnock's head-count revealed they were two votes short, so he made no nomination and Sawyer was elected unopposed.

Turnock had more success earlier when he needed to teach the new General Secretary the way of the world. His practice had been to find out which Ermins Group members wanted to be on which committee and then meet with Mortimer (with whom he had a good relationship from London Transport days).

> The outcome of the meetings with the General Secretary resulted in our Group having a majority on every committee. As a consequence, we got the chairmen we wanted, and could vote down any alterations the left proposed at the first NEC after conference. When Larry Whitty took over, I adopted the same procedure with him, although I did have a feeling of apprehension in the first year knowing his past association with Benn. We were taking a family holiday in Tenerife which clashed with the full NEC. I decided to fly back to attend the meeting. After arrival at Heathrow the previous afternoon, I called at Walworth Road only to find that what Whitty had drafted was way out of line with what we had discussed. He accepted he would have to alter it or face an unholy row the next day. The amended recommendations went through with only a few minor amendments that did not affect the balance. He did not make the same mistake again.[87]

Later, Colling followed Turnock as the Whip.

> I thought I'd only be on one year – having just scraped on – so may as well learn as much as I could in that 12 months and do as much as I could. I did everything Charlie wanted me to. He was enormously impressed. I was at every meeting he'd asked me to be at. Did what I'd said I'd do. Sometimes he'd give me a bollocking if I hadn't said the right thing! Organising the NEC was as important as winning seats. Often it was a case of getting a proposal in first. Then have that proposal discussed rather than something else. Worst thing was to waffle. If we turned up without a line, hard-left and soft-left would get together.[88]

In due course, Colling became Whip to the entire union group, 'not just the little band of moderates'; even the TGWU finally came under his wing. By 1987, Kinnock could rely on the whole NEC in a crisis except for Tony Benn, Denis Skinner and Ken Livingstone. As Labour Party staffer Mike Watts recalled: if they or Leader needed something, they would 'speak to the trade union whip, Colling, who would say: "I'll speak to my friends", which was code for "they'll vote that way".'[89] Nevertheless, even after Kinnock had a comfortable majority, a number of MPs from the constituency section could not be seen to vote with the Leader – though they could be absent. Neil Stewart from Kinnock's team described how:

> Gordon Colling or Eddie Haigh would take the lead on many policies on the NEC. I would have a list, marked up as: 'For; Against; and Abstain or Leave early'. This continued right up to the 1992 election. On the day of Dave Nellist and Terry Fields [the NEC meeting to take action against the two Militant MPs], Kinnock only had 13 votes in advance. He would have resigned if it had not gone through. We had to know the numbers, so I would talk to Gordon and he fixed it.[90]

There were occasions when something went wrong, as at the first NEC after the 1986 conference. Someone broke ranks, to the Group's disapproval. The Group's November 1986 minutes make reference to:

> misunderstandings and problems which had occurred over the appointment of various persons to chair the sub-committees . . . it was emphasised that the success which had been achieved in electing a more responsible NEC over the last five years had been due to a lot of hard work and collective action, and that this should not under any circumstances be placed in jeopardy. It was also pointed out that the success of the leadership of the party reflected a widespread political opinion and any success in the future will also have to be based on the same criteria. It was felt that many of the misunderstandings could, in hindsight, have been avoided but it was hoped that discussions would take place amongst members of the NEC to avoid these problems happening in the future.

Given that normal minutes were brief in the extreme, this was an unusually long and sensitive paragraph.

OMOV and the Group

Whilst those on the NEC struggled to make their votes effective and deliver a majority for the leader, the St Ermins general secretaries and trusties continued their regular monthly work. NEC slates constituted the main business, but there was a range of other preoccupations. In January 1983, a paper on 'A system for balloting in the Labour Party' was discussed – the long campaign for OMOV for the election of leader and deputy taking shape. The moderates got the Organisation Committee to endorse the principle, though it would not apply for some years. Following the resignation of Foot and Healey, the meeting discussed the procedures being used by unions to ascertain the views of their wider membership about the forthcoming contest. The Group noted the CLPD's support of Heffer for leader and Meacher as deputy, neither of which would draw their votes.

Late in 1984, the meeting discussed the proposal to allow CLPs to involve the membership in the selection of candidates, although this presented difficulties for unions as it weakened their input into local GCs. In mid-1985, the Group agreed that OMOV should be dealt with at the 1986 conference. In January 1986 the members agreed to seek the views of interested parties as to whether this matter should come up at that year's conference and, following such consultations, suggested it should not be brought up in 1986 but that the NEC should approve the principle and conduct a detailed investigation as to how it could best be implemented. In February 1987, the party duly sent out a consultation document for comment and in April the Group agreed that, given the recent Greenwich by-election with, they thought, an unsuitable (left-wing) candidate, there was an obvious need to ensure that a wider selectorate was involved in the choosing of parliamentary candidates. Kinnock favoured a local Electoral College, and his office was 'taking soundings' on this. The Group hoped that the 'Wembley situation' (where the unions had not co-ordinated their votes) would not be repeated and that an extension to the franchise would be agreed.

TUC General Council elections

The Group stepped up its efforts for the TUC General Council elections with the first use of the Automaticity process. In January 1983, they agreed 7 names for the 11 seats reserved for the 83 unions with under 100,000 members, and considered Godsiff's recommendation that they vote for the Musicians' Union and the National Union of Seamen (NUS) in return for their support for the Group's candidates, especially those for the NEC. This could be the year to which Godsiff was referring when he related how he often appealed to Ego rather than Principle when winning votes. 'John Morton [Musicians' Union] was key at one point. I went to see him. He'd been soft-left. I said – we can put you top of the poll. But you have to do so and so. His eyes lit up – and he delivered.'[91] In March, Godsiff presented a detailed analysis of TUC affiliation figures and the 29 candidates for the 11 seats, where the left was hopeful of making gains, the left unions having also been meeting, with ASLEF, the Association of Cinematographic, Television and Allied Technicians (ACTT) and the Fire Brigades' Union (FBU) involved.[92] The September results were heartening for the moderates, when seven of their slate were elected. The *Daily Mail* hailed this as 'Right turn' and 'Militants are purged'.[93] It was a substantial tilt: the enlarged General Council had a 31:20 moderate majority, as opposed to 22:23 before. By January, work had started on the 1984 slate, with a detailed assessment of the 1983 results. In 1984, the Group made another two gains, with nine of its slate elected (and the remaining two the runners-up), due partly to

> Much more discipline amongst those unions who supported all, or most, of our recommended candidates and considerable indiscipline amongst the unions with candidates on the 'left slate' cause by blatant 'self-interest' and also by the fact that they only ran a slate of ten candidates. It is quite obvious from the voting that a number of sitting members on the left slate did not vote for other candidates on the slate and were only interested in their own self-survival. The real cause for satisfaction was in the fact that the discipline exercised by our unions ensured that, almost without exception, all of our candidates advanced together.[94]

Although not minuted, the Group took delight in ousting two prominent left-wingers, Alan Sapper (ACTT) and Ken Cameron (FBU).

Discussions on the 1985 slate began in February, with the full slate of 11 (including Grantham, as APEX's membership had dipped below 100,000) finalised in July. All but one were elected (ASLEF's Ray Buckton being the left's sole success). This was not sufficient for the Group, which wanted a full house. In September 1986 they took great satisfaction that all 11 on their list were elected. However, they failed to appoint a whip as 'on a number of recent votes on the General Council, the moderate majority had not asserted itself due to a lack of cohesion and it was agreed that discussions should be held with interested parties with a view to trying to ensure that this problem is overcome'.[95] In July 1987, a Godsiff paper credited the success over the previous four years in winning all 11 seats to

> coordinated hard work and discipline based on mutual self interest, which has been greatly facilitated by the gradual emergence of a clear moderate majority among unions with under 100,000 members. It has also been helped by the fact that our recommended candidates have come from unions which reflect a wide spread of industrial interests, which had allayed the fears of a number of people that automaticity would lead to a 'take-over' by white collar unions in this section.

The union leaders had achieved more than a simple transfer of power. Their work had helped strengthen the moderate forces within individual unions so that political belief rather than simple 'deals' accounted for some of the results.

The Group and the party

The level of affiliation to the party became another problem, as unemployment soared and union membership declined. In January 1983, the Group strongly emphasised the need for affiliated unions to retain and, if possible, increase their affiliation to the party given the importance of NEC elections, and discussions were held with a number of unions.

By mid-1984, they had a new worry when the party started discussing reducing the unions' vote at conference from the existing 89 per cent. In the 1950s, the union–CLP balance had been about 75:25 but by 1981 it was nearer 90:10, which was unsatisfactory for constituency members. The 1983 conference had remitted a resolution calling for a rebalancing towards the CLPs and in May 1984 the NEC sought views on this. This timing was particularly unfortunate given that unions were preparing for the first round of ballots, under new Conservative legislation, on the retention of political funds. It was, therefore, agreed to write to the Labour Party pointing out that this should not be pursued until the balloting was over. On behalf of APEX, though expressing the views of the other unions, Grantham wrote to National Agent David Hughes in June 1984 stressing that no changes should be proposed 'until all affiliated organisations have completed the ballots on the retention of their political funds, as any controversy arising from such proposals could adversely influence such ballots'. It would clearly not make the unions' case to their members for continuing to affiliate to the party if, just at that moment, the party was reducing their influence. In July 1985, after every ballot had been won, the NEC drafted proposals for the 1986 conference to bring the two parts more into balance. Meanwhile, the Group emphasised the importance of maximising affiliation levels for the 1985 NEC elections.

Over time, the Group began to discuss conference resolutions, whereas in the beginning the focus had been on elections. In 1986, some pro-leadership resolutions were circulated and the Group agreed to support a TSSA resolution seeking a wide-ranging re-examination of the party's constitution and one from APEX on the Labour women's conference. The Group continued to take an interest in the wider party, but in November 1983 they were concerned that the work of the Solidarity Campaign had become moribund over recent months. Members no doubt compared Solidarity with the activity rate of CLPD, whose literature was always read carefully by Spellar and distributed to the Group by Godsiff. As this reflected the output of a dedicated team of hard-working volunteers, with detailed circulars, model resolutions, voting records from the NEC and methodical planning for conference, the more modest output of the centre-right group, dedicated less to activists and more to parliamentarians, would have looked poor by comparison. However, in February 1984 they showed more satisfaction with Solidarity and appointed three union representatives to its Steering Committee. The Group also agreed to support Labour Student Solidarity in 1985, and in 1986 had a report back from Solidarity's National Advisory Council. This was all in contrast with their view of *Tribune*, in respect of which they urged unions to consider its tone before placing advertisements in it. In spring 1987 the Group met with Solidarity to discuss NEC elections.

The Group also looked at developments in the union movement, discussing a left-wing union conference held in Sheffield, and other left-wing groupings. The St Ermins Group worked with some non-affiliated unions to counter the left, which led to the creation of another organisation, 'Mainstream', on 30 March 1985. In addition, representatives from some non-party unions met with the Group occasionally, joining the Swinton House meetings at 6.30 pm, after Labour Party issues had been discussed.

Turning to other business, the Group had a first discussion on the post-Mortimer general secretary candidates in February 1984, and about the equivalent TUC position after Len Murray announced his retirement in May 1984. This was followed by a letter from Godsiff alerting members to the fact that Gavin Laird (AUEW) was interested in the post. When it later became clear there were just two in the race, Norman Willis (TGWU) and Murray's Deputy, David Lea, there was the usual paper detailing the TUC's 10.135 million affiliated membership – which necessitated the winning candidate attracting 5.068 million votes. Godsiff's breakdown of committed support showed Willis with 50.78 per cent (plus a further possible 4.5 per cent) and Lea with 23.4 per cent. On that basis, the final figures would be 70:30. The actual figures were 7,362,000 to 2,678,000.

The following year, the new general secretary of the party was appointed. A senior elected union official might have been expected to apply and for a time the smart money was on the GMWU's effective political operator and Chairman of the

Conference Arrangements Committee, Derek Gladwin, but he was not asked. Had Kinnock said the word, he would have applied. In the event, it was another GMWU employee, Larry Whitty, who was also Secretary to TULV, who beat the party's Scottish Secretary, Helen Liddell, to the post. The Group subsequently agreed to give every assistance to him in dealing with the difficult problems he faced. A hefty overdraft and continuing staffing problems were just two of these. His proposals for reorganising headquarters were discussed in mid-1985, along with the action being taken against Militant in Liverpool. Another crucial topic was regional staff appointments, particularly regional secretaries, which were then in the hands of the NEC. The Group was relentless on these, understanding the importance of organisational staff to achieving the electoral and political changes it was planning.

One issue which concerned the NEC, and the Group, was 'black sections', where these were apparently being set up (when GCs still selected candidates) to influence the choice of MPs. The unions believed such groups were unrepresentative of the black members they purported to represent. The 1984 conference voted 5 million to 1 million against black sections, the Group supporting the NEC in upholding the party constitution against those CLP they considered were seeking to subvert it. In June 1985, the NEC was urged to assert its authority over East Lewisham CLP, where a candidate had been selected with the unauthorised participation of a black section delegate, contrary to the NEC ruling. Whilst the NEC would never learn of such urgings, these minutes are evidence of NEC members taking advice from fellow Group members.

Women's seats on the NEC were not the only female matter which engaged this all-male Group. They arranged a slate for the TUC Women's Advisory Committee and in 1983 they discussed the anti-union sentiments expressed at the National Conference of Labour Women, concerns shared by Margaret Prosser of the left-wing TGWU. Little seemed to have improved, as there were continuing murmurings from the 1984 conference. In 1986, following concern over open hostility towards union delegations, the party held a meeting with union representatives. In March 1987, the party issued a consultation note on the future of this conference and the Group agreed a response to improve the situation. In 1985, the TUC women's conference also led to complaints, with the union leaders taking their concerns about voting procedures to the TUC.

Voting for the NEC

Throughout all of this, the Group's preoccupation had been with increasing its vote on the NEC. 1983 was always going to be difficult, Weighell's 1982 action and his subsequent departure jeopardising the NUR's vote. Jimmy Knapp, his successor, was on the left, opening the possibility of left-wing gains. To make matters worse, the POEU, reflecting an internal shift to the left, decided not to re-nominate Golding which, the *Guardian*'s Martin Linton assessed, would have a profound effect on the Labour Party. Linton portrayed Golding as 'hardly a charismatic leader with his shambling look and his grey suits . . . but he is far the most politically astute among the trade union representatives that give the right its majority'.[96]

1983 saw considerable changes to the slates and to voting. It was the first year when a full list of how each organisation had voted would be published. CLPD claimed that this meant 'any repeat of the NUR saga will be on record . . . which will be a strong deterrent against any repetition'.[97] In fact, the major effect was to end Militants standing in the CLP section (their candidates withdrew and never stood again), as votes for them would be obvious to any delegate's own CLP.[98] Because the general election had seen Joan Lestor and Ann Taylor lose their parliamentary seats, they were no longer automatically eligible for the NEC – though this took time to be confirmed. Ann Clwyd MEP had earlier written to Grantham seeking support, but without success (she was pro-European but against expulsions). However, when Taylor – on the Ermins' list – was ruled out, the Group switched to Clwyd (which saw her elected in second place on her first attempt).

CLPD had been hoping for considerable gains in 1983. 1982 had been a bad year for them, not only for the loss of the NEC's left majority but because of 'deep divisions within the CLPD'.[99] Their Secretary, Vladimir Derer, in his January 1983 AGM report (when CLPD had 1,203 members) wrote that '1982 was a year of continual in-fighting' resulting from their debate about whether to register; the Militant issue spread everywhere. Sawyer, on the left's slate, was writing for 'Labour against the Witch-hunt' and CLPD pressed for opposition to witch-hunts to be the focus for conference activity. The left seemed set to recapture the NEC.[100] Its slate included anti-witch-hunters Margaret Beckett, Patricia Hewitt and Joan Maynard, together with Renee Short.[101]

The St Ermins Group was worried, not just because of CLPD. In July 1983 its number-cruncher predicted they were likely to lose two seats, and possibly all four, in the women's section and would achieve only a small margin for Varley over Albert Booth as treasurer. Assuming Kinnock and Hattersley won the leadership and deputy leadership, Godsiff's best guess was for 9 moderates, 5 soft-left and 15 hard-left, giving the hard-left an overall majority of 1. The actual results were better for the Group, even though Hoyle dislodged Howell. Judith Hart was defeated and Beckett failed to win. They lost Davis but Boothroyd, Clwyd and Dunwoody won – along with the left's Maynard. *Tribune* judged 'Kinnock holds the balance' (12:12).[102] It was, initially, unclear how the NEC would divide on key issues, with a new leadership in place (Hattersley having beaten the left's Meacher as Deputy). In theory, the right lost its overall majority, returning its balance, as in 1981–82, to the centre-left leadership loyalists. In fact, this centre-left grouping, when aligned with the right, narrowly outnumbered the left and Kinnock could command a majority.[103]

At the subsequent Swinton House meeting, there was satisfaction with the results, bearing in mind the tremendous efforts of the hard-left to defeat other sitting members. Godsiff's analysis showed:

> Due to indiscipline on the left and a lot of hard work we were able to minimise the damage in the union section and only Denis Howell lost his seat. Our three marginal candidates were all elected . . . The discipline amongst our Group compared with the indiscipline on the left was crucial in minimising our loss of one seat. The fact that the left slate only consisted of 11 candidates helped us considerably. Prior to Conference

we expected the left to gain three seats. In the event, the discipline amongst our Group, together with the indiscipline amongst the left resulted in a net loss of one seat and the important defeat of Judith Hart. We were lucky.[104]

They may have been lucky but they were not complacent; in February they started work on the 1984 slate. In looking at whom to support, the March meeting had a breakdown of Sawyer's votes on NEC decisions (such as Tariq Ali, selections following boundary changes and Militant). This showed him voting contrary to the leadership on 15 key votes. Meanwhile, a new candidate was needed as party treasurer, Varley having resigned mid-term, to be replaced by the runner-up Albert Booth. Turnock observed that at 'the first tests he joined the left . . . [over] two issues. One was the student conference; Booth voted with the left. The second issue [was] the proposed expulsion of six Blackburn members for Militant activity. Same voting'.[105] Booth had voted with Blunkett, Hoyle, Meacher and Sawyer against Kinnock and the moderates; he had to go. The Group noted that McCluskie (who was often helpful, wherever possible supporting Kinnock) was standing, so discussions began. On the basis that the Group would support McCluskie and that he would win, Godsiff's May 1984 prediction was that their position was 29,000 votes worse than in 1983 due to reduced affiliations. They therefore needed maximum unity of support from the unions which tended to support their slate. Dropping Clwyd (in view of her voting record), they ran Boothroyd, Davis, Dunwoody, Diana Jeuda and Renee Short – the latter supported in view of her 'excellent' voting record and who thus moved directly from the left's slate to the right's. By June, Godsiff was no more upbeat. 'The position from which we start is no better than last year. Nearly all unions have suffered drops in their membership and a number of moderate unions have reduced theirs. We had the advantage last year because the "left slate" had only 11 names on it and a number of left unions cast at least one of their votes for moderate candidates.'[106] Their nervousness showed, and a number of approaches were made to potentially sympathetic unions, with Godsiff preparing careful briefs for each union to help the particular Group member nominated to approach them. His emphasis was always on the marginal candidates, stressing to one general secretary, for example, that if he failed to get his delegation not to vote for Maynard, then to try and support the marginal Davis or Jeuda but certainly to avoid Beckett, who was a potential threat to one of the sitting candidates. Despite Basnett failing to vote for Sawyer (for which 'error' he promptly apologised to NUPE[107]), the 1984 results swung slightly to the left although McCluskie held off a challenge from Booth for the treasurership and Davis replaced Clwyd, thanks to the union votes. Godsiff's verdict was that, bearing in mind that on a straight calculation of figures between left and moderate they were 500,000 votes behind, the results were not at all bad. The balance moved to a 17:12 moderate majority. *Tribune* commented: 'Despite a paper majority for the left in the trade unions and an overwhelmingly left majority among the constituency parties, various deals between trade unions resulted in a seven-to-five majority for the right in the trade union section and a four-to-one majority to the right in the women's section.' The paper blamed the TGWU, claiming it had 'clearly struck some poor bargains' as it had voted for nine right-wingers as well as failing to support TGWU-sponsored Beckett.[108] Perhaps Kitson topping the poll, with a massive 5.33 million votes, explains the TGWU's decision, concentrating unwisely on the size of an individual's majority in contrast to Godsiff's preoccupation with marginal candidates. *Tribune* noted the GMWU's failure to vote for Sawyer, despite its normal support for NUPE. However, as Sawyer was comfortably elected, further votes would have been wasted – a point the paper failed to grasp. The Campaign Group thought that the result should have been better as the left had 'a commanding 300,000 majority'.[109] Other commentators noticed the imbalance between numbers and the results, Rodney Bickerstaffe complaining to Spellar: 'Every time I go to Labour Party conference thinking we've got a left majority and every time you do it!'[110] The Campaign Group noted the unsatisfactory result in the women's section where the left should have commanded a safe majority. They blamed the TGWU, which could have elected at least Margaret Beckett and Clare Short if it had voted strategically. However, other unions did not escape criticism – they had made misjudgements and did not take the election in the women's section seriously.[111] There may have been more to it than that. The Campaign Group Secretary (who presumably drafted those words) was the left's number-cruncher, Alan Meale. According to Spellar, they benefited from 'Meale's inability to count. Godsiff ran rings round him'.[112]

In the treasurership election, McCluskie's narrow 46,000 victory was partly due to the Dyers and Bleachers' surprise vote (a union liberated from TGWU pressure by Automaticity – though they might have supported McCluskie so that their left-wing nominee, Haigh, could then capture the vacated seat). Despite his provenance, Haigh turned out to be a 'hero' to the moderate's Whip, Gordon Colling: 'Eddie was hung out to dry on one issue. Had said to me "if I'm there for that issue, I will have to vote the way the union wants". I told him: "You go to the toilet, we'll spring the vote". And we did just that!'[113] (At times, the gents' toilet must have been a busy place. Kinnock also relates how often NEC members decided they needed to go, just when an awkward vote was coming.) By 1986, Haigh had joined the moderates' slate.

The new NEC had hardly got to work before preparation started for the 1985 slate. By May, ten of the names for the union section were agreed, with further discussions to take place for the remaining two places. Richard Rosser and Ted O'Brien were then added. The women's slate was finalised in July but Godsiff remained pessimistic, as

> the moderate unions trailed the left unions by 500,000 votes last year and [this] if anything will be accentuated through reduced affiliation and mergers. We need to ensure that the candidates we recommend have the widest possible appeal beyond our own Group and also maintain maximum discipline to secure the extra votes which our marginal candidates will need to be elected.[114]

He thought the women might do better because of splits among the left groups on their varying slates. The actual results, despite the left's expectation of making gains,[115] gave considerable cause for satisfaction as nine of the St Ermin's slate were elected in the union section. Despite intense competition for the marginal places, some favourable arrangements and the generous assistance of the moderate unions enabled the Group to displace Hoyle and get Colling elected (helped by Meale having put Colling on the left slate, even claiming his election as a success for their side).[116] One women's seat was lost, when Beckett (this time with TGWU support) beat Davis. Overall, the moderates would have a 15:14 majority on most issues, and on the big issues, where the credibility of the leadership was at stake, Godsiff thought the majority could be as high as 20:9.

Soon after, the CLPD Secretary wrote, under the subhead 'The decline of the Labour left', that in 1981:

> the left lost five seats on the National Executive, and Tony Benn was defeated in the deputy leadership contest because the hitherto left-wing NUPE cast its vote in favour of the right-wing candidate . . . [In 1982] the left was routed over the Register and the scene was set for the expulsions of Militant supporters . . . In the NEC election of that year there were further left losses . . . 1983 saw the left-wing candidates in the leadership and deputy leadership contest heavily defeated. An overwhelming majority of CLPs, and a sizeable majority of left Labour MPs, voted for Neil Kinnock in preference to Eric Heffer. Trade union delegations voted for Kinnock *en masse,* and only a few supported Michael Meacher for deputy leader. In 1984 the pace of erosion of the left's influence seemed to have slowed . . . Yet the left lost the . . . Treasurership . . . The miners' defeat early in 1985 and the isolation of Liverpool council . . . gave the leader and the NEC right-wing majority a new strength at the 1985 party conference.[117]

The *Bulletin,* circulated to the St Ermins Group, must have brought a knowing smile to the authors of these changes.

Despite the 1985 successes, the grass was not allowed to grow before work on the following year's contests started. In February, support was agreed for McCluskie as treasurer and for the five women, plus nine names in the union section, whilst discussions continued with other union leaders. July saw a detailed, 15–page briefing on the candidates and voting numbers, which showed that, whilst in 1985 the Group

> had to exercise considerable agility and flexibility in order to get nine of our candidates in the trade union section and three in the women's section elected, as we were over 600,000 votes behind the left in the union section and nearly one million votes behind in the women's section. There are indications that the situation in the trade union section will have improved the prospects of moderate candidates. They would have to maximise the support for our recommended candidates and to ensure that the credibility and trust which ha[ve] been built up over the last five years, thereby enabling major changes to be made in the composition of the NEC, was retained.[118]

Howell withdrew his nomination so as not to split the votes for recommended candidates (the Group wishing him luck for the 1992 Olympic bid he was overseeing), and Lestor was agreed as a reserve for the women's seat.

Godsiff's 1986 briefing paper was more optimistic as political changes within the TGWU could result in gains for moderate candidates. McCluskie had indicated he would continue as Treasurer even if he became General Secretary of the NUS, rather than move to the TUC General Council. However, despite the better omens

and at a time 'when the political climate has moved strongly against disruptive elements within the party and on the NEC', Godsiff as ever writes, 'it is essential that
unity and discipline [are] maintained among the moderate unions'.[119] On the eve
of conference, Godsiff noted that, of the 12 supported for the union seats, 9 'were
well placed to retain their seats' but maximum support was required for the 3 marginal ones. On the women's section, problems were anticipated and

> mindful of the widespread agreement on the need to ensure that an increased number
> of persons were elected who will be supportive of the leadership of Neil Kinnock,
> thereby enabling him to spend more time out and around the country campaigning
> on behalf of the party, it was agreed that every effort should be made to maximise the
> support for Anne Davis and Diana Jeuda, who were best placed to gain seats currently
> held by Beckett and Maynard. If support was needed to bolster Lestor, it would be
> taken from Renee Short or Betty Boothroyd, who were already guaranteed re-election
> with very large majorities.[120]

On the opposing side, Blunkett was urging support for Beckett and Maynard, who
would be successful 'if the constituencies and not the block vote of the trade
unions counted'.[121]

The actual results were evidence of the Group's efforts. The unusually long
minute in October 1986 gives an insight into the *modus operandi* of the Group. In
the union section, 10 of the 12 were elected, Rosser being beaten by the NUM's
Clarke despite considerable effort and organisation being expended on maximising his vote. After 'arrangements' had been made with some left unions, it
appeared, with half an hour left before the ballot closed, that Rosser would be
elected. Unfortunately, the left were then successful in persuading GMBATU[122] to
switch their votes to Eric Clarke. Had the GMBATU voted for Rosser instead of
Clarke, which they had originally intended to, Rosser would have been elected
10,000 ahead of Clarke. The women's section reflected some equally nifty foot-
work:

> In the women's section we gained an extra seat with the election of Diana Jeuda at the
> expense of Margaret Beckett. Again, 'arrangements' with certain left unions worked to
> our advantage, particularly the support obtained from ASTMS for Jeuda. Anne Davis
> was in contention up until Monday lunch-time but was finally beaten by the decision
> of the UCATT delegation, after three ballots, to support Maynard and not Davis.

Overall, Godsiff's plotting and 'arrangements' led to a gain of one seat in the
women's section and 'a more reliable replacement for Alex Kitson' (Jack Rogers of
UCATT) – a moderate majority of 18:11.

CLPD concurred, heading its report 'NEC elections – right gains significantly'.[123]
The Times' succinct 'Right wing tightens grip on NEC' took account of a further
moderate gain in the CLP section, where Eric Heffer was defeated by Tam Dalyell,
benefiting from his persistent criticism of Thatcher's Falklands role.[124] Shaw
described how, 'By 1986, the work, begun several years earlier by John Golding, of
constructing a solid bloc of leadership loyalists encompassing virtually all trade
union members of the Executive had been completed'.[125] CLPD later noted:

Since 1981 the political composition of the NEC has been changing. Increasingly nominees of the party's right wing have been elected. This partly reflects the shift of opinion in the country. But it is also due to successful electioneering by the right wing in the party and the trade unions. Its effectiveness was not matched by the left. As a result, the right wing has made substantial direct gains in the Trade Union and Women's Sections.[126]

After the 1986 results, Godsiff allowed himself the luxury of reviewing the NEC losses and gains, noting that 'the Conference in 1981 marked the beginning of the "fight back" by the moderates to stem the advance of the broad left'. He set out the changes which 'culminated in the election this year of an NEC overwhelmingly supportive of the parliamentary leadership and with a very large moderate majority'.[127] The Group took no respite, and the 1987 slate was in preparation by February, with the added complication of Turnock's retirement. The list was finalised in July, Joan Lestor taking the place vacated by Betty Boothroyd (who was about to become a Deputy Speaker in the House of Commons). Problems were anticipated, the September meeting urging maximum support 'for our three most marginal candidates' in the union section. The women's section was fluid although it was 'quite possible that all five could win provided the maximum discipline was maintained, but that any fall off in support could result in the loss of one seat'.[128] All five were deemed 'marginal' so maximum support was sought for all. (In previous years, votes could be switched from Boothroyd, who attracted widespread support and was bound to win, to help a worse-placed sister – something the former cheerfully accepted.) In fact, the 1987 results were the 'Best Ever'. All ten union seats were retained plus two gained in the women's section so that, for the first time, all five were in moderate hands. The number-cruncher commented that

> Bearing in mind we were more than 180,000 worse off than last year, these results give considerable cause for satisfaction and were due to the overall excellent discipline exercised by those unions who support our recommended candidates and the very considerable help given by unions in the arrangements which were made to protect our most marginal candidates.[129]

The new National Constitutional Committee

Early in 1986 the Group started thinking about the composition of what was to become the National Constitutional Committee (NCC). One of the Group's early objectives had been to rid the party of 'infiltrators'. St Ermins Group members of the NEC had been at the forefront of this unpalatable work. Ken Cure chaired the Appeals and Mediation Committee from 1983 to 1987, leading a number of difficult investigations. Turnock led some of the biggest enquiries – especially into Liverpool.[130] The NEC itself undertook expulsions – spending days on the Liverpool Militants, for example, and running into legal difficulties when the same people who had conducted an enquiry also then tried to hear the expulsions. The demand on the leader's time in these cases was wasteful, the publicity damaging. Natural justice demanded a separate body to adjudicate on cases once the NEC had decided to formulate charges. Hence the creation of the NCC.

In summer 1986, the Group welcomed the plans for such a committee and 'agreed that consideration should be given to the names of persons who unions would wish to nominate as a postal ballot would take place'[131] after the October conference. The balancing of unions' interests had to be carefully weighed. As there were to be only five union and two women's seats (the latter effectively union controlled), 'it was recommended that no union should consider nominating for both'.[132] Godsiff's paper in October noted that a number of unions wanted to make nominations but that there was 'an obvious need to ensure that those unions who do not have a nominee already on the NEC are sympathetically considered'.[133] Despite that hint, the Group agreed to support nominees of the AUEW, GMWU and TGWU and to consider Keith Brookman (ISTC) and Rose Degiorgio (APEX), whilst further consultations took place. The list posted out in November did not include Alan Quinn of the TGWU in view of his association with Militant, but urged full support for the others 'in view of the absolute necessity to ensure that the NCC has a clear majority of members who will act responsibly to ensure that the rules and constitution of the party are upheld' – code for vote to expel Militant. The January 1987 elections – unusually at that time by postal ballot – gave the Group four of the five union places (Quinn having been elected). It would, said Godsiff's paper, have been unheard of for any TGWU nominee to be defeated in a trade union election, though the TGWU's mistake in choosing such a candidate almost achieved the impossible. All the unions which normally followed the Group slate voted for Eric George rather than Quinn, other than the GMWU – without whose votes the TGWU flag-carrier would have lost. In the women's section, the GMWU supported the slate so both candidates were elected over the TGWU nominee, as 'favourable arrangements' had been concluded. The balance on the NCC was 7:4 for the moderates, a result which was warmly welcomed, though only achieved 'because of the discipline which existed amongst those unions which traditionally supported our recommended candidates'.[134]

Reviewing the Group's successes

After the 1987 autumn conference, the Group reviewed the impact it had made since 1981 across the NEC, NCC and TUC General Council. On the NEC, the Group had won 10 out of 12 union and all 5 women's seats; on the NCC, 4 out of the 5 union and both the women's seats; and all 11 in the TUC 'under 100,000' section. Outside observers concurred: the 1987 NEC providing 'a comfortable soft-left/centre-right base' for Kinnock.[135] It was a mammoth achievement for these dozen men, who had met monthly and laboured hard by persuasion and some darker methods (or 'hairy stunts' in Godsiff's words) to change the political complexion of the governing councils of the Labour movement.

From the disaster of 1981 to the June 1987 election was barely six years, but in this time the moderates felt the party's fortunes had been turned, even though an election victory was still ten years off. A Leader determined to change the party had been elected, and he was backed by an NEC determined to walk that road with him. Could it have happened without the St Ermins Group? It seems unlikely as, again and again, the moderates lacked the numbers but made up for it with discipline and cunning, both in marshalling votes for NEC seats and in utilising them on the NEC.

It is said by some that it was not organisation but the shock of the SDP departure, followed by the 1983 election disaster, which turned the party around. This underestimates the impact of Duffy's success in moving the AUEW to the moderate cause, which he achieved by late 1981, as well as the unions' determination to rid themselves of Thatcher. Their members had suffered from her industrial and other policies and they knew this before the 1983 defeat. As the archives show, their efforts and some of the major victories (Automaticity, seizing the NEC majority and Healey's deputy leadership victory) preceded the 1983 election. The moderate NEC members found that they had many years of neglect to correct, as the left's long control of the NEC had secured a staff immune to their objectives, a deep penetration of the party by Militant and an electorate hostile to Labour. They were also dealing with a large organisation which, like an oil tanker, was hard to turn round.

Commentators have stressed the importance of organisation in political parties[136] but few have glimpsed the professionalism and determination of this Group of union leaders. Some did understand it: 'The preconditions of Labour Party recovery would be brought about . . . by untrumpeted union men . . . who would work – much as [Bill] Rodgers had worked twenty years before – through the unions, to shift the NEC back to reason'.[137] Pearce refers to the 'regular gatherers at the St Ermine's (*sic.*) Hotel, Labour's favourite resort of conspiracy, and so known as "the St Ermine's Group" . . . The campaign, not just to re-elect Healey, but over a longer period to restore a moderate NEC and put the Labour Party back on the rails deserves a full study to itself. It came before red roses and mattered more.'[138]

Two politicians confirm this. Healey admitted to the author: 'Without the unions, change wouldn't have happened'.[139] The other was Kinnock, both in interview and in his inscriptions in a couple of books. In Tony Clarke's copy of his book, Kinnock wrote: 'Without you many parts of this book would not have been written' and on Turnock's monograph he wrote, 'to Charlie with thanks for sense, socialism – and some of the best laughs too!!'.[140] Kinnock's crucial 1985 Bournemouth speech, on Militant, was delivered with the massed ranks of a supportive NEC behind him on the platform.

Kinnock also acknowledged to the present writer not only the Group's diligence and discipline, but the unpopularity this sometimes brought them within their own unions:

> Self-discipline and collective discipline: they had a fundamental belief in the use of votes. At a later stage, they said, we've got to win the arguments as well as votes. What made them say that to me was that, even with good organisation, even with winning seats consistently on the NEC, they never had quite enough to ensure a guaranteed outcome when just one or two of the trade union group voted in another direction. In order to ensure unanimity, or something like it, in the trade union group, they had to win arguments, they had to win the vote and arguments. So they acknowledged [that] having a solid, disciplined group with particular organised political objectives in mind, would be crucial but sometimes it wasn't quite enough. The trade union people

were putting themselves on the line; they were representing their leadership stance but not the unanimous view of their annual conferences. Didn't automatically win them popularity and support within their own unions. So they took some risks.[141]

Thus whilst unions were blamed, following the Winter of Discontent, for Labour's travails, there seems little doubt that this committed band harnessed the resources and commitment to Labour within the movement to steer the party back towards electability for, without a compliant NEC, it is unlikely that Kinnock could have succeeded. The St Ermins Group continued for nearly another decade but its toughest assignment had been completed by 1987. Just as, in 1931, trade unionists including Ernest Bevin had played a decisive role in steadying the party, 50 years later it fell to another generation of union leaders to maintain the party created by the unions in 1900 as an electoral force.

Notes

1 Alan Bullock, *Ernest Bevin: A Biography*, ed. Brian Brivati (Politico's, 2002), p. 219.
2 Bryan Stanley interview.
3 'Russell Tuck was on the party executive – nice but not politically conscious. So Sid Weighell sent me. He couldn't go to the first St Ermins Group meeting as it clashed with the executive of the NUR'; Charles Turnock interview.
4 Roger Godsiff interview; Giles Radice (unpublished) diary; John Golding, *Hammer of the Left*, p. 179.
5 Roger Godsiff interview, 4 December 2001.
6 Daly, 'The crisis in the Labour Party 1974–81', p. 227.
7 Roy Grantham interview.
8 Bryan Stanley interview.
9 Tony Clarke interview.
10 Bryan Stanley interview.
11 *Ibid.*
12 Christopher Hemming, 'Labour's "penny-farthing" machine: was Labour's local organisation better than the Wilson spin suggested?' (unpublished, 2002), p. 7.
13 Rodgers, *Fourth Among Equals*, p. 125.
14 Bradley, *Breaking the Mould?*, p. 61.
15 The overlap continued until Prime Minister's Questions moved to Wednesdays and NECs to Tuesdays.
16 The March meeting discussed the leak, which apparently resulted from Duffy speaking to journalists. It was agreed that meetings would be conducted on the basis of complete confidentiality; documentation would be tabled at meetings and collected at the end; correspondence would be conducted using home addresses; Golding, *Hammer of the Left*, p. 181.
17 Gordon Colling interview.
18 Sandy Feather interview.
19 Weighell, *On the Rails*; Chapple, *Sparks Fly!*; Denis Howell, *Made in Birmingham: The Memoirs of Denis Howell* (Queen Anne Press, 1990). Howell makes just one reference to Swinton House, when he describes arriving 'at the headquarters of the Iron and Steel Trades Union for a discussion about trade union and Labour Party matters to be met by Sandy Feather, who asked me to telephone home at once'- to learn of the car acci-

dent which killed his son (*Ibid.*, p. 371).

20 Seyd, *The Rise and Fall of the Labour Left*, p. 117.
21 Shaw, *Discipline and Discord in the Labour Party*, pp. 358–9.
22 Pearce, *Denis Healey*, p. 557.
23 Kogan and Kogan, *The Battle for the Labour Party*.
24 Minkin, *The Contentious Alliance*, p. 325.
25 Panitch and Leys, *End of Parliamentary Socialism*, p. 194.
26 Golding, *Hammer of the Left*.
27 Golding, 'The fixers', chapter 13, p. 7. (The unions were as good as their word, placing a number of advertisements in the newsletter.)
28 Former MP for Lincoln. She later joined the left-of-Tribune 'Campaign Group' (*1983/84 Annual Report of Campaign Group of Labour MPs*).
29 Golding, *Hammer of the Left*, pp. 183–4.
30 *Daily Mirror*, 7 September 1981.
31 The Group had originally been known as 'Labour Liaison' (Sandy Feather interview).
32 *The Times*, 8 September 1981.
33 *Daily Mirror*, 25 September 1981.
34 With the exception of Hayter, who he erroneously thought would succeed; *Scotsman*, 29 September 1981.
35 *Report of the 1981 Conference of the Labour Party*, p. 95.
36 Golding, *Hammer of the Left*, p. 197.
37 *Financial Times*, 30 September 1981.
38 Betty Boothroyd, *Betty Boothroyd: The Autobiography* (Century, 2001), pp. 109–10.
39 Panitch and Leys, *End of Parliamentary Socialism*, p. 199.
40 Robert Porter, *Daily Mail*, 30 September 1981. He noted where the Group met, albeit calling it the St Ermine's Hotel.
41 *Report of the 1981 Conference of the Labour Party*, pp. 207–8, 212.
42 Golding, *Hammer of the Left*, p. 213.
43 *The Times*, 10 November 1981.
44 *The Times*, 24 November 1981.
45 Gordon Colling interview.
46 Roger Godsiff interview, 9 April 2002.
47 Roger Godsiff interview, 4 December 2001.
48 Charles Turnock, 'Rigorous route', p. 203.
49 Roger Godsiff interview.
50 Chapple, *Sparks Fly!*, p. 130; Howell blamed an inter-union dispute with ASTMS which cost Grantham his seat on the General Council: 'an act of petty vindictiveness' (Howell, *Made in Birmingham*, p. 271).
51 Eric Hobsbawm, *Interesting Times: A Twentieth-Century Life* (Allen Lane, 2002), p. 266.
52 *Ibid.*.
53 Chapple, *Sparks Fly!*; John Spellar interview.
54 Bryan Stanley interview.
55 Charles Turnock interview.
56 Chapple, *Sparks Fly!*, p. 173.
57 *The Times*, 9 December 1981.
58 Chapple, *Sparks Fly!*, p. 186.
59 Roger Godsiff interview, 4 December 2001.
60 Turnock, 'Rigorous route', p. 203.
61 Terry Pattinson, 'Obituary of Sidney Weighell', *Independent*, 15 February 2002.

62 *Report of the 1982 Annual Conference of the Labour Party*, p. 66.

63 *Ibid.*, p. 67.

64 Roger Godsiff interview, 4 December 2001.

65 Pearce, *Denis Healey*, p. 571; *Report of the 1982 Annual Conference of the Labour Party*, p. 280.

66 *Ibid.*, p. 275.

67 Golding, *Hammer of the Left*, p. 261.

68 Panitch and Leys, *End of Parliamentary Socialism*, p. 204.

69 Golding, *Hammer of the Left*, p. 256.

70 Boothroyd, *The Autobiography*, p. 112. The next year's deficit was £37.62 (following seven such dinners); accounts from Turnock's private papers.

71 His son-in-law, Brian Key, had been deselected as an MEP, bringing home the difficulties in constituencies (Richard Tomlinson interview).

72 Boothroyd, *The Autobiography*, p. 113.

73 Turnock, 'Rigorous route', p. 229.

74 Golding, *Hammer of the Left*, pp. 269–70.

75 *Ibid.*.

76 Gordon Colling interview.

77 Dick Clements interview.

78 Golding, *Hammer of the Left*, p. 230.

79 *Ibid.*, p. 221.

80 Benn, *Diaries 1980–90*, p. 180.

81 *Guardian*, 20 November 1981; *Tribune*, 27 November 1981.

82 *Guardian*, 27 October 1983; Golding, *Hammer of the Left*, p. 273.

83 Golding, *Hammer of the Left*, p. 227.

84 NEC paper, NAD/109/3/83, 23 March 1983.

85 Turnock, 'Rigorous route', p. 229.

86 *Ibid.*, p. 236.

87 Charles Turnock interview.

88 Gordon Colling interview.

89 Mike Watts interview.

90 Neil Stewart interview.

91 Roger Godsiff interview.

92 *Financial Times*, 18 April 1983.

93 *Daily Mail*, 7 September 1983.

94 Minutes of 17 September 1984, St Ermins Group.

95 Minutes of 24 February 1987, St Ermins Group.

96 *Guardian*, 14 July 1983.

97 CLPD, 'Guide for conference delegates', 1983.

98 *Tribune*, 7 October 1983.

99 *CLPD Newsletter*, Number 27, May 1983.

100 *Tribune*, 22 July 1983.

101 CLPD Circular, 20 June 1983.

102 *Tribune*, 7 October 1983. Similarly, 'A net gain of three' for the left had Kinnock holding the balance; *Financial Times*, 5 October 1983.

103 Shaw, *Discipline and Discord in the Labour Party*, p. 254.

104 Briefing paper on 'Labour Party NEC Elections 1983' for November 1983 Meeting of the St Ermins Group.

105 Turnock, 'Rigorous route', p. 232.

106 Briefing paper on 'Labour Party NEC Elections 1984' for 12 June 1984 Meeting of the St Ermins Group.
107 *Tribune*, 5 October 1984.
108 *Tribune*, 12 October 1984.
109 *1983/84 Annual Report of Campaign Group of Labour MPs*, p. 16.
110 John Spellar interview.
111 *1983/84 Annual Report of Campaign Group of Labour MPs*, p. 17.
112 John Spellar interview.
113 Gordon Colling interview.
114 Briefing Paper on 'Labour Party NEC Elections 1985' for 23 July 1985 Meeting of the St Ermins Group.
115 *Tribune*, 23 August 1985.
116 *1984/85 Annual Report of Campaign Group of Labour MPs*, p. 15.
117 'Secretary's statement', *CLPD Bulletin 11*, January 1986.
118 Briefing Paper on 'Labour Party NEC Elections 1986' for 22 July 1986 Meeting of the St Ermins Group.
119 *Ibid.*
120 Notes of the 23 September 1986 Meeting of the St Ermins Group.
121 David Blunkett Column, *Tribune*, 5 September 1986.
122 General, Municipal, Boilermakers and Allied Trades Union; the GMWU had been through a number of name changes, at this stage having merged with the Boilermakers' Union.
123 *CLPD Newsletter*, Conference Edition.
124 *The Times*, 1 October 1986.
125 Shaw, *Discipline and Discord in the Labour Party*, pp. 270–1.
126 CLPD letter to supporters, August 1987.
127 Paper on 'Elections to Labour Party NEC during period 1981–1986' for 21 October 1986 Meeting of the St Ermins Group.
128 Notes of the 22 September 1987 Meeting of the St Ermins Group.
129 Briefing Paper on 'NEC Elections – 1987' for the 27 October 1987 Meeting of the St Ermins Group.
130 Turnock and Cure were involved in reports on St Helens, Sparkbrook, Knowsley North, Brent East and Bristol South.
131 Notes of 19 August 1986 Meeting of the St Ermins Group.
132 Notes of 23 September 1986 Meeting of the St Ermins Group.
133 Briefing Paper on 'National Constitutional Committee' for 21 October 1986 Meeting of the St Ermins Group.
134 Notes of 24 February 1987 Meeting of the St Ermins Group.
135 Sked and Cook, *Post-War Britain*, p. 568.
136 Seyd, *The Rise and Fall of the Labour Left*, p. 113; Shaw, *Discipline and Discord in the Labour Party*, p. 224; Ben Pimlott and Chris Cook (eds), *Trade Unions in British Politics* (Longman, 1982), p. 24.
137 Pearce, *Denis Healey*, p. 535.
138 *Ibid.*, p. 557.
139 Denis Healey interview.
140 Charles Turnock, 'Labour needs 30 miracles' (unpublished, 1987), on its front cover.
141 Neil Kinnock interview.

11
Labour Solidarity Campaign

Giles Radice is given the credit for building up something called the 'Manifesto Group' which helped save the party. So far as I remember, it was Solidarity which did this job over the dead body of the Manifesto Group

Austin Mitchell, Solidarity Treasurer.[1]

Solidarity . . . tried hard [but] had neither the resources nor the leadership to be successful

John Golding, Solidarity Member.[2]

The Manifesto Group had failed to deliver the party leadership for Healey or to hold the PLP together. The party adopted the Wembley 40:30:30 formula for the Electoral College, leading to the Limehouse Declaration within 24 hours and the SDP within 2 months. Wembley also led to the creation of the St Ermins Group and to the better known Labour Solidarity Campaign. This was set up 24 days after the conference, partly in recognition that the moderates' failure to organise had allowed the left to engineer the very formula that would produce the schism. Solidarity was created to reverse that formula and to stem the flow of defections from the party. The vitriol within the party, and the condemnation of the 1974–79 governments, had left the moderates on the back foot. They now believed that they had to act if the party were to return to 'sanity' and electability. Their aims consolidated as: changing the Wembley formula, OMOV, expelling Militant, creating a tolerant party, getting a moderate majority on the NEC, keeping members in the party and arguing the case for representative (or parliamentary) democratic socialism – and achieving these by organising the natural majority within the party.

This chapter tells the story of Solidarity and it tests the above views of its Treasurer (Austin Mitchell) and a supporter (John Golding), one of whom praised, one of whom questioned, the role it played in 'saving' the party. Mitchell places it above the Manifesto Group, Golding below the St Ermins Group. Both may be correct.

Immediately after Wembley, centre-right MPs experienced the loss of colleagues – and the haemorrhaging of Manifesto Group numbers – to the SDP. Confronted with resignations from the PLP, the moderates had to act fast. Their response was a January statement signed by 150 MPs – Tribunites as well as Manifesto members – which, whilst accepting an Electoral College, disagreed fundamentally with the formula: 'All of us agree that the decision of Wembley was a mistake and should be rectified at the earliest opportunity'. These 150 were the pool from which Solidarity emerged, and comprised the invitation list for its February founding meeting.

Within days of Wembley, Spellar wrote to a number of senior MPs (who became the Solidarity leadership) and senior trade unionists calling for the creation of an organisation to replace CLV, involving general secretaries, MPs and party members. 'If the moderate majority in the party are to assert themselves and turn the tide then we will have to become as effectively organised as our opponents' wrote Spellar, proposing as priorities: a journal, regional conferences, control of the NEC and a 'statement of purpose' drafted by Hattersley.[3] This latter described how:

> For too long, the natural majority within the Labour movement – left, right and centre – has allowed unrepresentative minorities to impose their own narrow views upon the party . . . To leave the party now is both defeatist and divisive. Our prime task is to put the party back on course and save the country from the ruinous policies of Margaret Thatcher.[4]

Spellar's paper, slightly redrafted, was adopted by the Group together with a statement of purpose: 'The recreation of a Labour Party which is: genuinely representative of the millions . . . who support the movement; broadly based and tolerant of all democratic socialist opinion; safeguarded against infiltration and domination by extremist factions; determined to protect the democratic rights and electoral responsibilities of Members of Parliament.' The immediate objectives were: 'To reverse the Wembley decision; to obtain a moderate majority upon the NEC; to seek the adoption of moderate candidates; to confirm in office the elected leadership of the Labour Party'.[5]

It is interesting to note this early preoccupation with infiltration and the need to defend the position of elected representatives. The paper reflected the Group's analysis that, without a change to the NEC, few problems would disappear. The suggestion of finding reliable candidates mirrors one of the successful activities of the earlier CDS, in which Denis Howell was a key activist. The comment on the 'elected leadership' was a portent of Benn's challenge to Healey only weeks later.

Whilst Spellar put pen to paper, MPs knew they must act urgently to hold on to members and reassure them that the bulk of moderates were remaining in the party. Hattersley denied to the author that he had been the energy behind this:

> Solidarity wasn't my idea. Nothing about it was my idea. Denis Howell came into my office after the Wembley conference and said 'You've got to take the lead. You have got to do all these things.' I said: 'Why me, why not Denis Healey?' He said 'Denis Healey won't.' I suspect he had already asked him. Denis Howell called the meeting in the Grand Committee Room; Denis Howell sent out the notices; Denis Howell phoned round people; Denis Howell badgered me into phoning round people; Denis Howell attended the meeting and announced to them that I was the Chairman of this new organisation.[6]

An initial group of MPs, including Howell and three acting officers (Hattersley as Chairman, Ken Woolmer as Secretary and Austin Mitchell as Treasurer), met before the inaugural meeting. Preparations included the choice of a name.[7] This emerged in a meeting in Healey's room in the Shadow Cabinet corridor when, Woolmer recalled, a group was 'picking Healey's brains; it was at the time of Lech Walesa in Poland. It was Healey's idea: "only one name you can give it: Solidarity" he said'.[8]

On 17 February 1981, 102 MPs of the 150 signatories (including Healey and with support from 10 absentees) met under the chairmanship of Hattersley and agreed to establish the Labour Solidarity Campaign. A Steering Committee was appointed – drawn from the Manifesto Group, Labour First and Tribune – and the meeting agreed to advertise its presence, organise regional rallies, issue a newsletter and open an office. Within two days, its treasurer was soliciting funds from MPs, whilst others were building up contact lists. On the 18 February, the officers circulated a statement endorsed by the 102. This referred to those defecting, as well as to others 'who don't believe in parliament' trying to take over the party, and defined the organisation as being 'to give Labour new life as a tolerant party that believes in carrying out effective socialist policies through action in parliament'. The Group set itself limited objectives, as Geoffrey Smith noted when he described Solidarity, 'with backing from some of the reasonable left as well as from the right and centre', as being 'well placed to isolate the Militant Tendency and other representatives of the hard left'. But its aims concerned only 'the way in which Labour conducts its affairs, not [its] policies'.[9] This accurate portrayal belies that fact that, for Solidarity, there was no hope of changing policies until the composition of the NEC, and the pressures on MPs from hard-left activists, could be changed. In addition, the breadth of support of MPs meant that 'Members of the Campaign have widely different positions on current political issues'.[10] Indeed, short of agreeing that Thatcher was 'a bad thing', the Steering Group might have been hard pressed to draft any policy the 102 MPs could endorse. But that was its strength. By abstaining from policy, Solidarity could attract MPs from a wide spectrum, making it easily the major grouping in a PLP of 251 members.

Only the names Hattersley, Woolmer and Mitchell were initially on the headed notepaper. However, at the first recorded meeting of the Steering Committee, Hattersley welcomed Peter Shore's attendance and invited him to become Joint Chairman. Howell had pressed on Hattersley the need for a second figurehead – and another 'aspirant for leadership' of the party – so that the organisation did not look like an embryo 'Hattersley for leader' campaign. Shore accepted, stressing that the 'only people not organised in the Labour Party are the great majority'.[11] By this first meeting, the Group had already raised £400 together with the promise of a £6,000 donation. They knew they must spend fast (initially on advertisements in *Tribune* and *Labour Weekly*) to build momentum. The veteran journalist John Bevan (former CDS supporter and by then Lord Ardwick) agreed to edit a newsletter whilst an Organising Committee chaired by Jack Brooks[12] set about finding offices. At first, proceedings were a little informal, early minutes referring to 'a lot of humming and hahing' and 'a vague Treasurer's report which seemed to satisfy some people who were worried about finance',[13] but gradually the more formal requirements of an organisation emerged, not least when Mary Goudie became the National Co-ordinator.

Within the PLP, Solidarity's first aim was to stem the trickle of defectors. However, it had also to replace the former activists' grouping, CLV, many of whom had joined the SDP, and assure the wider party that the mainstream were remaining in the party and fighting – this being the critical period between the Limehouse Declaration of 25 January and the SDP's launch on 26 March. Its priority was therefore to establish a presence and to sign up supporters. Fringe meetings at all the party's regional conferences (between March and June) were quickly arranged whilst work began on the newsletter. John Grant, MP and former journalist, agreed to write for it and to drum up advertising revenue from unions. This was not only to meet costs but also to emphasise that all the centre-right unions, and their leaders, were remaining in the Labour fold.

Solidarity set out its stall as being 'broadly representative of the party's natural mainstream majority' which should now 'vigorously assert itself and reverse the narrow and intolerant decision which unrepresentative minorities have' imposed. Wembley, 'the most recent self-inflicted wound . . . must be overturned'. The founding statement flagged up the need for the NEC to 'more adequately represent the wide variety of party interests . . . We have no doubt that to leave the party now is both defeatist and divisive . . . our over-riding priority . . . is to get the party back on course . . . We pledge ourselves to fight enthusiastically and unswervingly to that end.'[14] The Group had to react to fast-moving events, not least the resignation on 2 March of 12 MPs from the PLP (as a prelude to moving to the SDP). In its response that day, Solidarity regretted

> the divisive and defeatist decision of the small group of dissident MPs, who have mistakenly opted to defect . . . and to abandon the real battle against both this appalling Tory government, and against the unrepresentative minority in our own ranks . . . A major fight back is now under way . . . We urge real Labour supporters everywhere to pledge their immediate backing for the Labour Solidarity Campaign.[15]

On 26 March a Solidarity press release described the SDP launch as 'a clear declaration of war on Labour, led by those who owe both their reputations and their careers to the Labour Party . . . it is now clear that the defections were plotted long before Labour's Wembley conference and the decision on the leadership election – a decision which Labour Solidarity wants to see rectified.' The defectors had been fortunate that Wembley had voted for such an untenable formula, giving the SDP this, rather than the less popular Europe, on which to make their stance. Hence the importance of Solidarity emphasising that Wembley was not universally applauded within the party.

In February and March, the priority was to emphasise these views and make it clear that this Group was not defecting. CLV's mailing list, held on the EETPU computer, was made available so that in February a circular could go from Mitchell inviting members to sign up to Solidarity. His letter claimed: 'There is no salvation outside the Labour Party . . . It is essential to fight back. Desertion reinforces weakness.' The CLV list, together with contacts from MPs and others, was used for the first edition of the newsletter 'which appeared in March with the leader 'The road back from Wembley'.[16] The contributors reflected the breadth of support, with Manifesto members (Radice and Hattersley) being joined by Tribunite MP Joe Ashton (on 'How to choose a delegate to conference') and Frank Field as well as the anti-Marketeer Shore. Shore criticised the NEC for encouraging some 'whose faith in democratic and parliamentary socialism is virtually non-existent', failing to safeguard the party's constitution and tilting the balance of power away from elected representatives. The party was being 'seriously threatened by both splitters and wreckers' whilst 'the majority opinion . . . is not being reflected'. Local government was represented by Jack Smart, Chairman of the Association of Metropolitan Authorities. The newsletter and publicity quickly attracted support-ers (including a young Tony Blair on 14 April 1981). By September there was a mailing list of 5,000.

Meanwhile, the Organising Committee found premises at 62 Charles Lane, in London's St John's Wood. The Campaign moved in at the beginning of June, the work having hitherto been done at the Commons or Goudie's home. Goudie was to be the lynchpin throughout Solidarity's life, taking no salary from the Group – and even her expenses not always reimbursed when the finances were stretched. In April, the Committee engaged a paid administrator (Chris Inman) for the remain-der of the year, with Goudie using her extensive contacts, built up over years of party and Fabian activity, to recruit volunteers.[17]

Goudie's priority was to set up fringe meetings at the party's regional confer-ences and the annual conference in Brighton. Her address book of members around the country – and her persuasiveness – brought in volunteers to book rooms, print flyers and distribute leaflets. The success of these gave Solidarity life, as party members could see the presence of the Group and hear Healey, Shore and Hattersley not only say 'we are staying' but also 'we are fighting our corner and we *will* take on the hard-left'. This was a message moderate members had long sought but had found neither from the Manifesto Group (which had no constituency presence) nor from CLV, which was too overtly pro-Europe and always had a hint of distance (justified when most of its leaders did defect). Solidarity filled a great need, its newsletter and fringe meetings testimony to its seriousness. The *Telegraph* acknowledged, 'the group has made a considerable impact on the party by staging fringe meetings at regional conferences'.[18] At the first of these, in Camden Town Hall during the London conference, Hattersley set out the task facing Solidarity: a re-affirmation of faith in the party, victory at the election and to oppose with all the vigour at its disposal, the enemies of democratic socialism – the Tories, the defectors and the unrepresentative minorities within the Labour Party who pur-sued their own sectarian causes. He attacked the bitter propaganda of the Rank and File Mobilising Committee, the devious manoeuvres of Militant, the divisive threats of litigation from the CLPD and all the disruptives' authoritarian extrem-ism dressed up in acceptable socialist language, calling on party members to play an increasing part in the movement, with a direct vote in the Electoral College. He turned on the left's category of alleged crimes committed by the last Labour government (an attack on the un-named Benn).[19]

A notable fringe meeting took place in Ely, on a sunny Saturday lunchtime in June. Peter Shore was to speak but when MP Ken Weetch checked the room, he found it was a long way from the Eastern regional conference. He asked Shore how he felt about outdoor meetings and, receiving an enthusiastic reply, set up a massively successful rally on the Green which, despite 'heckling from the Trots', gave real energy to the large, loyalist membership that existed in East Anglia.

Whilst practical and propaganda hands were turned to the mechanisms of setting up a new body and building its profile, Donald Dewar, Frank Field and Giles Radice penned a note on strategy in early March. This suggested that the Group's objectives should be, *inter alia*, encouraging members not to leave the party, making the party more tolerant and more representative, and arguing the case for representative democracy. The three MPs raised questions for urgent decision, such as the preferred formula to replace Wembley and whether it would include OMOV in the CLPs; whether to have a slate for the NEC or to propose a change in its composition (such as adding PLP and local government sections); and whether to ask for an enquiry into Militant (all of which would – eventually – be achieved, though not all within Solidarity's lifetime). They prioritised an office, newsletter, meetings' programme and supporters' list, all of which were quickly achieved. The following week – in a bid to involve unions – it was agreed to send a letter from Healey and the joint chairmen to general secretaries. Meanwhile, the officers found the party unwelcoming, with the General Secretary (Ron Hayward, whose sympathies lay with the left) objecting at the Shadow Cabinet to the advertisement placed in the party's house journal, *Labour Weekly*, which continued to refuse letters and advertisements from Solidarity. This would not be the only tussle with headquarters, which repeatedly omitted Solidarity from the list of friendly organisations in the pocket-diary. The party's 1984 European Campaign Pack list of contacts included the LCC but not Solidarity; on more than one occasion the Group's fringe meeting was omitted from the conference Diary of Events.

Meanwhile, the officers continued their work amongst MPs. A Recall Meeting (of the initial 102) was held at the end of March, when over 40 MPs signed in (including Tom McNally, who was later to defect). More MPs were added to the Steering Committee and MPs were asked to sign standing orders for £5 a month. There were soon 44 in operation, bringing in £259 a month. Regional representatives were nominated to help with fringe meetings, provide names for the database and involve local members. A second Recall Meeting, with Shore and Hattersley speaking, was held in mid-July, when the 35 signatories included Betty Boothroyd and John Smith.

It was not just in parliament that Solidarity was organising. In Hackney, Islington, Lambeth, Stevenage, Ealing, Teesside and Scotland, local groups were rapidly established, with MPs doing sterling service in speaking at these and the various fringe meetings. Hattersley took on much of this work; in Ken Weetch's words: 'He was a great traveller – the Marco Polo of Solidarity'.[20]

Whilst the Wembley formula and the SDP split were the catalysts for the creation of Solidarity, the aim of changing the former quickly slipped away. The Steering Committee did fix on an alternative of 50:25:25 (in preference to

30:30:40), with OMOV postal ballots for CLPs, but there was little energy behind this, not least because of the lack of support within the movement. Woolmer circulated a draft rule change in June but by August, according to *The Times'* political editor, Julian Haviland, Solidarity had 'tacitly agreed that this objective . . . is out of reach'.[21] Solidarity failed to get its model motion on the conference preliminary agenda, although one union (the UCW) tabled an amendment giving the largest say in the Electoral College to MPs. There was no support for this. For Haviland, Solidarity had failed 'both to organize and to persuade'. Despite this, he was generous in his praise of Solidarity's core of 60 MPs who 'possess a quality which is becoming steadily less common: they have little fear of Mr Benn's supporters'. Furthermore, with some 4,500–5,000 Solidarity supporters, as well as local groups, he acknowledged 'the fight goes on'.[22]

Whilst Wembley had to be put to one side, infiltration moved centre-stage. Alone in the party, Solidarity openly called for action on Militant. Its union friends wanted this, the EETPU's Frank Chapple writing to Ken Woolmer in August 1981 that his union conference had overwhelmingly passed a resolution expressing alarm at the degree of infiltration, and at the unwillingness of the NEC to take action. The Steering Committee had already asked Woolmer and Field for a paper on Militant and later the Group produced a leaflet, written by Harold Wilson's former press officer, Joe Haines, which was widely distributed.

Solidarity also enlisted the help of Lord Underhill and used the evidence of several defectors to compile a 17-page report on Militant's history, organisation and finance which Hattersley subedited, adding a few literary touches.[23] Militant remained a constant theme in the Group's work (disgust at its effects, and at the NEC's failure to act, attracting many to Solidarity). QC John Smith (and through him Derry Irvine, assisted by his junior barrister, Tony Blair) were to provide legal advice during the process of expelling Militant.[24]

The deputy leadership intervenes

Before Solidarity could set about its objectives (on Militant, Wembley or the NEC), it was hit within weeks by the announcement on 2 April of Benn's challenge for the deputy leadership – and the first use of the Electoral College. It could not have come at a worse time: the office was not yet open, mailing lists were incomplete and the SDP was siphoning off electoral and membership support. Furthermore, it exposed divisions within Solidarity, as not all had yet made the break with Benn. Solidarity's priority had been 'to strengthen its support on the left'[25] not to invite its members to walk one side or other of the dividing line. The Steering Committee viewed its major task as Healey's re-election (no mean feat) whilst also holding the Solidarity coalition together. On 15 April they agreed the careful line that 'Solidarity would support the collective leadership'. This drew Michael Foot into their strategy and enabled them to be seen as loyal to the left-wing Leader (for whom few had voted in October 1980). Healey's support for Solidarity had been given 'with Michael Foot's encouragement'[26] and helped bring the organisation close to the Leader in a way that had never been possible with the Manifesto Group.

[Solidarity] deeply regret[ted] Tony Benn's announcement . . . [which] can only produce a public conflict in the party . . . To insinuate that the present leadership cannot
be trusted to keep faith with the party's wishes is an attack on Michael Foot no less
than on Denis Healey . . . Solidarity . . . believes the team of Michael Foot, and Denis
Healey as his Deputy, provides the best combination for election victory.[27]

Even this careful enjoining of Foot's name was not enough to hold the fragile
coalition together. The effective support for Healey caused problems and the June
minutes show that 'the Steering Committee supported the collective leadership but
also recognised it must take into view the cross section of our membership'.

Peter Shore was outspoken. 'In an onslaught on virtually everything Mr
Wedgwood Benn stands for . . . [he said] that the Labour Party might never recover
if the far left's campaign for "the supremacy of party democracy over that of
parliamentary democracy" succeeded'.[28] Shore attacked Alan Fisher (General
Secretary of NUPE) for promising his union's support to Benn (little knowing that
NUPE members would in fact vote for Healey). However, it was not the person that
Shore feared, but a deputy leader being imposed on the PLP contrary to its own
preference.

Solidarity struggled to hold its disparate membership together. One draft
release, calling on the movement to keep the present balanced leadership team,
reminded colleagues that many who had not voted for Foot now loyally defended
him and considered that Healey was entitled to similar consideration. The battle in
the constituencies and the unions was hotting up, and a later draft reads 'The
Labour Solidarity Campaign unequivocally advises its supporters to vote to retain
Denis Healey as the party's deputy leader'. Though drafted on 3 June, it was immediately overtaken by events when Foot threw down his challenge to Benn to run as
leader, rather than as deputy. The Group then used Foot's own attack on Benn to
call on the party 'to keep the present balanced leadership team'. This was still too
much for some and Martin O'Neill resigned. He saw Solidarity becoming the
Healey campaign rather than the broader-based group he had wanted (and into
which he had even tried to draw Kinnock). He believed that, in being so committed to Healey, it would fail to attract a middle group. In September, he was to
vote for Silkin in the first ballot and then abstain. (He was not alone amongst
Solidarity members. Joe Ashton and Arthur Davidson followed suit, whilst Frank
Field voted for John Silkin and then Denis Healey.)[29]

However, Foot's tacit support for his Deputy (though he would abstain in September) allowed Solidarity to organise the campaign, which Healey undertook
with gusto. Whilst the May issue of Solidarity argued only 'Why Benn is wrong to
stand', in June it told readers to keep the Foot and Healey team.[30] The race intensi-
fied; in July the Steering Group agreed: 'The Joint Chairmen to write the front page
article including supporting Denis Healey, and the Editorial would also come up
in support of Denis'.[31] Whilst the choice of speakers for the conference fringe meeting (Healey, Shore and Hattersley) clearly indicated Solidarity's thinking, the
Group's decision to come out for Healey never happened. As requested, Grant:

penned a forthright pro-Healey leading article [but] our arrangement was that I
needed the approval of the co-chairmen for contentious pieces which committed

Solidarity . . . Hattersley agreed with the pro-Healey article. Shore . . . was away and
returned just in time to use his veto, much to my disgust. I had a heated argument with
him. In deadlock, we recalled the committee to decide . . . We had a wrangle . . . but
the majority favoured a toned-down version.[32]

Nevertheless, the September issue makes fascinating reading. The Chairmen's
front page praises the 'Foot–Healey' team three times but fails to name Healey
(the only one up for election) alone. Shore wrote merely that it would weaken the
parliamentary party if someone were imposed upon it who did not carry the
confidence of the majority. According to some of the Shadow Cabinet researchers,
Shore never publicly endorsed Healey (though he did vote for him). One page of
the September *Labour Solidarity* gave 'Three good reasons for saying no to Benn'
and another, on Healey, is headed, 'The man best fitted to work with Michael Foot'.
This reticence stemmed not just from qualms within the committee but from the
recognition that Healey's unpopularity with party members[33] could best be
overcome with the link to Foot. It is indicative of the difficulty of being a Healey
supporter that his campaign badges contained both names, 'Foot. Healey', to protect their wearers. Healey's unpopularity stemmed largely from his role in the 1976
IMF cuts; he also carried activists' resentments for all the shortcomings of the
1974–79 governments.

Whilst many MPs equivocated about supporting Healey (the only candidate
who could stop Benn), Roy Jenkins ran Labour's Doug Hoyle a close finish in the
Warrington by-election on 16 July 1981, providing stark evidence of the inroads
the SDP was making into Labour's heartlands. Yet little time could be spent campaigning against the SDP (or the Tories) as the summer of 1981 was used to amass
votes for Healey. The 'Sherpas' – advisors to the Shadow Cabinet – doubted that
the politicians did as much as the staff or unions. One Steering Group member did
'fuck all' and another of the supposed team 'was in the US all summer – so didn't
do anything'.[34] Healey himself campaigned hard and admitted, 'I learnt more about
the inner workings of the trade union movement in those six months than in my
previous thirty-seven years of party work'.[35] Other Solidarity members were similarly busy, with Goudie and Inman organising innumerable meetings, mailings
and leaflets. They were looking for votes for Healey and for the NEC. Whilst the
unions were successful in this, Solidarity failed to swing constituency votes for any
of its candidates (Jack Ashley, Hattersley, Radice and Shore). It was a reminder of
the distance Solidarity had to travel that the top-placed (Ashley) got only 219,000
votes to the lowest elected's 259,000. Solidarity's chairmen attracted just 176,000
and 183,000 – reflecting the left's pre-eminence on local GCs where votes were
decided.

The eightieth conference of the Labour Party opened in Brighton at 5.30 pm on
Sunday 27 September 1981, chaired by Alex Kitson of the TGWU. The outcome of
the deputy leadership ballot was still unknown but the result, three hours later, was
to mark a turning point for the party. Before the conference John Grant had predicted that if Benn won 'some people who have been supporting us will just pack
up and go. I am not sure they will join the SDP . . . it is more likely they will just
walk off the pier.'[36] Elsewhere there was talk of a 'UDI' within the PLP, with MPs

electing their own deputy leader.[37] It remains the view of many that a different result 'would have made the divisions in the party even more bitter. There would have been more defections' (Ken Woolmer); 'terminal disaster' (John Gyford);[38] 'there would have been a haemorrhage of Labour defections to the SDP ... I do not believe the Labour Party could have recovered' (Denis Healey).[39] As it was, the actual result denied the Conservatives, the Liberals and the SDP 'their most wanted prize'.[40]

The overwhelming response at 8.31 pm was relief, despite the narrowness of the margin (as Radice said: one is enough in politics). The Healey camp installed themselves in the Old Ship Hotel to savour a rare victory. The abstaining MPs (who had denied Benn victory) had a harder time, Kinnock being attacked as 'Judas' and Joan Lestor being on the receiving end of Margaret Beckett's sharp tongue.[41] For Solidarity, however, the result marked just the beginning of its work. Conference was notable for the five seats won on the NEC (though credit belongs to the unions) plus highly successful fringe meetings (with 800 at one) which offered mutual support and encouragement to delegates who were isolated within their own constituencies. Solidarity was in the vanguard of preserving the Shadow Cabinet's role in the manifesto, a major defeat for the left.

Despite the newness of the organisation, Goudie, helped by the unions, established an office in the Old Ship Hotel from which daily briefings were distributed to delegates by teams of volunteers. The mastheads on these read: Monday: 'A vital victory'; Tuesday 'The tide has turned'; Wednesday: 'Clause V: the case for partnership'; and Thursday 'Drive to victory'. The following day, Hattersley used a speech to Lambeth Solidarity to invite defectors to return, as the conference victories had shown there was 'not even a plausible excuse for desertion ... Now that the Labour Party can be seen as a broad based party once again, I hope that they will come back home and work with us'[42] – an unrequited hope.

Back to Westminster

Conference over, MPs returned to the harsh realities of Westminster. The immediate task was the Shadow Cabinet election, the first since the SDP defections had removed a chunk of Manifesto votes, so the Tribune slate might have been expected to benefit. The 1980/81 Parliamentary Committee (to give it the correct title) had seen four elected outwith the Manifesto slate, with a fifth (Benn) joining when Bill Rodgers defected. The 1981/82 balloting began with the Chief Whip, when Michael Cocks comfortably beat the left's Martin Flannery by 156:51. Ian Mikardo (whose 1974 election had led to the formation of the Manifesto Group) ran for the chairmanship but was easily defeated by Jack Dormand. There had been controversy about Benn's candidature for the Shadow Cabinet, with Foot warning him that, if elected, he would have to accept collective responsibility.[43] Despite this, the 'left within the left' – led by Benn – signed an 'oath of loyalty' expressing 'a commitment to the constitutional changes and central policies agreed at Labour conferences' and claiming their right 'to advocate the whole range of such policies', including unilateralism and withdrawal from the EEC.[44] This indicated that, even in the Shadow Cabinet, Benn would assert his right to support policies contrary to the agreed line. Solidarity worked hard to maximise support for its candidates. Whilst 5 MPs from outside its original 'list of 150' were elected, the 3 top positions were held by Solidarity's Shore, Kaufman and Hattersley; Benn was joint 20th, well below the elected 15 (Healey was on as Deputy Leader).

Solidarity began discussing a new paper entitled 'Where now?' Spellar wanted to widen the Group beyond parliament, and proposed a 'National Solidarity Organising Committee' comprising two MPs, two general secretaries, one person from the NEC and one from the co-operative movement. Frank Field drew up some 'First ideas for the Campaign' which recommended focusing on 'a blocking mechanism for the PLP in the choice of leader or deputy leader',[45] OMOV in each part of the Electoral College and a concerted effort to get Solidarity supporters on to the NEC. Peter Shore summoned the troops immediately after Brighton, writing: 'There is no possible alternative for those who oppose Bennism to fight back. This fight must be stronger, more formidable and better thought out and organized than anything attempted so far'.[46] Others believed that the structure of the organisation had to change. The Lambeth Group stressed: 'If Solidarity is going to have any effect at all in the country then it must stop being run by the PLP. Senior trade unionists must be brought on to the Committee and space made available for constituency and area groups of Solidarity . . . It is vital that the Solidarity Campaign takes itself out of Parliament within days rather than weeks'. Lambeth members were critical of the newsletter; whilst they understood its per force pro-Healey stance, they regretted its strident manner which appeared close to 'reds under the beds. There is far, far, too much at stake in terms of the future of the party to allow anyone to be alienated from Solidarity – whether left or right – who supports a democratic socialist position'.[47]

Another submission wanted Solidarity to campaign for OMOV and the creation of 'a new political image which is identified with the democratic spectrum of left and right, with additional [members] . . . from the Tribune Group' and a National Committee to include representatives from CLPs and unions, plus activities for supporters and some full-time staff. This note identified Solidarity's right-wing image as an obstacle and called for a new statement of aims which stressed 'the desire to . . . work with the democratic leftwing' and the recruitment of left-wingers to positions in the organisation. The author asked for a weekend meeting of contacts from around the country 'within the next month'.[48]

There was much soul-searching amongst the committee. Hattersley tabled a paper on whether Solidarity should adopt policies so as to give the Group a positive purpose. He ruled out anything on unilateralism or Europe (as that would 'destroy Solidarity both in the House and, perhaps more important, in the country'). Instead he proposed opposition to illegal or extra-parliamentary action combined with advocacy of 'genuine democracy' within the party, which he defined as (a) OMOV in CLPs and consultation in the unions for Electoral College votes; (b) CLP choice as to whether to go for full reselection; (c) PLP and local government seats on the NEC and a change in the women's seats; and (d) the exclusion of people who are members of organisations which are inimical to the party's aims.[49] Stanley Clinton-Davies questioned the value of 'a witch-hunt . . . [against Militant] because some of the soft-left groups would probably not continue to give us their support'.[50] Keeping the more left-wing MPs on board was a priority for those who saw Solidarity's right-wing image as its biggest handicap. However, if it could not agree on the EEC, unilateralism or Militant, it left the Group with little but OMOV in common. Nevertheless, some did want a position taken on policies although Hattersley reiterated that this would force some members out.

Above all, the electoral impact of the party's polling position was jeopardising their own livelihoods. The Liberal and SDP successes in London's Croydon North West and St Pancras North in the October parliamentary and Greater London Council by-elections made unhappy reading. At a Solidarity meeting in Rotherham, Shore warned that 'our party faces its gravest crisis since the 1930s . . . the SDP alliance with the Liberals faces us with a challenge that is now truly formidable'. He criticised Foot for keeping Benn as Chairman of the NEC Home Policy Committee[51] and said the party had inflicted hideous wounds on itself. He was determined to take on the far-left, declaring, 'No longer can we allow organized infiltration and organized conspiracy'.[52]

In addition to the by-elections, there was more bad news: the NEC endorsed a 12–month timetable for withdrawal from the EEC; the TUC General Council supported withdrawal without a referendum; Shirley Williams was fighting Crosby for the SDP; and the left was mounting a pro- Tatchell campaign. At the October Steering Committee Meeting, Solidarity Secretary Ken Woolmer therefore warned that 'outside the PLP the situation is very serious – we don't have several years to play with'. Donald Dewar reported that they had lost ground within the PLP, with a lot of people depressed or gone to ground. He predicted they would see more defections. Radice concurred, describing the low morale and the loss of party members whilst insisting that 'it is not right wing to object to Militant'. George Robertson concluded, 'it is slipping away'. Whilst at this meeting the MPs simply despaired, Roger Godsiff chided them that the unions 'want to see your leading lights reassert yourself – time is not on our side'.[53]

Following the discussion, Godsiff drafted a paper on 4 November 1981 on the 'Future of the Labour Solidarity Campaign' which recalled that Solidarity was set up to 'counterbalance the unrelenting activities of the "hard left" within the party' and, given the limited objectives the Group had set, he assessed that it had achieved 'a reasonable success' although this had been 'based on reacting to issues . . . precipitated by the hard left . . . therefore the Solidarity response has been perceived as negative . . . The need now is for the Campaign to rethink its role and to take a more positive approach . . . while acting as an umbrella organisation' for the Manifesto, Labour First and other groups, which could pursue their own viewpoints on policy. He wanted the organisation strengthened so it could influence individual CLPs.

The paper was debated by the committee, which confirmed that Solidarity would continue in existence, but would be better organised and with a drive to build contacts in CLPs and unions, organise more fringe meetings, and produce a reinvigorated newsletter and model resolutions. In the discussion (which started with news of John Grant's resignation from the newsletter and the party), Peter Shore described how things were getting worse and stressed the need to 'broaden their appeal and muster democratic socialists against the authoritarians. There are people seeking to make us [Labour] into a vanguard party. They are much more of a danger because there are many more of them than the Trots. Our immediate objective ought to be to put the NEC under pressure'.[54] John Golding recalled that Solidarity existed to stop the drift, keep people in the party and win seats on the NEC, but it was Foot who held the balance. The amended paper replaced phrases such as 'hard left' with 'undemocratic left' and firmed up the proposals. Whilst recognising that the organisation had seen a more representative NEC, the retention of Clause V and the maintenance of 'the balanced leadership of Foot and Healey', nevertheless it stressed that the crisis facing the party was deepening, with substantial numbers of voters deserting Labour, the changes on the NEC failing to produce a decisive majority for common sense; and the Electoral College remaining unchanged. Furthermore, the internal struggles meant that policy was not being addressed. The paper concluded that the Group had 'to counter attack and expose the whole political philosophy that lies behind the attempts to distort and undermine the traditions of democratic socialism . . . We have to expose and overcome Trotskyism in all its many forms and disguises within the party'.[55] Its priority was the defence of democratic socialism, the parliamentary process and the role of elected representatives. The Group's objectives were: (1) further gains on the NEC; (2) tackling infiltration, starting with an NEC-instigated inquiry; (3) exposure of party policy-making weaknesses; (4) increased CLP and union activity; (5) OMOV; (6) modernisation of the NEC and conference and reconsideration of mandatory reselection and the Electoral College procedures; and (7) attacking the government and winning the election. It was a tall order.

A week later (by which time Peter Tatchell had been selected for Bermondsey, Spellar having been kept off the shortlist) it was agreed to hold a Recall Meeting of MPs, tabling the new paper, to raise morale within the PLP (though trade unionist David Warburton warned that 'the newsletter makes Solidarity look like "a self-protection society for MPs" and they should get other names on it'[56]). However, before any Recall Meeting could be arranged, Frank Field resigned from the Group and the committee reconsidered whether press coverage of its document was advisable on the eve of the Crosby by-election. Field's resignation followed his plea that Solidarity should be wound up because it had not succeeded in building an effective bridge with the democratic left. However, his reason for going was that, as he saw OMOV as being the only constitutional change which could prevent the party being turned into a vanguard party, and as its achievement depended on getting support from all sections of the party, rather than being seen as allied exclusively to any particular group, he intended to devote his efforts to campaigning for it.[57] His resignation did not prevent him collaborating with the Group and he continued to pursue his OMOV campaign in the newsletter.[58]

Swirling around the depleted Group was more bad news. Tom McNally had left the party in October and John Grant in November, with George Cunningham and Bruce Douglas-Mann to follow before the end of the year. Whilst the right slipped away, left-wingers were selected for safe seats, whilst existing MPs faced difficult reselection battles. Stanley Clinton-Davies scraped home in Hackney Central by a narrow margin,[59] Willie Hamilton faced a second ordeal in Fife Central when he tied with challenger Henry McLeish, and Ilkeston's Ray Fletcher was deselected.[60] Even the Chief Whip was not safe: Cocks faced a vociferous challenge in Bristol. Meanwhile, AUEW General Secretary John Boyd protested to Foot over the exclusion of moderate candidates from shortlists.[61] All of this fuelled the MPs' desire to see CLPs allowed to choose whether to go through a full reselection. However, the 1981 conference having failed to halt mandatory reselection, the Group fell back on offering 'shoulders' for those in trouble. Ken Woolmer recollected how 'life was a misery. People can't imagine now the malevolence, and often violence, that went on against people. When you went to your monthly constituency meeting – your stomach was churning. A perpetual sense of stress. Deep anxieties. It was a time when – unless you were a fighter – the easiest thing was to back off.' However, he acknowledged that the friendly shoulder helped and 'quite a few stayed in the party because of Solidarity. It gave them a home and a sense of belonging. There was a fight. The vast majority of people faced by a crisis are frightened'.[62] Even John Silkin – no friend of the grouping – recognised the role it played: Solidarity 'gave many MPs an opportunity to affirm their support for Labour governments . . . it gave some MPs a feeling that . . . they were not completely alone as with heavy hearts they headed towards their constituencies and confrontation with their detractors'.[63] Reselection and activist hostility towards politicians were taking a heavy toll.

Meanwhile, Tatchell had been selected in Bermondsey to replace Bob Mellish, supported by many of the younger members though not – despite Foot's allegations – Militant. To London activists Tatchell seemed more radical and energetic than the old guard, but to the PLP he was a reminder that the party was changing and they were losing out. On 3 December 1981, Foot (unwisely) told the House of Commons that Tatchell was 'not endorsed' and would not be, starting a struggle with the local party he was to lose and creating more damaging attacks in the press.[64] Foot was pushed into this partly to stop MPs defecting. He failed in this and in stopping Tatchell.

Whatever doubts the Group had about re-fuelling internal debates, they felt that a fightback was the only option. After the SDP's success in Crosby, Solidarity decided to press ahead with the new document, as 'a concerted and nationwide counter attack against the undemocratic left as part of a determined drive to save the party'.[65] This was not their only statement. Grant had previously ghosted the lead article in the post-conference edition of *Solidarity* as well as one under his own by-line on the outcome of the conference. The former vowed 'We shall stiffen our Campaign'. In claiming Brighton as 'a watershed for the Labour movement', it nevertheless warned 'we cannot afford to be complacent'. Radice added: 'Now is the time to win the hearts and minds of the activists' whilst Warburton reviewed the NEC elections, the newsletter coining the term 'a solidarity of trade union leaders' to describe the St Ermins Group heavyweights (Boyd, Duffy, Grantham, Jackson and Sirs) who joined John Smith on the Solidarity platform at Brighton.[66]

However, a wider audience was needed for Solidarity's message. They therefore arranged a centre-spread in the *Mirror*, authored by Callaghan, on 'Here's how we can save Labour'. Repaying the loyalty that Foot, as his Deputy, had given him (especially during the IMF crisis and the Winter of Discontent), Callaghan had remained loyal to his successor, but now wrote that 'The crisis in the Labour party is caused by small, single-minded (and narrow minded) groups. Until they are defeated there will be no peace or unity within the party and its standing with the voters will continue to decline'. He welcomed the NEC decision not to endorse Tatchell (little knowing he would soon re-emerge as the official candidate) and the moves towards an inquiry into Militant. He outlined what had to be done: expel Militant, disaffiliate the Young Socialists, improve the system of electing the leadership, adopt a new process for reselection and have a meeting between the NEC and the Shadow Cabinet 'to re-establish confidence in each other and to place on record that each has its own responsibilities and that neither is subordinate to the other'.[67] Indeed, such a meeting did then take place in January 1982, leading to 'the peace of Bishop's Stortford' which promised an end to constitutional changes.

1981 ended with mixed news. The NEC voted not to endorse Tatchell and to set up an inquiry into Militant. But Douglas-Mann defected and the unhappiness within the PLP was palpable. Solidarity had ensured – albeit by a whisker – Healey's re-election and seen five places change on the NEC (though, lacking Foot's support, without the hoped-for changes in committee chairmanships). Benn had failed to be re-elected to the Shadow Cabinet. The outside world was stormy. Williams had returned to the Commons from Crosby whilst Jenkins – flushed with his Warrington performance – was encircling other seats. The SDP were winning local by-elections and holding a continuous lead in the opinion polls. A final Recall Meeting of MPs before Christmas gave unanimous backing to the statement of objectives and endorsed Shore's resolution that Solidarity 'believes that actions to re-affirm and reinforce the truly democratic and parliamentary traditions of the Labour Party must be fully and unequivocally supported, and calls on all members of the party to unite behind the leadership of Michael Foot and Denis Healey to defeat the Tories and return a Labour Government'. Not every intervention at the Recall Meeting was in harmony. Campbell-Savours thought their attacks 'have been too hard and that some of our comrades are having to look over their shoulders. The main thing of the future must be the danger of Militant'. Underhill believed 'It's in the CLPs that we must make ground and must direct the work of Solidarity' and Weetch warned 'If we do not get this party into some sort of order shortly more decent people will be leaving the party and some of us will not be here any longer'. An interesting exchange followed non-Solidarity member Stan Newens urging Solidarity 'to disband because we are making matters worse and it would be our fault if we lose the election', pledging 'he would always be a Marxist'. From the chair, Shore responded: 'We respect you for coming to this meeting and saying what you have to say to us, but it is those who are Marxist/Leninists who we have to worry about'.[68] This encapsulated the challenge that Solidarity faced – the desire of many Labour voters and members to expel Militant but a denial on the soft-left that it posed any threat.

Into its second year

By early 1982, Solidarity's place in the struggle was assured; its newsletter, advertising meetings in North Wales, Cheshire, London, South Wales, Lambeth and Teesside, foretold a year of activity.[69] Its front-page leader, 'An unpleasant necessity', signalled determination, calling for support for Foot in his conflict over the Tatchell candidature. Inside, it renewed calls for OMOV in the Electoral College. CLPD, London Labour Briefing and the IMG (whose efforts led to the deselection of councillors, divisions and defections) were lambasted. 'The Solidarity Campaign exists to destroy the SDP, defeat the Tories and help Labour back to power' it proclaimed – which needed compromises, although not at the expense of leaving Militant untouched.

In January, straight after the Bishop's Stortford conclave (with the Shadow Cabinet, unions and NEC brokering a peace accord), Foot spelt out 'My kind of socialism' in two long *Observer* articles, taking on Benn's arguments and giving comfort to Solidarity.[70] He staunchly defended past Labour Cabinets (in which he and Benn had served) against Benn's charge of betrayal, and reasserted the role of parliament in achieving democratic socialism. Meanwhile, Hattersley was calling for Militant to be thrown out of the party.[71] The following week the Solidarity-supporting Leeds South East MP, Stan Cohen, was replaced by the (then) left-winger, Derek Fatchett – the sixth such deselection.[72]

Solidarity sent out model resolutions, together with invitations to its key workers to a February forum in Swinton House. The committee wanted to focus on priorities for the party in the light of Bishop's Stortford, preparing for an election, and priorities for Solidarity. Whilst deciding to continue to push for OMOV, it was anxious not to be seen to be the first to break the Bishop's Stortford agreement.

Peter Shore opened the first meeting of 50 Solidarity key workers – including a dozen MPs – on 28 February 1982 by recalling the appalling Wembley conference. He saw Bishop's Stortford as, at best, a truce as 'the lion won't lie down with the lamb'. As for the NEC, speaking just days after it accepted Tatchell's candidature, he despaired. It was, he said, shocking that the NEC should have agreed to endorse Militant candidates. Solidarity's first aim should be further gains on the NEC, as only it had the power. His Co-chairman, Roy Hattersley, agreed that gains on the NEC were absolutely necessary although he feared that could take years. He urged the Group to win arguments and not rely on organisation as it had to win over the idealists and sentimentalists who hoped the trouble would go away. There was little disagreement amongst the dozen others who spoke, with warnings that the working class were leaving the party whilst middle-class membership was holding up. Good councillors were being lost, Liverpool Council was a disaster. Contributors recommended activity in constituencies, gathering evidence for the Militant inquiry and more effort to increase union delegations to GCs.[73] Goudie's later report identified 16 points from the forum to the March Steering Committee including the need for firm, positive leadership; a move away from a Westminster-based organisation; liaison with CLPs and unions; agreement for an NEC slate; a higher public profile; and encouragement of support from the soft-left.

The March issue of *Labour Solidarity* argued that nothing in the Bishop's Stortford truce precluded moves towards OMOV, whilst the Militant inquiry was vital to defend the constitution. In vain the newsletter advised that the NEC would be making a serious mistake if it endorsed candidates who were open supporters of Militant. The April newsletter reported that Jenkins' Hillhead victory witnessed the electorate voting against the left-wing drift in the Labour Party, Benn's name having cropped up every day on the doorstep. However, the Group's aim was not to denigrate party members but to show the SDP's true colours, pointing out that Jenkins had defended private health and independent schools whilst Rodgers (formerly GMWU-sponsored) now confessed his dislike of trade union sponsorship. Jenkins and Williams had fought a shrill and unpleasant campaign which misrepresented and abused their former party. The newsletter attacked the Tories but found time to highlight the speech of Militant supporter Pat Wall (about to become the Bradford North candidate) to his Socialist Workers' Party branch, concluding there was no place for his like in the Labour Party. The NEC, it said, had 'a duty to act'.

Meanwhile, responses to a questionnaire to Solidarity supporters had been analysed (by Shore's advisor, David Cowling). These showed an activist membership (over 60 per cent holding office in their CLP or union), half under 51 years of age and with a strong preponderance of men. Their views on politics made grim reading. Just 8 per cent were happy with the state of the party (against 90 per cent not), 2 per cent believing Labour was certain to win the election (with a further 9 per cent in the 'probable' camp and 38 per cent 'possible'). Forty-seven per cent had written off that eventuality. Asked the reason for the poor electoral prospects, 83 per cent cited the party's own divisions (particularly the activities of the undemocratic left). Ninety per cent saw the SDP/Liberals as a threat. Half thought Militant infiltration was already a problem. Only 3 per cent thought Trotskyism was compatible with Labour's aims and objectives (although 27 per cent agreed with Newens' view[74] that Marxism was compatible).

The Falklands intervenes

Between February and June 1982 the political map of Britain changed. While Labour continued to falter (despite an opinion poll hike after Bishop's Stortford), Jenkins swept to victory in Hillhead on 25 March. But on the very day he took his seat, 30 March, the first statement on South Georgia was made in the Commons.[75] By 2 April the Argentineans had invaded the Falkland Islands. Mrs Thatcher's determined response, and the despatch of the task-force, restored Conservative fortunes. A government previously challenged in the polls rallied in the May local elections, the SDP vote dipping for the first time in its year of existence. Similarly the Conservatives held the May Beaconsfield by-election (easily defeating the young Labour candidate, Blair) and, more notably, won the Mitcham and Morden by-election on 3 June when Bruce Douglas-Mann, the SDP's only MP to resign from parliament to contest his seat, lost by over 4,000 votes. The war had focused attention on parliament, re-establishing two-party politics, Foot's support for the military initiative giving the Labour Party credibility. The main domestic winner, however, was Mrs Thatcher's Conservative Party. By the Falklands victory on 14 June, the SDP/Liberal poll lead had melted away.

In the middle of this testing time, Solidarity supporters were keen to meet, as mutual encouragement helped compensate for their isolation within CLPs. One activist later described how Solidarity created a focus for party members who had just had enough; it helped people realise there was a constituency who were loyal, and moderate, and thus held the tide against the SDP.[76] On the eve of the final Falklands battle (6 June), therefore, key workers gathered in London where they heard Peter Shore warn that the 'Falklands factor' had acted to the detriment of the SDP rather than of Labour, the movement in the polls thus offering no comfort. He reiterated the importance of achieving a clear majority on the NEC to tackle Militant, which he described as a Leninist party – 'primitive, pre-democratic'. He feared the NEC would continue 'to fudge', in which case it should face 'an onslaught from us' as the NEC alone had the power to enforce the party rules by expulsions. Hattersley pointed to a dichotomy: on the one hand the public want us to stop fighting; on the other, they reject the hard-left. However, he was certain that, if the hard left had canvassed anywhere, they must certainly know 'it is they who lose us doorstep support'. For the rank-and-file attendees, there were local imperatives, with Lambeth's Nick Grant stressing that Solidarity had to move out of Westminster as it had promised; the Steering Committee needed union and CLP members on it. He urged the Group not to become another CLV, but get people like Neil Kinnock and Jeff Rooker in, 'even on their terms' and called on Solidarity's leading lights to address local meetings. Scotland's Bob Eadie called for work with regional councils of trade unions.[77] The pragmatic Secretary, Ken Woolmer, noted that nothing could be done without money; there was only £9,500 left and the Group needed £30,000 a year. Hattersley acknowledged the need to set up a committee of CLP representatives to meet quarterly, in addition to the weekly parliamentary meetings. Local groups should be created with help from MPs. There might also be a councillors' group and a trade union input. The Westminster weekly meeting could act as an executive, subject to direction of the quarterly meetings. He pledged a willingness for the Group to be guided from outside. In fact it was to remain Westminster driven.[78]

A larger crowd of over 200 Solidarity supporters met, under the chairmanship of John Smith, at Camden Town Hall on 19 June. Hattersley and Shore gave major speeches, the latter savaging the Conservatives' disastrous record – particularly on the economy – before pointing to 'the great paradox' whereby, despite Gallup showing people overwhelmingly hostile to government policies, Labour had a mere 25 per cent support against the Conservatives' 45 per cent. The Falklands was no excuse, he said. After the Wembley conference, Labour had shed 11 points in a single month. Even at the pre-Falklands conference (October 1981), Labour was only on 28 per cent. His conclusion: 'the party is sick'. That was why they had created Solidarity – to cure the party – though, over 12 months later, 'the fever and delirium are still there'. Blaming Labour's post-May 1979 'cultural revolution' and the loss of comradeship, Shore identified the current malaise as Militant.

Welcoming the Hayward/Hughes' view that Militant would not be eligible to be included on the Register, he pleaded for the party to have frontiers beyond which membership would not be appropriate. The NEC had a 'duty to *enforce* the constitution'. It was not a witch-hunt but a duty to police those frontiers. As 'a body of ideas . . . Marxism [had] always been one of the streams that flow into the broad river' of the party. But Leninism and Trotskyism, with their concern for revolution and 'the creation of a disciplined and elite, Vanguard party' were 'unacceptable to democratic socialists'. Their adherents '*despise* the democratic process' – witnessed in Pat Wall's call 'to his "comrades" to prepare for civil war, should Labour win the next election'.[79]

Hattersley considered it was imperative for the party to stress realistic manifesto commitments rather than fantasies; stop attacking the leadership – otherwise people would not vote for them; repudiate the 'cuckoos in the nest' (Militant); and to introduce OMOV, to give the party back to the members from the hands of caucuses.[80] It was just four days later that the NEC endorsed the Hayward/Hughes report and agreed to establish a Register. However, it also endorsed Militant candidates (Pat Wall becoming the prospective candidate for Bradford North on 28 July).

The speeches were well covered in the media whilst the atmosphere led to a successful collection – topped up by a percentage from sales of Susan Crosland's biography of Tony.[81] Perhaps more significant than the donation was her presence on the platform, illustrating Solidarity's Croslandite rather than Jenkinsite genesis.[82] Members wanted more literature and advice, organisation amongst unions, quarterly meetings for key workers and supporters from around the country being able to feed into the Steering Committee, as had been agreed at the two previous meetings. As the subsequent report to the Steering Committee noted: 'If we do not fully implement this Solidarity will collapse as our key workers will lose faith in the committee, and its intention to be less Westminster based'.[83] The organisation felt too top heavy to its supporters, with not enough grassroots input.

The officers then applied to go on the 'Register of Non-Affiliated Groups of Labour Party Members'. Whilst the Register was created to isolate Militant, it required other organisations to comply. Solidarity's application showed 5,265 members/supporters, no full-time but two part-time paid staff, a full-time volunteer (Goudie) and two part-time unpaid staff. Its finance came entirely from its supporters, with its modest assets comprising just six chairs, three desks, two typewriters, a filing cabinet and one table.[84] It was, in its own words, operating 'on a shoestring'.[85]

Mary Goudie had written to supporters in June outlining the recommendations of the Hayward/Hughes report, with a model resolution welcoming the lead given by Foot and the NEC. She circulated the full application in September, together with copies of *You, the Labour Party and the Militant Tendency*, which had been sent to MPs in July. This four-page, A5 Solidarity leaflet described Militant's history and current activities (undertaken by some 60 employees), detailing how the 'editorial board' was actually the organisation's Central Committee. Quotes from the Tendency's private document, *British Perspectives and Tasks*, included those foretelling how unions would be replaced by worker soviets when the revolution arrived, and plans for taking over constituencies to transform them on Marxist lines.

The August 1982 issue of *Labour Solidarity* focused on the Hayward/Hughes report and the importance of conference endorsing its conclusions. It included the NEC slate[86] and an article by Hattersley scrutinising 'Labour's Programme 1982', which 'contains much which is both genuinely radical and relevant' (the sections on social policy, industry and the economy) though he disagreed with its proposals for withdrawal from the EEC and for unilateral nuclear disarmament. Given that this Programme was to give rise to what Kaufman later termed 'the longest suicide note in history',[87] the Shadow Home Secretary's attitude seemed remarkably relaxed.

Autumn 1982

At the September TUC in Brighton, Solidarity held a successful fringe meeting at which both chairmen spoke, together with NEC member Gwyneth Dunwoody and trade unionist Bryan Stanley. Labour's conference in Blackpool (the 'Programme' aside) was a success for Solidarity. Its rally, chaired by John Smith, heard rousing speeches from Callaghan, Hattersley, Shore and Boothroyd, whilst a lunchtime reception for supporters offered mutual encouragement. The additional seats on the NEC, announced on the Tuesday,[88] were to deliver a working majority (and the key sub-committee chairmanships) on the NEC, whilst Solidarity's call to 'BACK MICHAEL – BAN MILITANT' was gleefully followed the next day with 'MASSIVE VOTE FOR REGISTER'.[89] Hattersley claimed to have witnessed members experiencing at last 'the will to win', despite his doubts over the 'overwhelming and unequivocal majority' in favour of unilateralism, lessened only by the 5:1 majority in favour of NATO.[90] There was no attempt to amend the Wembley formula. Apparently Basnett did not want any change and it seemed unlikely that Foot did. There being no challenge to Foot or Healey on the horizon, the issue was kicked into touch. Meeting in Blackpool after the Militant vote and the NEC results, Solidarity's Steering Committee agreed that Hattersley and Shore should tell Foot that they wanted a firm line taken on expelling the eight parliamentary candidates, the editorial board and the shareholders and organisers of the Militant Tendency. They were to wait many years before achieving all of these demands.

Whilst Solidarity was heartened by the NEC changes wrought by the unions, they were conscious of their own lack of success in the CLP section, where all their candidates fared badly. Even the best placed, Shore, with 179,000, lagged more than 100,000 behind the lowest-elected's 301,000 (John Smith garnered a mere 36,000).[91] Goudie's report to the committee suggested that the reasons were (1) the increased number of constituencies not affiliated or not sending delegates; (2) the slate being agreed too late; (3) insufficient contact with constituencies in the summer (when the office was preoccupied with the Militant evidence and the application for registration); and (4) increased activity by CLPD, including regular letters to CLPs, on policy as well as constitutional issues. However, she failed to mention either the political gulf between Solidarity and party activists, or the absence of OMOV for determining CLPs' votes. She did, though, re-emphasise the need for meetings of key supporters whilst broadening the membership of the committee to avoid being regarded as an MPs' organisation. Her work on recruitment was producing results: on 9 November, she reported 6,798 supporters. However, she questioned the future of Solidarity after the anticipated election, and whether it could attract sufficient funding to continue. Her paper stressed the need to respond to the underlying wishes of the members for a more direct influence on the organisation of Solidarity and reported they were under great pressure to hold another key workers' meeting. She feared that, unless they responded, some of their most important supporters would lose heart and interest. However, she acknowledged they could not hold a meeting without proposals for a new Solidarity constitution. The sensitive nature of the paper led to all copies being returned at the end of the meeting, at which the committee agreed its priorities were OMOV and reform of the NEC.

A further meeting again saw Goudie stressing that key workers had called for an input into the Steering Committee as agreed at two previous meetings.

> If we do not fully implement this, Solidarity will collapse, as our key workers will lose faith with the Committee and its intention to be less Westminster based. We should be working towards the setting up of a National Advisory Council made up from our key workers, and nominations from our Solidarity Groups in the country. The Steering Committee should remain the executive authority. At least 12 people, none of whom are MPs, should be co-opted from the trade union movement and local authorities. Unless we take some immediate steps, severe damage will be done to . . . Solidarity.[92]

It was therefore agreed that the January meeting become the inaugural meeting of the Solidarity National Advisory Council (NAC). Every proposal demanded finance, so in addition to agreeing to the inaugural NAC, and the production of an OMOV pamphlet, the Steering Committee set up a Finance Group, chaired by Denis Howell. Finance was a constant problem for the Group, which endlessly – but largely fruitlessly – sought donations for their work. Well-heeled business people perhaps doubted that Labour would ever become electable.

The trade unions were keen for Solidarity to concentrate on OMOV. By December, Haines had knocked the draft pamphlet into readable shape, whilst a model OMOV resolution was circulated to the mailing list. Wider distribution was not always straightforward, one reprimand from a CLP secretary complaining that Solidarity had sent, 'unsolicited', its newsletter and the Militant leaflet to members. 'The N E C has informed me that they are seriously concerned about the incident . . . [and] asked me to make enquiries into how a list of my membership became available to you.'[93] Goudie coolly replied that she had not heard from the NEC.[94] OMOV caused similar hiccups, with Stan Crowther MP demanding, 'When did OMOV become Solidarity Policy?' The response was 'December 1981, when it was adopted by both the Steering Committee and at a Recall Meeting of Solidarity MPs'.[95]

There was good and bad news for Solidarity in two by-elections in October. The good was Spellar's victory in Northfield – the first Labour by-election success for 11 years. The bad was the choice of the hard-left Harriet Harman – confirming the growing trend in the PLP – although in public Solidarity could only bemoan the low turn-out in Peckham.[96] 1982 ended on a regretful note, with Dale Campbell-Savours writing to Ken Woolmer on 27 December:

> Earlier this month I terminated my standing order to Solidarity. I did so as I feel that having seized the initiative on the issue of Militant and with an NEC poised to act, the party is better equipped to deal with the problems. I have never regarded Solidarity as a permanent exponent of more liberal forms of party democracy. I support its aims, recognising that whilst the party was in difficulty a clear case should be put for tolerance. I now perceive a readiness in the party to challenge intolerance. Solidarity should disappear as fast as it was given birth, claiming credit for action on Militant and re-formed only if the need were again to arise.

Woolmer thanked the MP for his financial and moral support and straight talking, but reminded him that OMOV was still to come.[97]

Election year

Pressure on MPs remained strong. Joe Ashton wrote, 'I am a "Tribune" supporter of Solidarity and because of this I would like to keep a low profile and not accept any speaking engagements'.[98] Even Robert Kilroy-Silk, under strong Militant pressure, felt it necessary to write: 'You are aware, aren't you, that I'm not a member of Solidarity but a member of Tribune';[99] Frank Dobson similarly protested, 'I am not a member or supporter of Labour Solidarity. You send me your literature, but that's up to you'[100] – despite both having been on the original list of 150 signatories.

The 16 January 1983 inaugural meeting of the NAC began with a briefing on Militant by James Goudie, Mary's lawyer husband and a Chambers' colleague of Derry Irvine and Tony Blair. He outlined how the party had chosen to deal with Militant as an organisational rather than an ideological question. The 1982 conference had not declared Militant ineligible, following Irvine's advice that the NEC had to do so before proceeding to any expulsions.[101] The difficult question was defining who were members of Militant, beyond the obvious editorial board and sales organisers. The meeting also heard a hint of what later became evident – Golding's acceptance of 'Labour's Programme' as the 1983 manifesto. Golding said he would support EEC withdrawal and unilateralism because the party wanted them, and even canvass for Peter Tatchell after losing the vote on the NEC![102] The importance of control of the NEC was evident and the meeting agreed that a full slate was needed. The NAC endorsed the OMOV strategy and model resolutions, subsequently distributed as an A5 leaflet, 'One person, one vote – true democracy'. One resolution was on OMOV for the CLP section of the Electoral College, the other in the selection of candidates.

The NAC having stressed the need to work closely with unions, Goudie wrote to friendly unions asking them to double their advertising rate in the newsletter to

£300. Meanwhile Donald Dewar moved Solidarity in Scotland up a gear in response to increased Militant activity. The moderates were not just fighting Militant but also the new 'Labour Against the Witch-hunt' group, formed to support Benn's attempt to halt action against Militant, and CLPD, which headed its campaign 'Resist the purge'.[103] Militant was a major preoccupation, with evidence continuing to arrive in Goudie's postbag. The party appeared more sanguine, its house journal, *New Socialist*, accepting Militant advertisements.[104]

Solidarity continued with fringe meetings at regional conferences, whilst the NAC met again on Sunday 27 March. Afterwards Goudie wrote to an absent Dunwoody that members were upset that the NEC had endorsed Militant candidates – a more visible presence than the editorial board – and thus rewarded the beneficiaries of infiltration.[105] This was symptomatic of the new NEC failing to live up to Solidarity's expectations. Members also wanted to see Shadow Cabinet members at NACs.

A Recall Meeting of MPs organised for May was cancelled as MPs fanned out for the general election, to campaign in the most hostile of climates. Much has been written about this election and its effect on the party, which will not be repeated, save to note that two Solidarity stalwarts, Woolmer and the recently elected Spellar, forfeited their seats in Labour's tally of losses. The 1983 election was led by Foot, whose poll ratings continuously trailed Thatcher's. Healey remained loyal to him but few others in the Shadow Cabinet respected his voter appeal. Alone amongst them, Kaufman had the courage personally to urge Foot to step aside. But this most romantic of leaders had been saved by Ossie O'Brien's Darlington by-election victory over a hapless, third-placed SDP candidate on 24 March, when national opinion polls had Labour on 32 per cent to the Conservatives' 44 per cent (and the Alliance's 22 per cent).[106] Labour fared much worse in the 9 June election – the trigger for all the policy, organisational and presentational changes which were to follow over the next decade. Without the Falklands, however, the crest of Thatcher's wave might have been lower, and it is unlikely that the SDP surge would have subsided so much. For the Labour Party, and for Solidarity, it was not just the final tally which caused despair, but the haemorrhaging of their core support, with trade unionists and skilled manual workers deserting in even greater numbers than in 1979.[107] Overall, Labour gained the lowest level of support since 1918, with only 27.6 per cent of the vote, giving the Conservatives a 144–seat majority.

After the election Solidarity had to pick itself up – at first fearing that a further leftward shift in the PLP[108] would make its work harder. In fact, in the subsequent Shadow Cabinet elections, Solidarity won 9 of the 15 seats, Healey topping the poll (with 136 out of 209 votes), followed by Kaufman, Shore, John Smith and Jack Cunningham.[109] In contrast Solidarity polled poorly in the NEC elections, where they failed to win a single seat in the CLP section, their top-placed candidate (Kaufman) securing just 180,000 votes to the 280,000 of Audrey Wise (the lowest successful candidate)[110] – demonstrating the gulf between the PLP and local activists.

A new leader and deputy

Before either the NEC or Shadow Cabinet elections could take place, the party needed a new leadership following the resignations of Foot and Healey. From the outside it appeared that: 'Solidarity was controlled by a secret caucus behind its public façade and that caucus had an intense loyalty to Roy Hattersley . . . The most powerful people who backed Solidarity did so on the clear assumption that Hattersley would be the next leader . . . [He] had the right's support guaranteed.'[111] Though writing well after 1983, Silkin failed to notice that Solidarity did not uniformly plump for Hattersley. Golding had intended to, but the candidate's behaviour switched him to the Kinnock camp.[112] Of the other 26 main Solidarity activists, 4 voted for Kinnock and 4 for Shore, Solidarity's Co-chairman, whom Howell and Hattersley had brought into the organisation specifically to prevent it being seen as a Hattersley campaign. For this reason Solidarity was studiously meant to avoid taking sides[113] although its co-ordinator booked the Old Ship Hotel for a late night party after the ballot, presumably for Hattersley supporters to celebrate. Given the predominance of Solidarity MPs in the Hattersley camp, whereas Kinnock won overwhelmingly elsewhere in the party, this is further testimony of the distance between Solidarity and party (and union) activists. Nevertheless, Solidarity did now have one of its joint chairmen as deputy leader and on the NEC.

While MPs were preoccupied with the leadership contest, others were looking to the future. One local member wrote that, 'The 9 June result seems to make Labour Solidarity's role ever more critical if we are to rescue the party over the next 3 to 4 years. There is an enormous amount to be done in the CLPs where the hard and naïve left groups still hold sway.'[114] Others continued to press for OMOV, assisted by branch members' increasing demand to have a say in their CLPs' choice in the leadership poll. The 'One person, one vote' leaflet was widely distributed and OMOV was chosen as the theme for the Sunday rally at conference. Solidarity held a fringe meeting at the Blackpool TUC Congress, and publicised its NEC slate, although the organisation 'kept a low profile over the summer'[115] because of the contest between its two leading lights. Some nevertheless entered the fray for the deputy leadership, Bristol's members claiming that 'The election of Michael Meacher . . . [would] be an unqualified disaster . . . he represents the hard left-zany left combination whose antics and dogmatism lost us millions of trade union votes at the general election'.[116]

In the autumn, a serious look at the future of Solidarity took place. Its finances could not sustain an office, so notice was given to terminate the Charles Lane lease from the end of December, returning the operation to Goudie's home. MPs were asked for £20 each to keep even a skeleton structure in place. Significantly, the post-election parliamentary party finally saw the amalgamation in December of the three moderate groupings – the Manifesto Group, Labour First and Solidarity MPs – into one: Parliamentary Solidarity. Hitherto, the Recall Meetings appear to have been the only gathering of MPs, but now this body took on a life of its own, complete with bank account, standing orders, cheque book and officers. The Chairman was Brynmor John, with Vice-Chairmen Gwyneth Dunwoody, David Clark (Labour First), Terry Davis (Solidarity) and Ken Weetch (Manifesto Group). The Secretary was the new MP Stuart Bell. The merger also brought Manifesto Group funds into Solidarity. A joint grouping would not be without problems – Denis Howell, for example, taking umbrage and resigning as Treasurer when he was not elected by Parliamentary Solidarity to be on their slate for the Shadow Cabinet.[117]

Whilst Parliamentary Solidarity consolidated, the wider grouping continued outside of Westminster, and towards the end of 1983, a number of papers were prepared for an NAC meeting on 14 February 1984. One recommended a new supporter membership (replacing the mailing list), together with encouraging the adoption of reputable candidates for parliament and local government, and improved representation on regional executives. An EETPU paper, 'Consolidating our progress', pointed to the leftward shift in the PLP (Meacher having attracted more PLP votes in 1983 than Benn in 1981), a number of retired MPs having been replaced by hard left-wingers; the Campaign Group had grown from a dozen to about 30, although the split on the left (between the Campaign and Tribune Groups) produced 'good' Shadow Cabinet results. Some ground had been lost on the NEC, whilst Militant were still active (their meetings advertised in *Labour Weekly*) and the soft-left dominated the leader's office.[118] The paper concluded, 'our supporters feel isolated and under siege; an occasional newsletter will not be enough to sustain them', and called for better organisation, especially in CLPs, and a renewed push on OMOV. Meanwhile, a paper for the Steering Committee concluded that there was a strong desire among key supporters that Solidarity should be kept with a newsletter, model resolutions, the NAC and the Sunday conference rallies but an end to regional fringes and the speakers' service.

Parliament–local tensions continue

1984 opened with further evidence of the Westminster/membership tension that plagued Solidarity. The NAC was set for mid-week, 6.30 to 9 pm, according to the invitation letter of 19 January 'in London to facilitate the attendance of MPs whose absence from Sunday meetings may be understandable but is still constantly criticised'. The reaction was immediate: Spellar wrote to Goudie on 24 January that this 'yet again demonstrates the way in which ordinary party members in the regions feel they are disregarded'. He criticised Solidarity activities for being 'stultified by national political events of all-consuming interest to parliamentarians, but of only relative interest to those in the constituencies' and predicted that a weekday meeting would 'deprive the NAC of much needed voices from the regions'. Barbara Hawkins remonstrated that the 'NAC is the best assembly for the non-parliamentarians. But mostly they do have jobs and mostly a long way from London. Teesside Solidarity urges a return to the week-end, whole-day, forum which can be truly representative of *workers* from the regions'.[119] Goudie reported to the Steering Committee that she had received a number of apologies and complaints because the meeting was being held mid-week. Nevertheless the meeting went ahead, Godsiff writing that he hoped that Solidarity would continue because it still had an important role in combating the 'illegitimate left' at constituency level.[120]

The Valentine's Day NAC meeting was cheered by the increased vote for Ashley and Kaufman in the NEC ballot, although Hattersley (appearing for the first time as Deputy Leader) reported difficulties in CLPs where the left continued to organise, admitting that Solidarity had done nothing since conference. This seems unlikely, as 9 of the 15 elected 1983/84 Shadow Cabinet places were held by Solidarity. Nevertheless, given that Hattersley had joined the NEC for the first time, and with a workable (albeit fragile) majority, it sees strange that a coherent plan of action was not more evident. The meeting established a new Steering Committee, including 11 representatives from Parliamentary Solidarity and 3 from the unions plus representatives from CLPs. Hattersley and Shore became Vice-Presidents. Goudie took the title of Secretary, Ken Woolmer having lost his seat.

At the subsequent NAC on Sunday 25 March, Hattersley stressed the importance of Solidarity existing independently in CLPs and unions, rather than being dependent on a few senior MPs, whilst also becoming more positive and moving into policy areas. There were mixed reports from around the country, Solidarity not having been very active since the election. Attention focused on reselection, with emphasis on the need to get OMOV through the NEC, to achieve which they would have to be very subtle, reassuring unions about their nomination rights under OMOV. The meeting agreed it was important not to concentrate just on saving MPs but also on selecting new candidates. CLPs wanted early reselection, which meant that work on OMOV had to commence quickly. Up to 25 MPs were at risk so they should emphasise to the NEC the appalling damage to electoral credibility if deselection occurred, causing internal rows. New officers were elected, with Terry Davis becoming Chairman. Meanwhile, from outside the meeting an indication of disquiet with Solidarity appeared in the pages of *Forward Labour*, with a snippet reading: 'LSC: Where art thou? Where is Labour Solidarity Campaign: You'd think they'd be hard at it in the constituencies. In case *they* don't know it, the Barmy Brigade *is* at it'.[121]

The first new-style Steering Committee Meeting took place in April, with attention drawn to the drastic state of the finances. It was agreed to approach supporters in the Lords for funds. By May, 52 parliamentarians had signed standing orders, although the bank account was still £1,000 overdrawn in July – a situation only saved by one £5,000 donation raised by the treasurer's persuasiveness. Politically the priority was OMOV. The committee agreed that Parliamentary Solidarity's Chair (Brynmor John) and Secretary (Stuart Bell) should meet Kinnock to press for this and to express continuing anxieties over reselection.

Discussions on the NEC slate took place in the spring, with names agreed earlier than previously and work with CLP contacts (which showed some support for Kaufman and Dunwoody but little for anyone else). The new Steering Committee immediately faced complaints that the MPs were failing to attend. It appears that Parliamentary Solidarity was fulfilling their needs, and there remained an unwillingness to engage with the wider grouping. Furthermore, when those present questioned what was going on in the House (such as on Early Day Motions or Shadow Cabinet elections), Brynmor John slapped them down with the reminder that these were the business of Parliamentary Solidarity. The MPs' attendance continued to be variable: John and Davis both made seven meetings; Robertson, Clark, Bell and Weetch four or five, whilst the other MPs attended from zero to three.

There were also complaints about the lack of visible activity. Boothroyd reported that members in her area had received nothing for a considerable time, and Helen Eadie questioned the absence of any newsletter, contrary to the NAC decision. She wrote to Terry Davis (Chairman of Labour Solidarity) on 26 June 1984 that MPs seemed to believe that:

> Solidarity could easily be re-kindled if there are pressing needs in the future whereas it is not easy to turn on the tap and come up with accurate records of where our support lies. By maintaining a very weak national machine, the most Solidarity can realistically hope to achieve will be influencing slightly the NEC elections but little or no influence over reselection. Many MPs will not be reselected and that will have been a high price to pay.

She warned that the current route could see Solidarity slipping away – in which case it would be preferable to wind it up. Davis' 8 July reply agreed on the effect of no newsletter, but claimed it was finance which prevented its appearance.[122] Whilst acknowledging her views on reselection, he felt that Solidarity should be more than an MPs' protection society and urged Eadie to remain with it. *Forward Labour*'s David Warburton wrote more openly: 'The sooner LSC realises that *its* job is to get to work in the CLPs the better. Any organisation, whether LSC or the hard left Campaign Group, which relies on pearls of wisdom from sympathisers in the Palace of Westminster tolls its own death knell.'[123]

Helen Eadie was rather optimistic in thinking they could influence the NEC elections. They were a disaster for Solidarity. In the CLP section, the lowest elected (MP Audrey Wise) was nearly 100,000 votes clear of Kaufman.[124] More ominously, there were only two names on Solidarity's slate.[125] In the union section Golding and Howell were defeated. However, the Sunday rally and two fringe meetings were successful. The NAC, in Blackpool, amended the Group's name to Labour Party Solidarity Campaign and introduced a £1 annual membership subscription (when this appeared as a supporter's subscription to the newsletter, there were complaints that yet again members would have no say over the organisation). Nevertheless, 137 had subscribed by November.

Reviewing the conference, Spellar bemoaned the constant appearance at the rostrum of Militant (suggesting that Liverpool's Eric Heffer in the chair explained the selection of both Militant and 'scouse' delegates) and the conduct of delegates, which shocked voters. Even before former Prime Minister Callaghan began to speak, Heffer had to call for good behaviour, saying 'I don't want anybody ... hissing, shouting or booing'.[126] For Spellar this made it essential to re-produce a sensible party, and to concentrate on the selection of candidates. Without a change, he warned of the suffering of those who would 'bear the brunt of our failure: the old, the poor, the sick, the homeless and the ill-housed'.[127]

Before the 1984 conference Solidarity had seemed optimistic about the 'Year of Progress', pointing to the party's improved fortunes following the arrival of the Kinnock/Hattersley leadership and the successful European elections (Labour seats near doubled to 32), whilst still affirming the need for increased efforts – particularly on OMOV (to which Kinnock had yet to commit) and entryism. But its November issue of *Labour Solidarity* (reduced to A5 format) was calling for 'active and efficient campaigning against . . . those who preach intolerance and whose success would cut the party off from its support in the country'. It professed itself sad to see the newly elected MP for Chesterfield, Benn, sharing a platform with the outlawed Militant (though this probably contributed to his poor Shadow Cabinet showing). However, the Group took comfort from Kinnock's recent conversion to OMOV for selections and his assessment that 'We won the argument but lost the vote' (by half a million votes). Its editorial line was that 'It is not so much a question of "if", but "when" victory comes'. On the other hand, the organisation was dismayed by those seeking 'defiance of the law' in their fight with the government on local government. Solidarity feared that non-compliance with the law won little sympathy with the electorate and conflicted with the party's history and philosophy. It feared that illegality – rather than the Conservative cuts – would become the story.

Parliamentary Solidarity, meanwhile, won two-thirds of the Shadow Cabinet places (including eight of the top ten places as well as the PLP chairman and chief whip). The left were unhappy: the 'Shadow Cabinet elections were a disaster for Tribune. Solidarity stood a full slate (so much for party unity) and was well organised. Ten of its members were elected (a net increase of one)'. Whilst Campaign Group member Meacher was elected with many Tribune votes, 'By not voting for the Tribune members, Campaign damaged the left as a whole . . . preventing . . . "inside left" candidates such as Rooker and Straw from being elected . . . Too many left wingers stood' (there were 51 candidates – a quarter of the PLP – of whom 29 were from the left).[128] The outcome was a measure of Solidarity's discipline, tactics and underlying strength.

At the end of November, a further NAC took place, with 35 present. This reiterated the importance of getting reliable candidates selected, as well as a good NEC slate. The threat of deselections was much in evidence, with Field, Shore, Kaufman (and even left-wingers such as John Silkin) facing difficult challenges.[129] The predicted purge of moderates did not in fact take place. Some MPs no doubt retired a little earlier than planned but elsewhere Militant was pushed out of contention (by Adam Ingram in East Kilbride and Steve Bassam in Brighton).[130]

Despite patchy reports of local activity, some Solidarity groups were functioning, London's having met in the Commons, a West London group in Ealing, and others in Scotland, the Wirral, West Midlands and Teesside. There were regional fringe meetings, in Wales, Scotland and across England. Student Solidarity was set up during 1985 'as a rallying point for moderate Labour students, and to counter hard-left student groups within the party'.[131] It had a place on the main Steering Committee (held by Andrew Cook, from the EETPU) and was given £100 to get underway. It held at least one fringe meeting and produced newsletters but did not continue for much more than a year.

The Steering Committee's preoccupations in 1985, finance apart, were OMOV, resolutions for conference and the NEC slate. Joe Haines redrafted the OMOV leaflet, whilst the cause was helped by a split on the left when the LCC gently distanced itself from CLPD and the hard-left. The LCC move towards OMOV was surprising given its role in helping defeat the 1984 amendment which would have offered constituency parties the option of allowing every individual member a direct vote.[132] CLPD opposed too great an extension of the franchise, calling the 'right wing proposals for one member one vote' an 'attempt to dilute the party's policies through media influenced results. This is unacceptable – particularly the postal ballot'. (Though CLPD did acknowledge that perhaps members who had attended one-third of their branch meetings, and had at least a year's membership, might be allowed to vote for a candidate at a meeting.)[133]

The NEC's role in taking OMOV (and the isolation of Militant) forward was going to be crucial, so attempts for an attractive slate continued. However, one of the best known of Solidarity's standard-bearers was unwilling to help, John Smith writing to Goudie on 9 May: 'I have given some further thought to the NEC elections and I have come to the firm view that I do not wish to be a candidate'. Despite this, a slightly longer list than in 1984 was offered (Ashley, Kaufman, Radice and Robertson). It had no more success. The last elected (Wise) had 317,000 votes, with Tam Dalyell the runner-up; best-placed Solidarity member Kaufman polled 214,000 – a full 100,000 short. (The moderates did less well on the union side too, Anne Davis losing to Margaret Beckett.)[134]

Parliamentary Solidarity continued its activities, with 48 MPs and 5 Lords in membership and re-electing its officers in January 1985. Relations between the two parts remained distant, Goudie having to write on 10 November to ask to address the Parliamentary Group as 'it's over a year since I last came formally'. Attendance by the MPs at the committee was variable, a list for 29 February 1984 to 16 January 1985 indicating that whilst Brynmor John had managed ten meetings, and Davis and Robertson eight and seven, seven of the others had made either three, two or even just one meeting. The Steering Committee asked the 'Secretary to send a stiff note with the next notice because of the bad attendance'.[135]

The weekend meetings were no greater attraction. Seven MPs did not attend a single NAC, though Chairman Davis made three, Hattersley four, and John, Dunwoody, Robertson, Clark, Shore, Dewar, Smith, Millan and Radice either one or two. The mismatch between the parliamentarians and supporters was continuing. At the January 1985 NAC, there were proposals for a restructured – and smaller – Council, presumably to give it more teeth, but little seems to have changed. The 35 attendees concentrated on a major concern – matching reliable candidates with receptive CLPs – and on the traditional issues (OMOV and Militant) plus model resolutions on the economy and law and order. NAC meetings were arranged for February, June and September – a difficult period for the party with the miners' strike at the beginning of the year, the failure to re-take Brecon and Radnor, the loss of the supposedly safe Lambeth Vauxhall seat on the Greater London Council, local government problems and Militant activity. In parallel to Solidarity and St Ermins, Spellar was meanwhile engaged on the establishment of yet another group (Mainstream), taking Solidarity into friendly unions, some not affiliated to the party.[136] There was an NAC at the end of the year, when 22 of the 74 present were MPs, including Hattersley, Shore, John Smith, Cunningham, Kaufman, Dewar and Radice from the Shadow Cabinet, plus Boothroyd and Dunwoody from the NEC.

Whilst 1984 had seen just two issues of *Labour Solidarity* (one two-sided A4, one eight-page A5, both photocopied), there were three issues in 1985, albeit still photocopied rather than the red-bannered, typeset versions of the first two years. In January, the miners' strike – which caused the party so much trouble – was covered, with an attack on the Campaign Group for seeking a debate in the House which would have embarrassed Kinnock (a man 'growing in stature every day').[137] Solidarity took too much heart from the party's performance in the May local elections, which indicated that Labour could be 'the largest party after the next election ... [with] every chance that Neil Kinnock is heading for No 10'.[138] The Student newsletter hailed Kinnock's Bournemouth anti-Militant speech as 'brilliant and courageous' and welcomed the enthusiastic response from delegates.[139] The December 1985 *Labour Solidarity* applauded the NEC's decision to launch an inquiry into Liverpool, and reported that applications to join the party had flooded in after Bournemouth, along with a surge in opinion poll ratings. The Group, having made the case for parliamentary socialism for so long, felt vindicated by Kinnock's re-assertion of 'the democratic, reformist roots of our party. His condemnation of impossibilism ... was a vital return to the fundamental principles of Labourism. The traditional pragmatic majority in the Party can now feel that they are on the offensive with an ideology which ... is popular.'[140] Although the OMOV motion (moved by Spellar, seconded by the National Union of Labour and Socialist Clubs and supported by Robertson) had been remitted, it seemed its day would come.[141]

Kinnock did not rest after Bournemouth, penning an 'Open Letter to the people of Liverpool' describing how 'My patience has run out on Tendency tacticians'.[142] He then delivered a Fabian lecture in London's Friends' Meeting House, where he attacked

Democratic centralism (which employs the most undemocratic methods) ... Vanguardism ... [of a] self-appointed elite ... and the dishonesty of those who opt for a parasitical life inside the mass Labour movement ... [which] involves systematically abusing the open and tolerant Labour Party. Their belief that the ends ... justify the means (a neat and nasty tactic called 'revolutionary truth') provides a licence to lie about their organisation, their funding and their aims. [Anyone committed to Militant should be] put out of the party ... Democracy must always defend itself and democratic socialists cannot permit their party to be defaced by a secretive group whose whole purpose is to contradict the values, feed off the vitality of and disgrace our party.[143]

This was music to Solidarity ears and the sweeter from the left-leaning Kinnock, who was clearly intent on change.

However, the divide between party activists and the PLP remained. So whilst Benn, Heffer, Meacher, Richardson, Skinner and Wise were all elected to the CLP seats on the NEC (plus Beckett and Maynard for the women's places), alone of these Meacher was also elected by fellow MPs to the Shadow Cabinet.[144] There was similarly no congruence on the left between MPs' and activists' views, Robin Cook and Denzil Davies being chosen in the MPs' ballot but failing to make the NEC (for which other left-wing Shadow Cabinet members, such as Prescott, were not even candidates). Benn was more than 20 votes adrift of one of the 15 Shadow Cabinet places, in contrast to Kaufman's top position with 122 votes. Solidarity's slate took nine seats (losing Dunwoody).[145]

1986 saw a more concerted campaign to win an NEC place – building on Kaufman's existing vote[146] and, it was hoped, John Smith's public profile. However, Smith would not commit himself, Stuart Bell writing to Goudie on 6 January that 'Some of the senior figures, such as John Smith & Jack Cunningham would wish to reserve their position to see how well a national campaign can develop around their candidatures'. This did not facilitate the development of such a campaign. Meanwhile, Shore was unable to get the necessary nomination from his CLP. By June it was clear that Smith would not stand. The slate therefore comprised Ashley, Bell, Kaufman, Mitchell, Radice and Robertson.[147] Whilst none was successful, Heffer was defeated – replaced by Dalyell – with Ashley and Kaufman as two of the three runners-up.[148] (In the women's section, the unions replaced Beckett with Jeuda, to the delight of the moderates.) At the year end, Solidarity was again producing slates for the new National Constitutional Committee but whilst the St Ermins Group delivered both women's seats and 4 of the 5 union places, Solidarity made no impact on the 3 CLP places, attracting, at most, the votes of 43 constituencies.

Solidarity remained active in 1986, and held fringe meetings at various regional conferences.[149] The main event was the Sunday rally at Blackpool when Hattersley's speech won wide publicity.[150] The NAC continued to meet, with Anne Davis replacing her husband Terry as Chairman at the January 1986 AGM. The tighter system of subscriptions saw 594 supporters in January (rising to 665 by September) – not enough to provide the necessary finance, and at the beginning of the year Goudie and Hattersley had to guarantee a £1,000 overdraft. The NAC met in April and then at the October conference, when the subscription was doubled to £2. Its final meeting in 1986 was due to discuss the future of the organisation but this was postponed until February; meanwhile it continued to experience the difficulty of running activities without funding.

Local meetings may have been declining, but Solidarity's great cause, OMOV, was gaining ground, with the party launching a consultation on extending the franchise for selection and reselection as a result of the EETPU motion remitted in 1985. Haines revised the OMOV pamphlet into 'They say it can't be done: one person one vote', complete with model resolutions and rebuttal arguments against the opponents' case. The issue was promoted in the Students' March newsletter as 'real, grass-roots democracy', and the Steering Group circulated another resolution on OMOV for the Electoral College. Solidarity took heart from the expulsion of the Militant Eight from Liverpool, though recognising that the fight was far from over. In London the party was still in trouble so a number of members launched

'Londoners for Labour' at the end of 1986, including the ever-organising Spellar and, as Secretary, Godsiff.

Electorally Labour was doing better, holding every council (except Liverpool) in the May elections and with their overtly family man, moderate Nick Raynsford, taking Fulham from the Conservatives in April (the SDP's Roger Liddle coming third), the first good news since the 1983 debacle. Everything the government did heightened the opposition's desire for victory, from the abolition of the Greater London Council and allowing US planes to take off from England to bomb Libya, to the disregard for the niceties of protocol when Thatcher alone of European leaders chose not to attend Olof Palme's funeral. She had survived Westland and the miners' strike and helped marginalise the five-year-old SDP (whose third-party presence in the House never allowed them to land a blow on the government). However, Labour's problems continued, its hapless far-left candidate in the Greenwich by-election, Deirdre Woods, losing spectacularly to the SDP's Rosie Barnes.

This was the atmosphere in which Parliamentary Solidarity organised for October's final Shadow Cabinet contest before the election. Benn's vote fell even further (from 62 to 50) while Kaufman and Smith took the two top places (113 and 103 respectively), being joined by eight others from their slate (as well as the Chief Whip and PLP Chairman). Solidarity clearly represented the bulk of the PLP, its leading lights seen as the workhorses on the opposition front-bench. There was some friction between the two arms of Solidarity, not least because the parliamentarians had money whereas the main Group did not. In parliament, paper and photocopying were free, notices of meetings could be distributed internally, and there were neither staff to pay nor newsletters to print. Despite this, some 50 parliamentarians paid £10 a year, allowing the build-up of a useful reserve. In November, when the central organisation had difficulty paying for the conference rally, Goudie asked the MPs' Treasurer, Weetch, for £300 towards this, leading to a 'cool' exchange of letters, a meeting of the respective officers, and – finally – the cheque.

In late 1986, there was more discussion on the future of Solidarity, with another Spellar paper which identified current work as: OMOV, Militant and Shadow Cabinet elections. He attributed the fall-off in local activity to the fact that 'the NEC is dealing with Militant and that the party is getting its act together'. Nevertheless, he saw 'the need for an organisation to determine the slate and to send out information'. Solidarity had kept many people in the party who had been 'disillusioned and horrified'[151] (especially from 1981 to 1983), and these members were now putting their effort back into the party. Spellar therefore recommended concentrating on local groups or on providing information.

With Militant having been defined as ineligible for membership, and its leading lights expelled, the party set up the NCC in response to a judicial ruling that the NEC should not be both 'prosecutor' and 'judge/jury' in cases of alleged breach of rule. The NCC started work early in 1987, with a healthy Solidarity/St Ermins majority. However, some in Solidarity (such as Dunwoody) remained concerned about other groups which could replace Militant and mused over reintroducing a 'Proscribed List' as had existed until 1973. A paper was prepared for the Steering

Committee, but attention turned to the forthcoming election and the future of Solidarity, especially in view of its funding problems. While the future of the Parliamentary Group seemed assured (and possibly increasing in influence[152]), without a higher profile and regular newsletter, the main Solidarity Campaign was not viable (although it had notably longer tentacles into the party than the rival Campaign Group).

1987 – and two defeats

At the 1987 AGM, no fundamental decisions were made, although Hattersley's stress on the need for a higher profile was endorsed and with it the continuation of a newsletter. Dunwoody replaced Anne Davis as Chair, an Organiser (Andrew Cook) was added to the Secretary (Goudie) and a reformatted Steering Committee agreed, with four regional representatives, four from the Parliamentary Group, two from the unions and one from Student Solidarity. The Group dispersed, not to meet again until after the 11 June election.

The election results were sorely disappointing, Labour gaining only 20 seats, leaving the Conservatives on 372 with Labour well behind on 229. There was not much to celebrate after eight hard years of opposition. The moderates knew that further changes were needed within the party, not least in collaboration with the soft-left. Within a month, Spellar was pressing for closer discussions – even 'amalgamation' – with sections of the LCC. The Steering Committee met as soon as the House was back, organising its slate. This was when disaster struck Solidarity: it lost five of its ten Shadow Cabinet places[153] and was even shifted from its long-held pole position. Bryan Gould, having masterminded the party's election campaign, topped the poll, with 163 of the 220 votes, with Prescott and Meacher second and third. Solidarity managed only 4th, 5th, 9th, 11th and 14th places.

Thus not only was the general election worse than had been anticipated but: 'We have a real crisis. For the first time in thirty years or more, the old, as distinct from the actual, centre right of the party is not in control of the Shadow Cabinet', wrote a chastened George Robertson. Throughout the Manifesto Group's history, its majority was assured, a situation continued under Solidarity whose slate had comfortably filled the bulk of the seats. Now the soft-left had eclipsed it. 'On the NEC and on the Shadow Cabinet having the backing of Solidarity is now meaningless and both the left and the leadership can afford to ignore us', despaired Robertson. Not only had they lost five seats, but they had gone to those he characterised as 'almost identikit Solidarity types – Gould, Brown,[154] Dobson, Straw'. Robertson felt the time had come to wind up Solidarity. Given his key role first in the Manifesto Group and latterly Solidarity, it is worth quoting at length from his analysis of the organisation's successes and weaknesses.

Recalling that Tribune had orchestrated the hounding of 'honest, decent party members' when 'the last Labour Government was being rewritten as worse than Ramsay MacDonald', he went on:

> Solidarity grew out of the . . . revulsion in the PLP . . . at the vicious, irrational, irresponsible climate in the post 1979 period. It built on the work of the Manifesto Group

... [and CLV and] as a defence organisation for beleaguered MPs, councillors and sane Party members ... It stiffened people at a time of unprecedented pressure and vitriolic attack. Amid the defections to the SDP it kept the broad church of the Labour Party intact. Reselection would have been much bloodier without it, the SDP might have had other recruits, Benn would certainly have beaten Healey, the NEC would not have been regained [so] early ... and the 'dream ticket' would not have triumphed ... Without Solidarity ... [the party] would barely have existed ... During all that time ... the Tribune Group campaigned for mandatory reselection, against purging Militant, for Tony Benn (with the very 'bravest' voting for John Silkin), for giving the NEC the final say on the Manifesto, for the Electoral College and for the 40 per cent to the unions ... Times have changed ... what was the soft left, and which now controls the Leader, the NEC and the Shadow Cabinet, ... have assaulted Militant ... pushed ahead with OMOV and established [the NCC] ... The real division ... is now between the hard-left and the rest ... So, what is there left for us in Solidarity to do? With a number of our supporters slithering over to Tribune ... and espousing a line identical to ours, what is the point of us remaining simply as a 'right' wing rump to prove that they are in the centre? ... There is still a role and a future for our people. If Solidarity had not existed ... the left would have ruined the party. If we were to give up then the resolution of the new image makers would soon fade.[155]

However, he considered that unsuccessful slates and small meetings were no response so he advocated a return 'to the pre-1976[156] position where there was no formal centre-right organisation', just a newsletter, links with the unions, *Forward Labour* and co-operation with some in the LCC and Tribune to isolate and defeat the hard-left (particularly on OMOV).

This was heady stuff but followed Spellar's suggestion of collaborating with the once-hated LCC. A Steering Committee was called for mid-September but, despite its importance, attendance was low. Robertson's paper was leaked to the *Sunday Times*, which ran it as 'Labour right admits defeat'.[157] Brynmor John reassured members that the Group was alive and well although, ten days later, the Steering Committee agreed to propose to that weekend's NAC that Solidarity be dissolved as its objectives had been achieved, and for it to be replaced by a regular publication to continue its message.

Spellar chaired what became the final NAC on Sunday 1 November at Swinton House when Goudie reported on the Steering Committee. Most participants saw a continuing need for an organisation, Willy Bach warning: 'If we disbanded, we would be back to where we were in the 1970s'.[158] The Group represented the majority of Labour voters and needed to maintain contacts. There were internal elections – and reselections – to be organised. (There were reports that Prescott might challenge Hattersley as Deputy, which may have influenced people.) Whilst some felt that, as Militant was receding, a looser grouping around a newsletter would suffice, others hankered after a machine which could organise. Former Number 10 staffer (and daughter of an MP) Jenny Jeger warned that if Solidarity closed, other groups would not, and stressed the need for a link between Westminster and what goes on outside. Spellar thought a re-emergent 'Labour First' could encompass Solidarity and *Forward Labour* as a source of information to 'our people'. A lengthy debate led to agreement on: (1) a newsletter; (2) a skeletal national organisation meeting twice a year; (3) local groups where desired; (4) CLP mailings; (5) Parliamentary Solidarity for slates; and (6) conference fringe meetings. A smaller executive was agreed, with representation from the unions (Spellar), NEC (newly re-elected Anne Davis) and PLP (Robertson) plus the newsletter editors and officers.

1988: Solidarity closes down

The old Steering Committee endorsed those decisions the next day – though nothing more is recorded for 1987 other than the winding up of the West London Solidarity Group (its funds being sent to the centre). In February, the final bullet was placed in the barrel of the gun, with a letter from the Chair, Gwyneth Dunwoody, and Secretary, Mary Goudie, to the mailing list. This sums up the achievements of the Group for which they had both worked so hard:

> Solidarity was born out of . . . revulsion against the vicious and irresponsible climate
> . . . Tolerance was under siege, moderation was under attack and the SDP was drain-
> ing away support . . . Solidarity stiffened the resolve of decent party members at a time
> of unprecedented pressure and vitriolic attack. In many ways it was the decisive factor
> in keeping the broad church of the Labour Party intact.

The letter repeated Robertson's list of achievements, adding the case for OMOV, and continued: Solidarity 'has never been . . . an alternative to the party. Our success has been as a pressure point for sanity . . . Realignment . . . is already under way and most of us want to be part of it'. The letter invited views as to whether to continue or suggestions on how to maintain 'the pace of progress'.

The press picked up the story, quoting an unnamed member: 'Our dilemma is that there are no battles left to fight. Kinnock is moving our way on defence, Europe and the economy and we've clobbered the nasties.'[159] Replies poured in, voicing the grassroots' views of the organisation which was, almost to the day, celebrating its seventh birthday. All but 5 of the 29 recorded responses called on Solidarity to continue, some prompted by the Benn–Heffer challenge to Kinnock and Hattersley, as the following heart-felt extracts demonstrate:

> As there is to be a struggle for the leadership I hope [Solidarity] will remain active.
> Whilst I cannot envisage leaving the party, should the superannuated nobleman
> and/or the *ancien terrible* have any success, my activity may be confined to paying the
> minimum sub.

> I would hope Solidarity continues its tolerance and moderation. We have now seen the
> intentions of the left-handed supporters as envisaged by Benn and Effer [*sic.*] . . . it is
> imperative that Solidarity remains to counteract these.

> Although we have won some important battles, *the war has still got to be won!* The
> leadership campaign emphasises the need for fresh support for Neil Kinnock against
> the *hard left* Campaign Group.

> I was of the opinion that it would be better to wind up as we had won the battle against
> the 'head-bangers' but it would be better to keep the public informed until after the
> contest.

PLEASE KEEP GOING.

The threat from infiltration and Militant remains. 'Eternal Vigilance is the price of Liberty' . . . continue.

Solidarity is still useful as a pressure group for OMOV. (How many party members will feel frustrated that they have no vote in the forthcoming leadership/deputy contests?) Will it not be necessary to support Roy Hattersley's candidature?

Carry on. We have always to watch the 'far-left' and we have to be ready to challenge them. It would be a sad day if Solidarity ceased.

Now Benn and Heffer have decided to contest the leadership, Solidarity should continue so as to ensure victory for Kinnock and Hattersley.

Labour Solidarity is needed: the hard-left are mobilising.

There is a need for *more* solidarity to rally support against the attack from Benn, Heffer and their Militant supporters. We should not sit back and count our successes. Continue, for *tolerance, moderation* and above all *sanity*.

The NEC changed because some unions have become 'less left' but the heart of the movement has hardly changed. It is mainly 'left orientated'. Solidarity must be re-vitalised.

We can feel pride in what has been achieved in thwarting the attempts of those who sought to highjack our party. It is easy to forget the threat which faced us in 1981 when the infiltration from Militant was very real. To the eternal credit of those who formed Solidarity, that threat has receded. However it has not been routed. The decision of Tony Benn and Eric Heffer could give a boost to the extreme left. Therefore remain and support Kinnock and Hattersley.

One CLP women's section admired the efforts put into Solidarity for the benefit of the Labour Party and urged it to carry on. From Liverpool, where Militant had pushed out members, 'these people are still in charge. Now we have a leader who is bringing the party back to its senses and we are proud to call ourselves Labour. We all want to see OMOV [but] we see once again the stupid antics of the left in proposing Benn and Heffer..They don't want a Labour Government.' Two long-standing party members had similar views, W. M. Herbison hoping it would continue as 'I have found the info it has provided helpful at GMC'. Marjorie Durbin wrote: 'its excellent work should not yet be abandoned. Its main objective (one member, one vote) has still to be attained'.

Two Steering Committee stalwarts also wrote in, Anne Davis saying, 'I thought the AGM had agreed that we should continue with the newsletter and occasional meetings and support for local activity . . . I don't think we can sit back and feel secure'; Barbara Hawkins wanted to: 'continue . . . as a broader federated structure of like minded groups . . . the battle for sanity has still to be won'. Sandwell Solidarity's view was that:

> We must continue. Our task is far from complete, witness the Benn, Heffer challenge. The left are waiting to seize the reins of power. The left must be swept aside or the possibility of becoming the government will never be achieved. The Kinnock/Hattersley

support within the NEC is not because of a change of heart among party members . . .
the left is still predominant. So the need for Solidarity is greater.

Four MPs favoured continuing, with defeated Shadow Cabinet member Archer
ruefully acknowledging that:

> the Solidarity 'slate' no longer has a function in PLP elections . . . However . . . there is
> a need for a forum within the PLP for discussions [for] those who would not be at
> home in the Tribune group . . . Secondly, there is still a job to do at constituency level;
> we need some mechanism by which MPs visit areas where mainstream Labour people
> feel isolated.

Boothroyd wrote: 'I would like to see it remain . . . as would other Blackcountry
friends'; Bruce Millan: 'I have been very reluctant to accept the proposition that
Solidarity should be wound up.' Finally, Parliamentary Solidarity Chairman
Brynmor John: 'I cannot accept the relatively benign view you have taken of the
party'. Solidarity's problem, he wrote, was that some of its leading lights were more
concerned about 'who' rather than 'what' the party was about and found themselves 'in positions which they do not want to jeopardize and in which they feel
perfectly cosy. That is why they feel the party is in a much better state'. He dismissed
any idea of realignment, especially when 'the Tribunite left, and particularly the
leader, is constantly humiliating people in the right and centre . . . the Labour Party
is becoming jelly. No one knows what we believe in.' The Group should contest the
battle for ideas as 'there is still a large element wedded to unreality'.

In addition, there were five letters in favour of winding up, two of which drew
different conclusions from the Benn/Heffer challenge. One felt that ending
Solidarity would 'put the current leadership election challenge in its proper perspective' whilst David Bean wrote: 'the time has come, with dignity and honour, to
call it a day. The leadership elections make this more urgent. If Roy is to win it can
only be as the candidate of the whole party, not as a factional candidate'. The
remaining letters read: 'the Labour Party has overcome most of the difficulties . . .
[so] there seems little point in continuing'; 'the job has been just about done' and,
lastly, 'Solidarity has done a fine job and achieved much . . . it should stand in
abeyance with "trustees" to call it together should the need arise'.[160]

Solidarity's luminaries gathered in Hattersley's room to review the responses.
A paper dated 11 May summarised these as: go into 'abeyance'; an information network so that like-minds can know what is going on; new thinking; a reluctance to
keep a high profile organisation, the objectives of which are not clear; team up with
non-Solidarity people who now accept what we set out to do; maintain an organisational structure particularly for slates; and finally, much of what Solidarity was
founded for has been achieved – although more needs to be done, especially on
OMOV.

Despite the balance of the written responses from around the country, the paper
proposed: (1) that Solidarity be formally wound up and this (and this alone) be
announced; (2) that in one to two months a newsletter be started with (a) news
and gossip from the party; (b) articles on stimulating issues; (3) that it have a new
name; (4) that it have an editorial committee, with a broad membership; (5) that

it organise meetings at annual and regional conferences; (6) that this be announced *at least one* month – maybe more – after the wind-up of Solidarity.

The work of some core activists did continue, under the banner of a new 'Labour First', which still exists today. But in spring 1988, the then 'owner' of that title – Brynmor John – had, by some misunderstanding, failed to receive his invitation to the final crucial meeting. It was doubly unfortunate, given his firm views, that he was therefore absent when the decision to wind up Solidarity was taken.[161] But taken it was, with the Secretary writing to the party's General Secretary for a form 'to de-register Solidarity'. She and Dunwoody wrote to all their supporters at the end of June, with thanks for their responses from which they concluded (despite the evidence above, but presumably based on discussions with the MPs):

> the consensus was that now was an opportune time for a change of approach. We were created when the Labour Party seemed very likely to tear itself apart. Now – despite the conduct of a small unrepresentative minority – the overall determination is to re-create Labour as a party of government and to rally round the leadership ... We have therefore decided to dissolve the Labour Solidarity Campaign.

After more thanks, they asked recipients to cancel their standing orders. £200 remained – which Goudie sent to the party in July.

A statue remains

That was not quite the end of Solidarity. The parliamentary wing had long held its own funds, in a separate bank account, where it then lay dormant for some years, recalled just in the memory of its last officers. Then something rather strange happened. One day, Donald Dewar asked Stuart Bell[162] whether he would mind using the residue to help fund the bust of Nye Bevan, as the PLP had failed to raise the required £5,000. These two, plus George Robertson and Ken Weetch, agreed and so they – and Blair – in addition to the traditional Bevanites were present for the unveiling (which made 'some people – notably Dick Clements – very cross').[163] The £885 made all the difference and the story is deliciously summarised in a note from Alan Haworth, the PLP Secretary: 'Thus did the heirs of Gaitskell contribute massively to the bust of Bevan'.[164]

Is that the greatest achievement of 'the heirs of Gaitskell' – funding the bust of the once-reviled Bevan? Solidarity's brief life – 1981 to 1988 – witnessed a fundamental turnaround in Labour's internal dynamics, not yet obvious to the electorate, but encompassing the underlying changes which were needed to create what within ten years became an election-winning machine. Solidarity could not claim sole credit. It was the St Ermins Group which produced the change on the NEC, although both helped defeat Benn for deputy leader. Before ranking Solidarity's achievements and failures, it might be useful to summarise its strengths and weaknesses.

Its major single strength was (until 1987) its widespread support within the PLP. Of the 251 MPs, 150 signed the post-Wembley statement, attacking the Electoral College's 40:30:30 composition. Whether this number, the 102 who attended the launch meeting, the 80 to 90 who consistently voted the Solidarity slate, or the 37 who paid their £10 to Parliamentary Solidarity is the correct gauge of its strength, Solidarity was the clear voice of the bulk of Labour's elected representatives. Added to this, the Group had support from most of the unions, was led by two acknowledged parliamentary performers (Hattersley and Shore), and was blessed with the ever energetic, dedicated (yet unpaid) Goudie. It abstained from policy and could therefore encompass a wide spectrum of opinion.

Some of these strengths were also weaknesses. Its lack of policy denied it a cutting edge in the hurly-burly of political debate. The rivalry of its co-chairmen for the party leadership in 1983, as well as Shore's refusal to campaign for Healey in 1981, left it devoid of clear direction. Other weaknesses stemmed from its lack of finance, early defections to the SDP, obstruction from party staff, and the timing of the deputy leadership election: too early in its existence to have reached a settlement with the 'soft-left'. Its biggest handicaps, however, were its right-wing image and the gulf between its views and those of party activists. It also had an internal weakness, never resolved, in the split between MPs and its ordinary members which reduced its ability to win hearts, minds and votes locally. It was hindered by the failure of its star names – Smith, Shore and Hattersley – to stand for the NEC. Even where CLPs could deliver a Solidarity vote, there was no slate to compete with the attractions on the left. It had no figurehead to compare with the charismatic Benn.

Furthermore, some of the trade unionists who were working so hard within the unions – and sometimes courting unpopularity for it – questioned the effort made by the MPs. Kinnock reflected this:

> They really didn't like the way politicians, or some of the politicians, took stances and got attention but took no risks. That was one thing. But the main thing was what was common to Solidarity people other than Giles Radice, George Robertson, Phillip Whitehead and one or two others, they didn't put the work in. I repeatedly thought that was quite sensible, especially when I was driving to some meeting on a Friday night, and other people were putting their kids to bed. They didn't cover the ground. The other outfit, Solidarity, wouldn't do the work. No-one could ever accuse Giles or Phillip of not doing the work. Even if they weren't doing the GCs, they were writing the pamphlets and doing all the rest of it. But there were too many others who were dinner party and armchair fighters – that's no bloody good to anybody.[165]

Given Solidarity's strengths and weaknesses, what were its failures and achievements? It failed in its initial aim – to reverse the Wembley formula. It failed to halt mandatory reselection and was unable to get its candidates elected to the NEC (or NCC) – though Kaufman finally made it in 1991. It failed to stop the NEC endorsing Militant candidates, and did not see OMOV achieved in its lifetime. It neither won the 'hearts and minds' of activists nor built bridges with the soft-left.

Solidarity's achievements, however, were rightly acclaimed by Robertson and others in 1987 and 1988, especially measured against the state of the party in 1981. It stemmed the flow of defectors to the SDP, offered succour to beleaguered MPs and helped reduce the impact of reselection. It contributed to Healey's success in the deputy leadership contest, and to making the case for the retention of Clause

V, leaving the Shadow Cabinet (or Cabinet) an equal say with the NEC over the manifesto. It articulated – at first virtually alone – the case for OMOV, and won that argument (its implementation following later). Alone and against formidable opposition, it argued against Militant and maintained pressure for action.

Its publications, fringe meetings – particularly its rally at conference – and regional activity helped keep otherwise isolated members within the party, reassured they were not alone. With a mailing list of at one point over 6,000 (and later some 500 subscribers), it provided a presence on the ground, even if it could not compete with the long-established CLPD. Within parliament, Solidarity helped isolate Benn between 1981 and 1983, and regularly won nine or ten places on the Shadow Cabinet from 1981 to 1986. By articulating the moderate case, it gave cover and rationale to what the unions were delivering on the NEC. Without continued pressure and authority from Solidarity, and the speeches of Hattersley and Shore, the union-created majority on the NEC would have struggled to push through the changes (including dealing with Militant) which were vital to Labour's re-emergence.

So who is right in the quotes which open this chapter: John Golding or Austin Mitchell? The former ignores the role Solidarity played in keeping members in the party and the political cover it gave to the changes wrought by the unions, without which general secretaries might have found it hard to carry their executives. Mitchell is nearer the mark. The Manifesto Group failed to hold the PLP together, but at that stage had no 'St Ermins' to effect the changes on the NEC – and no support from the likes of Mitchell. Before the SDP, it was those who refused to stand up to the hard-left who helped produce the schism which finally woke the party from its slumbers. It is clear whom Labour leaders thank, as the names of today's Lords (Clark, Clarke, Goudie, Graham, Woolmer, Radice, Robertson) testify. However, what both Mitchell and Golding omit is any recognition of what was happening in the constituencies, where the soft-left was to mellow and take the reins, producing the PLP which shunned Solidarity for a younger, pragmatic, Kinnockite majority. Perhaps, without Solidarity, there might have been no party for the Kinnockites to inherit.

Notes

1 Austin Mitchell, 'Party people: review of Dictionary of Labour Biography', *The House Magazine*, 4 November 2002 Mitchell was Treasurer of the LSC.
2 Golding, *Hammer of the Left*, p. 181.
3 Undated note on 'Wembley conference: revolution or coup' and note 'For consideration of members of the Trade Union Group'.
4 Draft statement attached to Spellar note, 'For the consideration'.
5 Ken Woolmer, handwritten amendments to Spellar note, 'For the consideration'.
6 Roy Hattersley interview.
7 Suggestions included the Democratic Labour Movement, Labour Movement Action, the Representative Labour Movement; and the Labour Representative Movement.
8 Ken Woolmer interview.
9 *The Times*, 27 March 1981.

10 John Grant, *The Post*, July 1981.

11 Steering Committee Minutes, 24 February 1981.

12 Lord Brooks of Tremorfa; Callaghan's Agent, Chairman of the Welsh Regional Council of the Labour Party and Leader of South Glamorgan County Council.

13 Steering Committee Minutes, 26 February 1981.

14 'Get the party back on course: official statement of the Solidarity Campaign', *Labour Solidarity*, Vol. 1, no. 1, March 1981, p. 2.

15 Reprinted as 'Their mistaken option', *Labour Solidarity*, March 1981.

16 *Labour Solidarity*, March 1981.

17 Including Jennifer Beever, Richard Tomlinson, Alison Butler and Evan Durbin's widow, Marjorie, with Kay Graves, Jo Wilkins, Sally Graveling and Betty Clarkson helping out – sometimes paid, sometimes for the cause.

18 *Daily Telegraph*, 20 April 1981.

19 Roy Hattersley Speech, Solidarity Meeting, 7 March 1981. Other speakers were Roy Shaw, Leader of Camden Council, and John Grant, who appealed for funds for a 'sustained campaign, a long hard struggle against the resources of Militant and the SDP. There's a price to pay for the kind of Labour Party we want to see. It's a hard slog and cash will help'.

20 Ken Weetch interview.

21 *The Times*, 1 August 1981.

22 *The Times*, 27 March 1981.

23 Crick, *The March of Militant*, p. 195.

24 *Ibid.*, p. 208; Dominic Egan, *Irvine: Politically Incorrect?* (Mainstream Publishing, 1999), p. 101.

25 Julian Haviland, *The Times*, 1 August 1981.

26 *Ibid.*

27 *Labour Solidarity*, May 1981.

28 *The Times*, 27 April 1981.

29 *Report of the 1981 Labour Party Conference*, p. 343.

30 *Labour Solidarity*, May 1981 and June 1981.

31 Steering Group Minutes, 22 July 1981.

32 Grant, *Blood Brothers*, p. 107.

33 Even a moderate party (Braintree) voted for Benn. 'People who voted Benn here were the "Starry Eye'd" not the sinister. They really did see Benn as he would like to see himself – as the repository of some native, indigenous, radical, tradition: "Foot Writ Young"'; John Gyford interview, 25 April 2002.

34 Sherpas interview: political advisors to the Shadow Cabinet, 1979–83 (Tony Page [Varley], David Cowling [Shore], Richard Heller [Healey], Patrick Cheney [Howell]).

35 Healey, *The Time of My Life*, p. 482.

36 *The Times*, 24 September 1981.

37 *Guardian*, 28 August 1981; *Sunday Times*, 30 August 1981.

38 Ken Woolmer interview; John Gyford interview, 25 April 2002.

39 Healey, *The Time of My Life*, p. 482.

40 Peter Shore, *The Times*, 1 October 1981.

41 Harris, *The Making of Neil Kinnock*, p. 165.

42 *Financial Times*, 3 October 1981.

43 *Ibid.*

44 *Guardian*, 31 October 1981.

45 Paper on 'One year on – first ideas for the Campaign', 23 September 1981.

46 Peter Shore, *The Times*, 1 October 1981.
47 Letter from Councillor Nick Grant, Chairman, Lambeth Solidarity, to Ken Woolmer, 9 October 1981.
48 Paper on 'The future of the Labour Solidarity Campaign', 20 October 1981.
49 Paper prepared by Hattersley for the 28 October 1981 Meeting of the Organising and Steering Committee.
50 Minutes of 28 October 1981 Meeting of the Organising and Steering Committee.
51 With the five new right-wingers on the NEC, this could have been changed with the votes of Foot and his allies. It upset Shore that his old friend was failing to address the issue he took so seriously: the onward march of Bennism.
52 *The Times*, 31 October 1981.
53 Minutes of 28 October 1981 Meeting of the Organising and Steering Committee.
54 Minutes of 4 November 1981 Meeting of the Organising and Steering Committee.
55 'The future of the Labour Solidarity Campaign' December 1981.
56 Minutes of 11 November 1981 Meeting of the Organising and Steering Committee.
57 Letter from Field to Woolmer, 10 November 1981. Field had already written on the importance of OMOV, such as in *Labour Solidarity*, October 1981.
58 *Labour Solidarity*, November 1982.
59 *Sunday Times*, 15 November 1981.
60 *Labour Weekly*, 11 December 1981.
61 *Guardian*, 21 December 1981.
62 Ken Woolmer interview.
63 Silkin, *Changing Battlefields*, p. 38.
64 Tatchell, *The Battle for Bermondsey*.
65 *The Times*, 19 November 1981.
66 *Labour Solidarity*, October 1981.
67 *Daily Mirror*, 10 December 1981.
68 Minutes of Solidarity Recall Meeting, 16 December 1981.
69 *Labour Solidarity*, January 1982.
70 10 and 17 January 1982.
71 *Observer*, 14 February 1982.
72 *Guardian*, 22 February 1982.
73 Notes from 28 February 1982 Meeting of Solidarity Key Workers.
74 See page 144.
75 Thatcher, *The Downing Street Years*, p. 177.
76 Chris Savage interview.
77 Scottish Solidarity did not mince its words. Its newsletter included 'We say to the leeches, the Bennites, the vulturous S.D.P. and the people of Britain, THE LABOUR PARTY IS NOT DEAD!!', together with a cartoon of a bed-ridden, invalid party, with symptoms of 'Militant and Benn' and the prescribed cure: 'Surgery!'; issue 1, February 1982.
78 Notes of 6 June 1982 Meeting of Solidarity Key Workers.
79 Text of Speech by Peter Shore to Solidarity Meeting, Camden Town Hall, 19 June 1982.
80 Notes of 19 June 1982 Meeting of Solidarity supporters.
81 Susan Crosland, *Tony Crosland* (Jonathan Cape, 1982).
82 John Gyford interview.
83 'Report of Solidarity Forum held 19 June 1982'.
84 Solidarity Application to be included on the Labour Party Register, submitted 21 July 1982.
85 *Labour Solidarity*, November 1982.

86 Ashley, Hattersley, Barry Jones, Kaufman, Radice, Shore, John Smith (for the first and only time), plus Boothroyd, Anne Davis, Dunwoody and Summerskill.

87 Golding, *Hammer of the Left*, p. 289.

88 *Report of the 1982 Annual Conference of the Labour Party*, p. 66.

89 Slogans on Solidarity handbills. The text continued: 'The vote on the Register is not a left–right issue. The decision of the TGWU and the Mineworkers to support it make that point. Militant are in breach of the party constitution . . . They want to use the party, not fight for it. Support Michael Foot and the NEC'.

90 *Sunday Times*, 3 October 1982.

91 *Report of the 1982 Annual Conference of the Labour Party*, p. 66.

92 Steering Committee minutes, 17 November 1982.

93 Letter from Robin Page, South Herts CLP Secretary, to Mary Goudie, 20 December 1982; David Hughes (National Agent), letter to Page, 24 November 1982.

94 Goudie to Page, 11 January 1983.

95 Crowther, letter to Goudie, 3 December 1982; Goudie to Crowther, 11 January 1983.

96 *Labour Solidarity*, November 1982.

97 Letter of 16 January 1983.

98 Letter to Alison Butler at Solidarity, 2 May 1983.

99 Letter to Goudie, 21 April 1983. When Kilroy-Silk left the Commons for television, causing a by-election, Austin Mitchell wrote: 'Letting down those who helped him against Militant is inconsiderate'; *New Society*, 8 August 1986.

100 Letter to Goudie, 5 May 1983.

101 David Bean, together with Nick Butler and Rosaleen Hughes, had in April 1982 met with Reg Underhill, who suggested that Solidarity should obtain legal advice to put before the NEC. A subsequent phone call to Mary Goudie was taken when she was at Irvine's house, which led to his involvement.

102 Notes of 16 January 1983 Meeting of Solidarity National Advisory Council.

103 *New Socialist*, January 1983, p. 40.

104 *New Socialist*, May 1983, p. 21.

105 Mary Goudie, letter to Gwyneth Dunwoody, 29 March 1983.

106 *Sunday Times*, 27 March 1982. O'Brien lost the seat in the general election.

107 Only 39 per cent of trade unionists voted Labour; Chapple, *Sparks Fly!*, p. 202.

108 Predicted, for example, by the *Daily Telegraph*, 23 May 1983, though not by Channel Four's *A Week in Politics*, 11 June 1983.

109 The other Solidarity members were Archer, Jones, Radice and Dunwoody.

110 *Report of the 1983 Annual Conference of the Labour Party*, p. 100. Only three MPs were elected to both bodies: Dunwoody (courtesy of the unions), plus left-wingers Heffer and Meacher.

111 Silkin, *Changing Battlefields*, p. 40.

112 Godsiff, who had the union figures, and Golding, with the MPs', went to Hattersley's home to break the news, which the candidate took badly. Godsiff said: 'You have to decide whether you want to be Deputy to Neil Kinnock', to which the renowned author retorted: 'Why should I be deputy to that Welsh windbag? I could be Deputy Editor of the Observer at £40,000 a year'. The amazed messengers left. Golding had gone intending to tell Hattersley that he would support him regardless of the figures, but after that reaction he went straight over to declare for Kinnock (Roger Godsiff interview, 4 December 2001; Golding, *Hammer of the Left*, pp. 320–1).

113 For example, a handwritten letter from Anne Davis to Mary Goudie, dealing with both Solidarity and Hattersley, then adds: 'I am sorry to mix Solidarity business with Roy's

campaign – sorry. I know I shouldn't!'; 21 September 1983.

114 Peter Jones, letter to Mary Goudie, 14 June 1983.

115 *Labour Solidarity*, August 1983. Only two issues of the newsletter were produced in 1983.

116 *Bristol Labour Solidarity*, no. 4, autumn 1983.

117 July 1984. This seems never to have taken effect as the papers show his continued activity in the Group.

118 Presumably a reference to Charles Clarke, Patricia Hewitt and Dick Clements.

119 Barbara Hawkins, letter to Mary Goudie, 7 February 1984.

120 Roger Godsiff, letter to Mary Goudie, 6 February 1984.

121 *Forward Labour*, April 1984.

122 In fact, the next issue – a simple two-sided photocopied version – did arrive in July, largely funded by the EETPU, the union for which her husband, Bob Eadie, worked.

123 *Forward Labour*, October 1984.

124 330,000 to 141,000. Ashley did slightly better with 183,000; *Report of the 1984 Annual Conference of the Labour Party*, p. 69.

125 *Labour Solidarity*, July 1984.

126 *Report of the 1984 Annual Conference of the Labour Party*, p. 150. Similarly when Hammond spoke, interruptions forced Heffer to plead, 'This is a Labour Party conference, not a rabble . . . there is a tradition of this movement which is basic tolerance' (*Ibid.*, p. 40). By contrast, a 'standing ovation and prolonged applause and cheers' greeted Arthur Scargill (*Ibid.*, p. 35).

127 John Spellar, Paper on 'Solidarity: the next step', 12 October 1984.

128 *Clause IV*, December 1984.

129 *Guardian*, 10 December 1984.

130 *Observer*, 17 March 1985.

131 Minutes of Labour Party Students Solidarity Campaign Steering Committee, 30 March 1985.

132 *Guardian*, 20 June 1985.

133 Neil Rhodes, in CLPD Circular, March 1985.

134 *Report of the 1985 Annual Conference of the Labour Party*, p. 85.

135 Minutes of the Steering Committee, 20 February 1985.

136 *Labour Solidarity*, May 1985.

137 *Labour Solidarity*, January 1985.

138 *Labour Solidarity*, May 1985.

139 *Student Solidarity News*, October 1985.

140 *Labour Solidarity*, December 1985.

141 *Report of the 1985 Annual Conference of the Labour Party*, pp. 190–4.

142 *Liverpool Echo*, 29 October 1985.

143 Text of Kinnock Fabian Lecture on 'The future of socialism', 12 November 1985.

144 *Report of the 1985 Annual Conference of the Labour Party*, p. 85, and PLP papers.

145 Stuart Bell, who organised the slates, recalls that Dewar was elected by one vote when Bell got John Gilbert out from his Lisbon hotel late at night to fax through his proxy in time; Bell, *Tony Really Loves Me*, p. 99, and PLP papers.

146 Bell and the EETPU having identified the 106 CLPs which supported him.

147 *Labour Solidarity*, July 1986.

148 *Labour Weekly*, 3 October 1986.

149 *Labour Solidarity*, June 1986.

150 *Labour Solidarity*, October 1986.

151 John Spellar, 'Labour Party Solidarity Campaign', undated paper.
152 'If the split between the Tribune and Campaign Groups continues, the next PLP will see the broad left majority . . . whittled away from the soggy end of the Tribune group until the centre/right absorbs enough of that to take control'; Ken Livingstone, *Tribune*, 28 November 1986.
153 Shore, Archer, Jones and Radice lost their seats (Healey did not stand).
154 Gordon Brown – arriving there ahead of Tony Blair.
155 George Robertson, 'The future of Solidarity', September 1987.
156 Shorthand for the creation of the Manifesto Group, though it actually operated from 1974.
157 *Sunday Times*, 18 October 1987.
158 Minutes of Solidarity National Council, 1 November 1987.
159 *Sunday Times*, 21 February 1988.
160 All letters: March 1988.
161 Brynmor John, letter to Mary Goudie, 17 May 1988.
162 Bell, *Tony Really Loves Me*, p. 100.
163 Alan Haworth, 26 February 2003, communication to the author.
164 Memo to PLP officers on 'Nye Bevan bust', September 1996.
165 Neil Kinnock interview.

12
Forward Labour

At the start of the moderates' 1981 post-Wembley fightback, the only public indication of union activity was *Forward Labour*. Written, edited, produced and mailed by GMWU official David Warburton, some 18,000 copies of this gestetnered, stapled 4– to 10–page, near-monthly newsletter were distributed over its lifetime, to a mailing list growing from under 100 in 1981 to over 800 by its final, 36th issue in January 1988.[1] Despite Pearce's implication that *Forward Labour* was an organisation,[2] in fact it was Warburton – albeit with a faithful group of about 20 party activists and trade unionists – who spread the message.

Warburton's story is typical of many of the right's stalwarts. As a young activist, he was a constituency secretary and agent, then rose to become a union national officer, retaining strong party links throughout his union career. He remains a Labour councillor in 2005. He was staunchly pro-Europe (and Treasurer of 'Trade Unions for Europe', alongside President Vic Feather and Secretary Roy Grantham) and thus close to Roy Jenkins and Shirley Williams from the 1975 European referendum. Despite not being a general secretary, he was active in TULV (set up at the instigation of his own General Secretary, Basnett), serving on the renamed 'Trade Unionists for Labour' National, Organisation and Finance Committees. He was thus well known to trade unionists and politicians, and would have been a prime catch for the fledgling SDP.

That was not his style. Instead, as with his friends in St Ermins and Solidarity, he set out to help regain the party for his type of Labour. His method was the written word, producing a popularist newsletter to encourage members both to stay and to keep active in the party. He provided a mixture of information and intelligence, the listing of slates to be championed locally, together with large doses of humour – particularly trained on the 'mindless left'. Above all, he helped recipients of his slightly scurrilous yarns know they were not alone in their despair at the party's fortunes.

The intelligence comprised polling data and analysis, usually from David Cowling, together with what was happening in unions, TULV or the TUC, and a breakdown of conference votes. Warburton also monitored the left's activities, revealing how 'Labour Liaison 82' was pushing Atkinson and Wise for the NEC in an attempt to remove Kinnock and Lestor. Individuals were singled out – such as the parliamentary candidate Diane Abbott for saying, 'We are not interested in reforming the police, the armed services, judiciary and monarchy. We are about dismantling them and replacing them with our own machinery of class rule'.[3] Militant was well covered, with pieces on its activities, war chest, record in Liverpool and the left's 'Greenwich Amendment', which sought to undermine the Register set up to deal with Militant.

Fire was also turned on the Conservatives, with campaigning material on the cost of unemployment, inflation, the Falklands War, the Franks report into its origins and 'big business funding of the Tory Party'. Former colleagues, now in the SDP, did not escape Warburton's pen. If his target was the government, and Labour's far-left, he could not resist the odd swipe at his own side. He chided Solidarity for being too Westminster based and on one occasion accused the Mainstream union group of paranoia.

The satirical style gave the author great pleasure, with snippets such as 'Winning elections isn't all that important' (quote from a CLP delegate at Wembley), 'Can we afford so broad a church?', 'Labour councillors: fellow socialists or puppets on a string?', 'The invisible miners' (noting that the NUM affiliated 105,000 members to the Yorkshire region of the party – some 45,000 more than the number of miners in the Yorkshire coalfields), 'Double talk from Benn' (comparing what he said with what he did) and 'God bless the sense of Wales' (the party's Welsh conference having voted for an enquiry into Militant).

Some was more knock-about: 'Labour is OUR party. 1982 must be the year to stop the rot! There are 3 million reasons why we must stop the wreckers' (referring to the number then unemployed), 'Everybody's No 1 carpetbagger – Leslie Huckster' (a reference to MP Les Huckfield busily touring the country in search of a safer seat), 'The Gospel according to St Mullins' (Chris Mullin was then editor of *Tribune*), 'Varley vaults ahead as Meacher stumbles' (the challenge for the treasurership), 'Putting teeth into Labour's bite', 'Fight like tigers – against the snakes', 'TRIB – ULATIONS! Yuk! Tribune gets worse' and 'Hark the herald' (about Ken Livingstone's *Labour Herald*).

Warburton enjoyed indulging his taste in humour: 'Militant is an objective voice in the party. I believe that it is genuine in its support for Labour and seeks to influence views in the traditional style of socialism. I also believe in fairies and that the moon is made of cheese'; 'Make Thatcher Governor of Falklands'; 'I'll now ask Neil to give us a short address; Neil: 10 Downing Street'; 'Twit of the month'. His spoof small ads section included offers of 'The smallest book in the world – *Democracy and the Militant Tendency*'; 'Wanted: an understandable defence policy. Send to SDP/Liberal Alliance quickly'; 'Lost: Grassroots support. Can you help the Rank and File Co-ordinating Tendency Faction?'; and 'Rare books – *Around Europe on 60p a Day* by Roy Jenkins and *How to Win Friends and Influence People* by A. Scargill'. It helped cheer up 'the troops' and was surprisingly well received by local activists.

From the start, Warburton used his journalistic contacts to best advantage, giving them early copies of each edition so that, retold on their pages, his ideas –

and particularly the slates – reached a far wider audience than he could manage alone.[4] The slates in *Forward Labour* were similar to those of the St Ermins Group[5] and Solidarity – but this was the only outlet for the former, which operated in secrecy. The slates proved vital in the 1984 battle for the treasurership, when *Forward Labour* was an early supporter of McCluskie (hitherto seen as a bit too left for some). Given that McCluskie's margin over the left's Albert Booth was a tiny 48,000 (or 48 constituencies), he would not have won without the CLP support which Warburton helped build up. Nevertheless, only one in four CLPs voted for McCluskie and his position remained tenuous for some years. In 1986 Warburton styled himself 'Convenor of Forward Labour campaign for McCluskie' when the Treasurer faced challenges from Gavin Strang and Ken Livingstone. Even in 1987, with a near 5 million majority over Strang, the CLPs still voted for McCluskie's opponent by 311,000 to 272,000 – albeit an improvement on the 1984 result.

At times *Forward Labour* ranged politically wider than the other moderate groups – for example, adding Lestor and Kinnock to its 1982 slate, when the left was trying to remove them for having abstained in the 1981 deputy leadership contest. In 1984, whilst endorsing Solidarity's Ashley and Kaufman, it suggested that Dalyell, Blunkett, Gould and Cook 'might also be supported'.[6] This was the first year *Forward Labour* had given support to Blunkett – according to Warburton, making this slate the first on which the future Home Secretary's name appeared. Occasionally there were bigger differences with Solidarity (the CND's Joan Ruddock appearing on Warburton's list in 1986, for example, in preference to Solidarity's Radice and Robertson). Success in NEC elections was widely trumpeted, though even as he celebrated Kinnock having the sort of majority that Wilson, Callaghan and Foot could only have dreamt of, Warburton nevertheless warned NEC members not to rubber-stamp proposals emanating from Westminster.

Organisationally, Warburton played a key role in Healey's 1981 campaign, not least by assiduously courting the 19 small unions which had escaped the Bennites' attention, 18 of which voted for Healey. The Deputy Leader embarked on the campaign with virtually no organisation (as Radice, one of the only two other major players, confessed, 'otherwise I'd have hardly got involved. I'm an unlikely campaigner'[7]). The *Forward* mailing list was the main source of contacts, especially as Solidarity was hesitant in backing Healey for most of the contest. *Forward Labour* was the only overt supporter of the incumbent Deputy – proclaiming 'It's got to be Healey' straight after the Benn challenge emerged.[8] During the campaign Warburton would meet Healey in the latter's Sloane Square flat every Wednesday to go through the figures, particularly adding knowledge from CLPs gleaned from *Forward Labour* contacts. Interviewed, both Healey and Kinnock rated his organisational abilities, the latter judging: 'He was bloody good at organising. Pleasant bully with good left-wing background. Which he never relinquished. What a shame he's not got a bigger country to run – 'cos this guy is ultra capable'.[9]

In the main *Forward Labour*'s strength was propaganda, not organisation (it never held fringe meetings, for example), as it was very much a one-man-band. Its first issue in March 1981 was sub-titled 'Bulletin for democratic socialists' (changed to 'Against extremism' in issue 2). The theme of its first article was 'The

road to recovery', identifying its audience as the main core of the party who 'share
a commitment to defeating the Tories . . . by, first of all, re-gaining our party from
those who have used it as a battleground for their own aims since May 1979'. With
a touch of self-flagellation, Warburton blamed his soul-mates for allowing the
problem to develop by seeking 'consensus whilst others relished conflict. We
preached tolerance while others pursued intolerance. We sought rational discussion while others practised arrogance'. The call to arms was to fellow members: 'We
– who represent the basic heart of the Labour Party – must put a stop to the nonsense which has done us so much harm.' In a style more in common with the
Mirror than the *Guardian*, a two-inch-square box simply urged: 'If you think like a
socialist, speak out like one!' Headed 'Naughty! Naughty!', another snippet ironi-
cally chided left-wing MPs for criticising the right for writing in the capitalist press
whilst some of their own number were simultaneously using 'such pro-socialist
papers as *The Times* or the *Guardian*'.

    Forward Labour's ambition had been to reverse the Wembley formula; its launch
issue detailed the voting pattern which led to the 40:30:30 outcome, which the
majority of unions opposed, and indicated the shift needed to amend the proportions to 50 per cent for the PLP. As that objective disappeared, Militant became its
prime target. This attracted widespread support, including from 56 MPs on its
mailing list although it was initially coy about naming them. Nevertheless names
appeared gradually, starting with Callaghan, John Smith and Shore and adding
Boothroyd (a family friend), Dunwoody, Ashley, Jack Cunningham, Robertson,
Summerskill, Golding, Varley, Woolmer, Archer, Hattersley, Radice and half a
dozen others, together with Gordon Adam MEP. Some senior trade unionists were
content to be named, including Duffy, Sirs and Tuffin. By the time Kinnock formed
his first Shadow Cabinet in 1983, *Forward Labour* could boast that it was read by
seven of them.

    Forward Labour was not slow to comment on political events, whether Warbur-
ton's own favoured cause of the Palestinians or developments within the party.
However, the central thrust was the need to win an election. Writing of the size of
this challenge in 1985, Warburton stressed that the party had to gain 117 seats and
increase its share of the vote from 28 per cent to 40 per cent – at a time when the
opinion polls had Labour on 34–37 per cent. Even after Kinnock's Bournemouth
speech, with the Conservatives on 32 per cent, Labour managed only 38 per cent.
Following the 1987 election, when Labour won 229 seats, the newsletter emphasised that the party had come second in just 153 and third in 245, taking less than
one-third of the total vote.

    Internal party issues – especially finance and publications – were regularly cov-
ered, with ideas for an elected party chair (chosen by conference) and a reformed
NEC structure, and comments on political fund ballots and the campaign strategy.
However, OMOV was only fully embraced after the 1987 election, and even then
with some hesitation due to its impact on the union role in the selection of candidates.

    Perhaps *Forward Labour*'s most newsworthy achievement was its instigation,
in the immediate aftermath of the 1983 election, of what became the Kinnock–

Hattersley 'Dream Ticket'. Although this expression did not emanate from its pages, *Forward Labour* was the first to advocate that the two front-runners should stand for both leader and deputy leader – each supporting the other for the number two position. Within days of the election, a new edition appeared headed 'Labour needs a new leadership' and balloting readers on their choice of candidate. The questionnaire polled views on all the likely candidates (Hattersley, Heffer, Kinnock and Shore for leader; plus Denzil Davies, Kaufman and Meacher for deputy) and offered a two-way balanced Unity Ticket of Hattersley/Kinnock or Kinnock/Hattersley. The 284 responses showed 232 (82 per cent) in favour of the Unity Ticket option (with, on a straight choice, 43 per cent for Kinnock, 38 per cent for Hattersley and 13 per cent for Shore – perhaps surprising for this anti-left grouping). Of the 23 MPs who responded (12 per cent of the PLP), 10 went for Hattersley, 7 for Kinnock and 5 for Shore. Trade unionists voted 42 for Kinnock, 39 for Hattersley and 8 for Shore. *Forward Labour* then pushed for the balanced ticket, which united soft-left and moderate-right, carrying advertisements for both and criticising Meacher for opposing this balanced left–right settlement, judging that his election as deputy to Kinnock would be 'an unmitigated disaster'.

Despite the help given to Healey in 1981, and the support for Kinnock–Hattersley in 1983, it was all to end in tears for *Forward Labour* and Warburton's own career in 1988. At the end of 1987 Warburton gave the usual advance copy of the January issue to journalists. The *Telegraph* ran a major article on its 'attack on Kinnock's leadership'.[10] *Forward Labour*'s – for once signed – front-page story, 'Make or break year?', criticised Kinnock for making no major speech since the election and taking no initiatives, evidence of the distance between the leadership and movement which was 'demoralising'. The Leader's low key strategy was, the piece opined, an example of either 'bad advice or an excuse for lethargy'. Warburton's remarks attracted attention not simply because it was the post-Christmas quiet period, but because they emanated from such a Kinnock loyalist. An onslaught fell on *Forward Labour*'s editor, well out of line with the mild rebukes of the offending article. It was just the excuse the new GMWU General Secretary, John Edmonds, needed to trim the wings of his number two and take political affairs out of his hands. Warburton resigned the editorship (which Basnett had tolerated and even encouraged) and resumed industrial, rather than political, responsibilities in the union. For a time after June 1988, the title continued under what was to become Labour First (mark two) which, based in theory at Brian Nicholson's address, took over the remnants of the dissolved Solidarity, continuing the numbering from the original and casting Warburton in the role of President.

The original *Forward Labour* was never an organisation, so in some ways sits uneasily with the other groups covered in the book. But it was the main communication between moderates seeking to change the party and a largish group of supporters within the wider movement. It helped promulgate slates, passed on intelligence, played a key role in the 1981 and 1983 leadership contests, added vital extra votes to those being amassed by the union general secretaries and 'flew the flag' for party members for whom winning an election was central to their membership. As such, it was a tool in the armoury of the moderates.

Notes

1 Eight hundred were distributed directly but recipients in unions photocopied it, bringing the circulation up to over 2,000, according to its editor.
2 Pearce, *Denis Healey*, p. 557.
3 *Forward Labour*, no. 13, February 1983.
4 See, for example, the *Scotsman*, September 1981; *The Times*, 31 August 1982; *Guardian*, 10 August 1984.
5 So much so that Diana Jeuda's name, habitually mis-spelt in the St Ermins papers, similarly appears as 'Jueda' in *Forward Labour*.
6 *Forward Labour*, no. 23, October 1984.
7 Giles Radice interview, 26 November 2003.
8 *Forward Labour*, no. 3, June 1981.
9 Neil Kinnock interview.
10 *Daily Telegraph*, 29 December 1987.

Part IV

Three decades: 1974 to 2004

13

Reviewing 1974 to 1988

In 1979 when Labour lost the election after five years in power, few would have foreseen its internal wars and the electoral ravages that were to mark the latter years of the twentieth century. Indications of future fissures were in view, but little to signal the dimension of the coming eruptions. The May 1979 election – following the Winter of Discontent – was portrayed in the media more as a result of a Labour Party–trade union rupture than as an indicator of an internal party conflagration. Yet it was an internal re-formation that was occurring, with a sharp disparity between the PLP (where the moderate Manifesto Group held sway) and the activists (pushing a left-wing agenda) – and with no over-arching structure, encompassing the entire party tradition, to maintain equilibrium or to shape a constructive path forward.

Earlier party splits – whether in the 1930s (over the government's response to the Depression), in the 1960s (when CDS rode to the rescue over defence) or in the 1970s (over Europe) – had been about policy. By the late 1970s and into the 1980s, the left had decided that the very nature of being in office, which caused leaders to betray the led, required constitutional changes to bring the government into line with party demands by making it accountable to the party at CLP and national level. Whilst the left was not alone in its disappointment with the 1974–79 governments (about which even the former Chairman of the Manifesto Group, Giles Radice, despaired both then and since), its recipe for change struck at the parliamentary/non-parliamentary settlement within the Labour Party and served to fuel the self-serving and careerist tendencies of individual MPs, steering a number of them to choose their own future rather than the party's interests. A climate of fear developed which weakened the parliamentarians' response to the party's move away from electorally attractive policies and conduct. Whilst the constitutional proposals reducing the MPs' role encompassed the Electoral College and control over the manifesto, reselection had the greatest effect. This undermined the authority, job security and hence confidence of each MP. They were, in a word, frightened. The Manifesto Group was weakened by being right wing and pro-Europe. The climate of fear forced it (and Labour First) to keep its membership list secret. This only added to the pressure on any MP identified with such a grouping. Some of Manifesto's members even resented the creation of its CLP-based sister organisation, CLV, as this drew attention to the moderates' existence.

After the loss of office in 1979, any semblance of party unity fell away. A downward spiral led to more public disagreements, further weakening the standing of the PLP. Then, as the trigger to the biggest split the Labour Party has ever seen, the adoption at Wembley of an Electoral College to select the party leadership drew the (unpopular) unions into a more public parliamentary role whilst reducing the role of elected MPs. The aftermath of Wembley is seen in the Limehouse Declaration and the SDP, but away from the media's gaze equally significant groupings (as far as the party's internal dynamics were concerned) were being created within a mile of the House of Commons. One was the St Ermins Group, the other Labour Solidarity Campaign. Both were unlike what had gone before and both have been virtually airbrushed out of history books. Philip Gould claims the 'modernisers' saved the Labour Party.[1] One of those modernisers, Peter Mandelson, believed 'it was the transformation, the rebirth of the Labour Party over the last two or three years' that finally clinched the victory for Blair.[2] More recently, the Fabian Society's then Chair, Paul Richards, whilst chastising those who date Labour Party history from 1997 (or just possibly 1994 – the year Blair was elected Leader), claims that 'Kinnock began the long march back to electability' in 1983.[3] Neither Gould/Mandelson nor Richards provides the full story. Gould fails to distinguish the party's presentation and policy modernisation from the earlier requisite political changes which facilitated these. Richards is nearer the truth, though Kinnock's modernisation owes much to the traditional right (his opponents in his earlier incarnation). This book does not argue that the groups described here were the sole saviours of the party as an electoral machine. It does argue that they made their crucial – necessary if not sufficient – contribution to saving the Labour Party between 1981 and 1987: a contribution which has hitherto been undervalued and underestimated.

As the preceding chapters relate, the march on Militant, the changes in the composition of the NEC (which delivered for Kinnock the majority he required for his reforms) – and indeed the delivery of Kinnock over Hattersley – were all begun before 1983 and owe more to a band of trade unionists than to the pollsters, advisors and parliamentarians who subsequently closeted themselves around Kinnock, Smith and Blair. Alone amongst these three leaders, Smith had spoken out against the Electoral College and the other constitutional changes and participated in saving the party during its darkest days. Even he played his most notable role somewhat later when, as Leader, he oversaw the final introduction of OMOV in 1993. Earlier, he failed to exploit his popularity, declining to stand in the annual beauty parade of the NEC elections. Instead, it fell to the heirs of the 1900 trade union leaders, who had in their time recognised the need for power in the House of Commons, to re-assert the centrality of the need to win power into the party's thinking and to provide some leadership. Both the NEC and the parliamentarian leadership had failed to give this lead, the parliamentarians concentrating initially on being in government and subsequently on opposing Thatcher, dealing with the

Falklands War and the miners' dispute, and responding to the SDP challenge in the Commons.

The major change that happened to the Labour Party – the new political make-up of the NEC leading, *inter alia*, to action on Militant – resulted from the St Ermins Group's work and was neither conceived of, led by or, initially, even blessed by the party leadership. This is in contrast to CDS in the 1960s, which worked on behalf of the leader, and it is at variance with some of the academic writing on party dynamics and change.[4] The St Ermins Group's intervention stems partly from the particular roots of the Labour Party, secured as they are outside of parliament, from the desire of unions to have an elected presence in the Commons. Thus there was an external force on the party willing it back to electability and, when the party machine failed to respond, taking action to make the necessary changes.

The group of trade unionists who rose to the challenge in the 1980s had much in common with their 1900 predecessors (and indeed with Ernest Bevin who played a similar role in 1931). Most left school at 14 years of age and made their way up through their trade and trade union, being dedicated to the well-being of their fellow workers. In the preceding decades, old-fashioned deference, allied with the unwritten 'rules' of the Labour Party, meant that in the main such trade unionists left high politics, and policy, to the politicians. That changed noticeably during the Wilson and Callaghan years, when NEC–government relations worsened and as the union movement (with its own disappointments in those governments) ceded influence to left-wing MPs on the NEC, allowing the party machinery (kept under leadership influence by Gaitskell and initially Wilson) to slip away.

Partly under pressure from radicals in their own unions, the 1970s generation of union leaders failed to discern within CLPD a more fundamental attack on the party structure and dynamics than mere expression of left-wing policy. Furthermore, from 1979, union leaders' attention was focused on industrial priorities as Thatcher's privatisations, public sector contraction and increased unemployment created a full-time agenda for them. However, from the late 1970s, a newer group of union leaders, who were to metamorphose into the St Ermins Group, was beginning to meet even before the cataclysmic events following the Wembley conference. Wembley was less the trigger for the organisational response[5] than was the creation of the SDP with its *electoral* threat. This gave rise to the SDP's subsequent claim that it took their defection to bring the party to its senses. In fact, Foot's election as Leader in 1980 – when the moderate majority in the PLP failed to deliver for Healey – was the trigger for the party's electoral misfortunes and hence the unions' organisation.

It is, perhaps, surprising that the PLP – which was to experience *directly* the electoral consequences of the party's troubles – was so ineffective at halting the whirlwind. The history of the Manifesto Group demonstrates how the right controlled the PLP – except where their votes were obvious to CLPs and where re-selection meant that MPs could not ignore their activists' views. Thus in the 1976 deputy leadership and 1980 leadership ballots and in 1980/81 when the PLP gave way over the Electoral College (though opposed to the device, neither the PLP nor the Shadow Cabinet took on the arguments), the moderate majority was unable to capitalise on its numerical advantage. Indeed, its success in internal elections only emphasised the disjunction between the PLP and the NEC, there being almost no overlap between the MPs elected by their colleagues to the Liaison Committee or Shadow Cabinet, and those chosen by CLPs for the NEC. The NEC/PLP divide, which started under Wilson, worsened by the year. From 1979, the PLP's standing in the wider party and its internal insecurities meant it was near neutered, whilst the unions' attention was elsewhere. It took some outside force – in this case the moderate union leaders – to have the courage and determination to break the impasse, as the MPs were not up to the task.

Labour Solidarity – created after Wembley and the loss of MPs to the SDP – sought to make up for the shortcomings of the Manifesto Group. It was politically more broadly based (including Shore, Mitchell and O'Neill), had a higher public profile (spearheaded by Hattersley and Shore), a membership beyond parliament and a programme of events outside Westminster. Unlike the Manifesto Group, its public profile was evidence that it was fighting back, the former's few publications being more academic than polemic, more persuasive than rallying.

However, Solidarity contained weaknesses: the absence of policy (a severe handicap in a party of policy and at a time requiring a positive agenda); a 're-tread' image as it lacked young spokespeople; insufficient local presence; and, above all, a political stance out of line with the activists in the wider party. Its inability to engage with and persuade party activists – key to any grouping seeking to lead a political party – repeated the shortcomings of the Manifesto Group and denied it any success in the CLP section of the party's NEC. Solidarity failed to achieve even its first objective – to reverse the Wembley Electoral College formula – partly because Benn's challenge saw it used so quickly and partly because Healey won under the very formula reviled by its opponents (largely thanks to those unions whose influence had been so feared but who were no Bennites). However, Solidarity largely failed in this original objective because there was no appetite for change. Solidarity had other weaknesses, such as the lack of a single, charismatic figurehead coupled with the disadvantage of having to promote the unpopular Healey in 1981, and it was weakened up to 1983 by its two co-chairmen fighting for the ultimate crown. Its concentration on Westminster and Shadow Cabinet elections rather than the party in the country made its relations with the all-important unions difficult. As one of the key players in St Ermins, Godsiff, has commented: 'the vast majority of subscribers to the Solidarity Group were MPs who were fearful of their own political careers rather than actually wishing to organise the fightback at a local level against the Bennites and Militant or to offer an intellectual position to challenge the hard-left's view of the world'.[6] Solidarity MPs, like their colleagues in the Manifesto Group, also failed to understand the depth of hostility of younger party members to the old guard, whether in parliament or in the unions. The very strengths of trade unionists (long serving, loyal, cohesive) were seen as the weaknesses of 'old, white, men' by the post-1960s student generation now active in inner city parties. It was a dialogue of the deaf, with old and new barely talking, much less understanding each other's perspective. Solidarity showed itself as incapable of dealing with these new circumstances as was the older parliamentary leadership. It was therefore not able to provide the dialogue so needed by the party.

Despite these handicaps to Solidarity's success, it had a number of achievements, even if not quite those claimed by some MPs (such as Mitchell's comment which opens chapter 11). It succeeded in offering support to moderates and it provided the only public arguments against Militant and in favour of OMOV (which would in due course transform the party). Unlike the Manifesto Group, it tried to take the debate outside Westminster, and it furnished grassroots members with ammunition and courage to take on the left, though it is possible that *Forward Labour*'s 18,000 copies did more to raise morale than the 24 issues (perhaps 20,000 copies) of Solidarity's slightly more staid newsletter.

The Group of Ten[7] was not able to carry this coalition forward and neither could Solidarity; it took the 1983 electoral disaster for even Labour First, let alone the Tribunites, to join Solidarity. Even then it failed to attract new MPs to its ranks. Blair and Brown joined Tribune, not Solidarity, in 1983 (particularly surprising in Blair's case as he had been an early Solidarity supporter, was a close legal colleague of James Goudie and Derry Irvine, a family friend of Mary Goudie and has not emerged since as a typical Tribunite). However, this might be explained by old-fashioned ambition and careerism. Even a serial 'non-joiner', like Bryan Gould, realised he had to be on someone's slate to get elected to the Shadow Cabinet; so he signed up to Tribune. He, Brown and Blair were all to achieve rapid success in this ambition, further proof of the need to hunt with the pack.

Because Solidarity could not break the left's hold on the party machinery, it was left to those outside Westminster to make the changes. We therefore return to our story of those trade unionists who started meeting before Wembley but, immediately afterwards, congregated in the St Ermins Group and decided that the priority was taking control of the NEC and then to fashion the party outside the House into an election winning entity. This would mean expelling Militant, changing head-office personnel and concentrating on winning back public support. Their first service to the party was not to defect in the aftermath of Wembley; their second was to take control of the NEC by 1982; their third was to help deliver the leadership to Kinnock, in whom they saw someone equally committed to the task of returning to government. The story told here shows how much effort went into this venture – at least 100 hours of business meetings between 1981 and 1987 – but also demonstrates the trust, discipline and organisational planning needed to deliver the conference votes. This was done in secret and for no ulterior motive. Whilst some of their number do now sit in the Lords, most of the names remain unfamiliar even to the Cabinet let alone the wider world.

Whilst there was a phalanx of union leaders whose determination allied with their standing in the union movement enabled them to amass the necessary votes, two other elements assisted the process. One was the undoubted arithmetic clarity and accuracy possessed by APEX researcher Roger Godsiff, who supplied the tactical path for his union masters to tread. The other was the particular role played by the EETPU. Frank Chapple (having already seen off the communists in his own union) and later Eric Hammond provided clear direction, as well as their boy Friday in the shape of John Spellar. The latter, backed by the support of his bosses, was able again and again to deploy the resources of the EETPU to service or subsidise the activities of the various groups described in these pages. Whilst the ISTC provided the Swinton House venue for the St Ermins Group (as well as for the Solidarity NAC, Labour First Mark Two and Londoners for Labour), it was the EETPU which provided the envelopes, postage, printing and equipment for Solidarity, plus staff time and postage for Londoners for Labour, Labour First Mark Two, Mainstream, and Labour Defence and Disarmament. APEX similarly provided printing, supplies and staff time for Solidarity, St Ermins, Londoners for Labour and the reborn Labour First. Godsiff and Spellar often despaired of the politicians in Solidarity but never refused the wherewithal for them to do their job. In addition, each put in hours of their own time to contribute to Solidarity's successes. Whilst Spellar reached senior ministerial office, Godsiff has been ignored by the party – perhaps partly embarrassed by the role many of its current leading lights were playing whilst he was contributing to the saving of the Labour Party.

The St Ermins' stalwarts had another characteristic: they did not believe in taking prisoners. Just as one of their number, John Golding, was content to allow the party to fight the 1983 general election on as left-wing a manifesto as Benn wanted, so that blame for the ensuing defeat could be comfortably hung round the left's neck (true vengeance for the 1979 defeat having been blamed by the left on Callaghan's timid manifesto), so others believed that dealing with the soft-left was time wasted.[8] In other ways, they were flexible and could deal with the union left, being willing to vote for even far-left candidates in NEC elections where this could produce resulting votes for their marginal candidates, or where such a vote would make no difference to the outcome. The rationale for each decision was what it could achieve. Having decided that control of the NEC was crucial, they set about amending the way the TUC General Council was elected (partly a good thing in itself, but partly to free up the negotiation of votes and to release unions' dependence on the left-wing TGWU), whilst targeting the NEC seats controlled by the unions: the treasurership, the women's seats and the union section. They would if necessary support a left-wing candidate (such as Glenys Thornton in London) to untie another group (in this case the co-operative movement) from an alternative, and then use traditional practices – such as support for an incumbent – to lock other unions into position. Occasionally they would break unwritten rules, such as when the AUEW supported Eric Varley against their own member, Norman Atkinson. Once, when one of their number 'went solo' and broke another tradition by failing to support the Triple Alliance, he was to pay the price of his own job as General Secretary of the NUR. That Weighell still believed many years later that he had done the right thing for the party is testimony to the Group's conviction that the future of the Labour Party was more important than any single individual. This concentration on the sole aim of bringing the party back to 'sanity' so that it could win elections enabled the Group to function as a tight-knit team, despite their varying views on policy, from Europe and defence, to the Middle East.[9]

The St Ermins' unions thus achieved a crucial change in the NEC composition which was then used, firstly, to push through action on Militant, and subsequently to support the leadership which it had helped deliver to Kinnock. Would the party have survived without the Group and its accomplishments? It is easy to forget, when the 2001 government won a majority of nearly 200, how close the party – with a mere 200 MPs and ongoing internal feuds – was to meltdown. In the words of Bryan Gould: 'There was a moment when it was touch and go. The Labour Party was at real risk at one point'.[10] In 1983, it came within a whisker of being eclipsed electorally by the SDP–Liberal Alliance. The implication was serious. As one respected commentator wrote at the time, outside the big cities, the party 'faced something that looks appallingly like terminal collapse in its support in much of the rest of Britain'.[11]

To gain some perspective of what happened to the Labour Party after that 1983 defeat, it is useful to look at the Conservative Party, which faced a similar electoral disaster in 1997 with just 31.5 per cent of the poll. Without the equivalent of the trade unions to ride to its rescue and to insist on the party re-focusing away from its core vote and existing members, and on to the wider electorate, the opposition remained more like a rabbit fixated by car headlights. Having made no meaningful changes by 2001, the car ran over it all over again. By comparison, it is possible to argue that without the unions forcing the Labour Party to change, it could have continued its downward path. More MPs would have peeled off had Benn – as was the wish of party activists – won the deputy leadership in 1981, a result denied them by the St Ermins Group of unions, Labour Solidarity, *Forward Labour* and the soft-left abstainers. Such further defection could have fatally wounded the party's chance of subsequent electoral revival.

In other ways, the traditional right was much less successful in impacting on the party. They failed in the period covered to alter the party's policies on withdrawal from Europe and defence, and they remained unable to win constituency support for their NEC candidates. Solidarity also failed to match CLPD's tactical skill in using resolutions to force its issue (OMOV) on to the conference agenda. Both this and the policy changes had to await Kinnock's and Smith's leaderships. However, given the short timeframe over which these groups operated, and lacking support from the soft-left, it is perhaps forgivable that they failed to undo a decade's damage to the party structure. The book does not argue that these groups were the sole saviours of the party as an electoral machine. It does argue that they made their crucial – necessary if not sufficient – contribution to saving their Labour Party between 1981 and 1987 when it was desperately unpopular even to say aloud the things they believed in, let alone embark on the tasks they set themselves. Without a majority on the NEC, Kinnock would probably not have made his 1985 Bournemouth speech. Without their determined work on Militant, the expulsions might not have taken place. And without their clear focus on the need to win elections, for the sake of their members and the good of the country, it is doubtful whether the party, within a decade of the 1987 election, could have soared to its electoral heights.

Notes

1 Now Lord Gould of Brookwood, this former pollster, advisor to Neil Kinnock and Tony Blair, even subtitled his book 'How the Modernisers Saved the Labour Party' – this being code for Blair, Brown, Mandelson and, of course, himself; Philip Gould, *The Unfinished Revolution* (Little, Brown, 1998).

2 Anthony Bevins, *Independent*, 2 May 1997, p. 1. (However, in 1990 Mandelson said: 'We have now effectively completed the building of the new model party ... now geared to the realities of government rather than the illusions of opposition'; *Guardian*, 16 February 1990.)

3 Paul Richards, 'Why study Labour history?', *Labour History*, autumn 2003, p. 3.

4 For example: 'political parties do not respond with changes unless their leaders order them to do so'; Frank L. Wilson, 'The sources of party change: the social democratic parties of Britain, France, Germany and Spain', in Kay Lawson (ed.), *How Political Parties Work* (Praeser, 1994).

5 The significance of the Electoral College, now universally accepted, was at the time much exaggerated.

6 Roger Godsiff, letter to the author, 27 November 2003.

7 See p. 30.

8 Godsiff commented that the Solidarity MPs spent 'interminably long' trying to keep O'Neill – of whom he had never heard – on board whilst 'the whole world was crashing around our ears', a priority he failed to understand; Roger Godsiff, letter to the author, 27 November 2003.

9 Warburton was highly involved in the Palestinian cause; Clarke and Spellar equally devoted to Labour Friends of Israel.

10 Bryan Gould telephone interview, 16 December 2003.

11 Peter Kellner, *New Statesman*, 17 June 1983.

14

Epilogue: from 1988 to 2004

The trade unions, having set up the Labour Representation Committee (the forerunner of the Labour Party) in 1900 so as to get working people into parliament, took fright in 1981 when they glimpsed the possibility of Labour becoming unelectable. The story told thus far is of a concentrated and concerted effort to change the ruling council of the party – its NEC – so that it would again focus on winning elections and representing ordinary people. One part of the process they saw as expelling Militant. Another was diluting the influence of left-wing activists by extending decision-making – through OMOV – to the wider membership.

There were other problems to face. The divide between Labour's enthusiastic supporters and the rest of society had increased markedly since the party lost office in 1979.[1] Even within the party, there was a gulf between the activists and its parliamentary wing. The public distrusted a party at war with itself as they witnessed Labour MPs arguing against each other on TV and radio, apparently oblivious to the real opponents, the Conservatives and SDP/Liberals (later the Social Democrats). Memories of the left's dominance and of the unions' role in the Winter of Discontent remained fresh – fuelled by the year-long bitter miners' strike in 1984/85. Furthermore, Labour's policies – unilateralism, EEC withdrawal, renationalisation – were deeply unpopular with the electorate.

The 1983 election, led by the left's choice of Michael Foot, had shocked many on the left, as they felt the electorate's hostility and had to fight the SDP for even second position in the popular vote (achieved by a whisker). The Labour Party just survived and its new Leader, Neil Kinnock, was ready to start making changes. He was deeply hampered by the miners' strike, which positioned the government on the side of the police, decency and law and order, against the union movement (in fact only the NUM) and the opposition. The 1987 election was dominated by Labour's policy to remove US nuclear bases from the UK and Kinnock's undertaking to withdraw Polaris nuclear submarines from patrol (raising doubts about the party's commitment to the country's defence) and attacks on the 'loony left' (shorthand for policies on gay and minority rights and nuclear-free city centres) and higher taxes. Nevertheless, the campaign was fought with professionalism and a growing seriousness. Internally, little had changed in the party's policy, image or cohesion. Tony Benn and the left remained the activists' favourites in the annual NEC contests, with Benn challenging Kinnock and continuing to lead an internal (albeit smaller) opposition.

After the election defeat, Kinnock was determined to speed up reform and to extinguish the party's image of being both extremist and divided.[2] He won permission from the 1987 conference to re-think the entire range of policies in a process known as the Policy Review. Its approach was new, involving the Shadow Cabinet and PLP as partners with the NEC, thus working to repair the previous two decades' rift. By 1991, four Policy Review reports had been agreed and these formed the basis of the 1992 manifesto. Together, they completely repositioned the party's stance on the market and working with industry, high taxation and uncontrolled public expenditure, trade union responsibilities and – vitally – defence. Solidarity's members played key roles in the Policy Review process (especially John Smith on the economy, Gerald Kaufman on defence and George Robertson on Europe). Meanwhile, many of the former St Ermins Group targets – Margaret Beckett in particular but also Patricia Hewitt – moved to the Kinnock wing of the party and helped develop the party's new credence.

The NCC ploughed through the expulsion of the remaining Militant members while Kinnock won the argument (if not the vote) for OMOV, which was recommended for the 1988 leadership contests by the Ermins-dominated NEC. The NEC was now operating in line with the party leadership and the PLP.[3] The decline in party warring produced electoral results. In 1989 this – and a professional campaign led by Kinnock advised by Philip Gould – saw Labour win 45 seats in the European Parliament, reducing the Conservatives to 32. It gave hope that the government could be beaten in 1992, producing the greater shock and depression after a defeat which saw only 271 MPs returned to Westminster.

Kinnock and Hattersley resigned, to be replaced by John Smith and Margaret Beckett (now fully emerged as a moderniser). The moderates had regained the leadership (in the shape of Solidarity's John Smith) for the first time since Callaghan's 1976 election, albeit now in alliance with a former Campaign Group MP. OMOV had still not been introduced for the selection of candidates (although it was used in the 1992 Electoral College which produced the new leadership team) and Smith committed himself to this as a sign both of the party's change and also finally to cut the apparent dominance over party selections by the unions and activists.

The period from 1987 had required the party to heal the NEC/PLP wounds, attract back working-class support by concentrating on their interests, reassure the country that it would be held hostage by neither outside aggressors nor internal unions and that, above all, it was a party at peace with itself and not torn by internal divisions. These changes did not, in the main, happen by persuasion but by organisation. Lewis Minkin's forthcoming study on the role of leadership and party management demonstrates how such changes were wrought.[4] The St Ermins Group had changed the political balance of the NEC but the mechanisms of policy development had then to be re-engineered, as did the power relationships between the various elements of the party: the leadership (and its staff), PLP, NEC, conference, unions, activists and members.

These were internal moves, which then had to be communicated both to party members and, more crucially and more challengingly, to the electorate. Kinnock recognised the policies had to change, power be taken from activists and the unions lose prominence. By the 1992 election much had been achieved, with John Smith (elected Leader in July 1992) finally overseeing OMOV's adoption in 1993. It appeared to pay off, with spectacular local and European election results in 1994, which took the number of Labour MPs to an all-time high of 62. The discipline required to make all these changes, and to win public support, remain etched in the collective brain – not least the requirement for an NEC to be totally loyal to, and support, the party leadership, together with the effective outlawing of public displays of internal differences. Hence the birth of both control (over the parts of the movement) and spin (showing only the positive agenda to the public) which were to become the mark of the party. After John Smith's death and the election in 1994 of Tony Blair, the new Leader wanted not just to control the members. He genuinely wanted to persuade them and have them embrace, not simply accept, a vision of the party which was truly attractive to the electorate. Hence his internal party referenda, first on Clause IV and later on the draft manifesto.[5] His desire to win was matched by a desire to be able to govern without the exhausting and draining battle with the party he had witnessed under Callaghan, Foot and, initially, Kinnock. He knew the party had to stay united, in his words, 'to govern as New Labour'[6] and he rapidly knew that any chance of a second term depended on the Leader and membership remaining facing in the same direction. His office, even in opposition, took on itself the earlier St Ermins Group role of ensuring a supportive – some would say compliant – NEC and of policing external communications to close off any possibility of public dispute.

Furthermore, Blair was determined that the party's loss of contact with the electorate would never happen again, being constantly briefed with opinion poll data which reflected current concerns and people's perceptions of the party's policies and presentation. OMOV having been won for the Electoral College and candidate selection, it was subsequently brought in for the CLP seats on the NEC. Meanwhile, in 1998 the NEC itself was restructured so that the PLP/EPLP (Labour's MEPs) together voted for three seats, the government had three places (chosen by the Prime Minister), MPs were debarred from the other places, which were expanded to include two local government representatives. The women's seats – the Trojan Horse so effectively used by the St Ermins Group – disappeared, to be replaced by quotas in the other sections. The result looked much as APEX, and later Solidarity (and indeed the current author), had dreamt of for up to 20 years.[7]

The Electoral College remains firmly in place – albeit with the percentages changed to thirds, the MPs never regaining their pre-eminent position.[8] Indeed, as MEPs were added to their section, the PLP percentage was lower than a third, particularly in 1994 when there were a record 62 Labour MEPs. Despite this, not only is there no suggestion that the College should be removed or changed, but it has failed to wreak the havoc on the party that the SDP and Labour's moderates predicted. As the three Leaders elected by it (Kinnock, Smith and Blair) each won in all three sections – Blair by large majorities – it has in fact strengthened the arm of the leaders in a way its instigators would have detested. It is also almost impossible to remove an incumbent as that requires one-fifth of the PLP to openly nominate an alternative candidate, and even that opportunity occurs only once a year when nominations are sought before the autumn conference.

The St Ermins Group and Solidarity members have reason to be pleased with their handiwork. NEC support for Kinnock's changes to the party's policies and presentation, together with the removal of Militant and the introduction of OMOV (which disempowered the activists in CLPs and brought greater democracy to union working), led to a strengthened party with its eyes focused firmly on election victories. These were denied both Kinnock and Smith (who lived for only 22 months as Leader), their determination and dedication being rewarded only in 1997 and 2001 under Tony Blair.

The question remains as to whether the new NEC structure, and the government–party relationship, does serve the movement well. The NEC, having ceded policy-making to the National Policy Forum, is left with little role and has failed to retain its pre-eminence over organisational issues (candidate selection methods, campaign organisation, staffing) as these are now led by Number 10. Furthermore, the creation of a so-called 'party chairman', appointed by the prime minister and with a Cabinet seat, has given unparalleled power to the government over a political party. (The constitutional party chair, according to the rule book, remains the chair of the NEC, who is selected by the NEC from amongst their number.[9]) The motivation behind these moves lies deep in the memory of the 1970s and 1980s, but without having learnt another lesson from this period: that the unions came to the rescue of, not to bury, the Labour Party. Early on in the 1997–2001 government, the leadership quickly had to resort to union assistance to achieve its aims, particularly stopping Ken Livingstone being the mayoral candidate in London and ensuring Alan Michael was the First Minister nominee in Wales. The unions loyally delivered – only to see their original judgement vindicated. Since then, the government–union relationship has varied but less attention has been paid to the government–party relationship. One lesson quickly forgotten has been that when these two elements fall out, much havoc can be wreaked. The Labour Party paid a high price for the travails of a disillusioned membership in the late 1970s. This book identifies the role played by unions in beginning to repair that damage. The question remains, has either group learnt how to prevent such problems recurring in the future?

Notes

1   Steven Fielding, *The Labour Party: Continuity and Change in the Making of 'New' Labour* (Palgrave, 2003), p. 8.
2   Keith Laybourn, *A Century of Labour: A History of the Labour Party 1900–2000* (Sutton Publishing, 2000), chapter 7.
3   *Ibid.*, p. 127.
4   Lewis Minkin *Domination and delivery: The politics of Blair's party management* (Manchester University Press, forthcoming). See also Meg Russell, *Building New Labour: The Politics of Party Organisation* (Palgrave, 2005) for a description of such changes.

5 John Rentoul, *Tony Blair, Prime Minister* (Time Warner, 2001), chapter 14.
6 Speech outside the Royal Festival Hall, at 5 am on 2 May 1997, having just been elected Prime Minister.
7 Hayter, *The Labour Party*.
8 Rule 4B of the *Labour Party Rule Book*.
9 Clause VII, 1B, of the *Labour Party Rule Book* reads: 'There shall be a chair and vice-chair of the party elected by the NEC from among its own members' who are elected at the first meeting of the NEC each year, and act as chair and vice-chair of the subsequent year's conference.

Appendix: Interviews

Peter Archer	Former MP. Labour First; Manifesto Group. Now Lord Archer of Sandwell	27 January 2003	House of Lords, London
David Bean	Advisor to Peter Shore; Solidarity member. Now Sir David Bean	28 May 2002	Bar Council, London
Cllr Jeremy Beecham	Solidarity; Leader of Newcastle City Council. Now Sir Jeremy Beecham	12 October 2001	Esher
Stuart Bell MP	Secretary, Parliamentary Solidarity. Now Sir Stuart Bell	22 January 2003	House of Commons, London
Stephen Bird	Labour Party archivist	28 February 2002	Labour Party Archive Centre, Manchester
Arthur Bonner	Former London Regional Secretary of NGA; Londoners for Labour; Trade Unionists for Labour	6 November 2003	Sloane Club, London
Chris Bulford	POEU Research Officer	12 April 2002	Islington, London
Steve Bundred	Former member of Greater London Council	30 November 2001	London
Nick Butler	Solidarity. Advisor to Peter Shore.	2 March 2003	Streatham, London
Roger Carroll	Former No. 10 Advisor	17 January 2002	Reform Club, London
John Cartwright	Former MP. CLV; Chairman of Manifesto Group; Member of NEC	6 March 2003	Maidstone

Jim Cattermole	Former Labour Party Regional Organiser; CDS	16 May 2002	National Liberal Club, London
John Charlton	CLV; Solidarity	26 June 2003	Glasgow
Patrick Cheney	Political Advisor to Denis Howell MP	21 March 2002	London
David Clark	Former MP. Labour First Vice-Chairman; Solidarity. Now Lord Clark of Windermere	2 December 2003	House of Lords, London
Tony Clarke	St Ermins Group; NEC. Now Lord Clarke of Hampstead	11 February 2002	House of Lords, London
Dick Clements	Michael Foot's office; Neil Kinnock's office; former Editor of *Tribune*	15 July 2002	High Barnet
Gordon Colling	St Ermins Group; NEC	1 November 2002	Bedford
George Cunningham	Former MP	24 May 2002	Hampton
Jack Cunningham	Solidarity; former MP and PPS to Jim Callaghan. Now Lord Cunningham	5 February 2002	House of Commons, London
The late Jim Daly	CLV and Radical Centre for Democratic Studies	3 May 2002	Chiswick
Richard Faulkner	Advisor to Sid Weighell; Solidarity. Now Lord Faulkner of Worcester	11 March 2002	House of Lords, London
Sandy Feather	St Ermins Group	6 November 2002	Sudborough
Frank Field MP	OMOV campaign; Solidarity	26 March 2003	House of Commons, London
Roger de Freitas	Son of the late Helen de Freitas	30 April 2003	By telephone
The late Derek Gladwin	GMWU. Later Lord Gladwin of Clee	29 November 2001	Hose of Lords, London
Roger Godsiff	APEX; St Ermins. Now Roger Godsiff MP	4 December 2001 and 9 April 2002	Westminster
Robin Gordon Walker	Son of the late Lord Gordon-Walker	14 October 2002	By telephone
Mary Goudie	Labour Solidarity. Now Baroness Goudie	7 January 2003, 11 November 2003 and 11 February 2004	House of Lords, London
Bryan Gould	Former MP; Tribune Group	16 December 2003	By telephone
Mrs John Grant	Widow of the late John Grant, former MP	5 March 2003	Deal, Kent

Nick Grant	Lambeth Solidarity; former Head of Communications at Labour Party	13 November 2003	Reform Club, London
Roy Grantham	St Ermins; TULV; former General Secretary of APEX	2 July 2002	London
John Gyford	CLV; Solidarity	25 April 2002 and 16 November 2003	Witham
Alan Hadden	St Ermins; NEC; NCC	23 January 2002	By telephone
Paul Harriott	National Union of Labour and Socialist Clubs	16 March 2002	Pitlochry
Roy Hattersley	Former MP. Deputy Leader of the Labour Party, 1983–92; Co-chair of Solidarity; NEC; Manifesto Group. Now Lord Hattersley	5 May 2004	St Martin's Lane, London
Alan Haworth	PLP Secretary. Now Lord Haworth	25 January 2002	Westminster
Denis Healey	Former MP. Deputy Leader of the Labour Party, 1980–83. Now Lord Healey of Riddlesden	16 October 2002	House of Lords, London
Richard Heller	Advisor to Gerald Kaufman MP and to Denis Healey MP	22 January 2003	Bloomsbury, London
Joycelin Hobman	Labour Defence and Disarmament Group	8 May 2002	Kentish Town
John Horam MP	Former Labour MP. Manifesto Group Chairman	14 January 2003	House of Commons, London
Norman Howard	TUPO; St Ermins Group; Solidarity; former POEU officer	14 February 2002 and 5 January 2003	Kentish Town
David Hughes	Former Labour Party National Agent; author Hayward/Hughes report	16 June 2003	Hayes
Chris Inman	Solidarity employee	17 December 2001	By telephone
Neil Kinnock	Former MP. Leader of the Labour Party, 1983–92. Now Lord Kinnock	7 June 2004	European Commission Office, London
John Lloyd	EETPU	18 March 2002	EETPU, Bromley
Dickson Mabon	Former MP. Manifesto Group Chairman	3 July 2002	Eastbourne
Edmund Marshall	Former MP. Secretary of Labour First	12 November 2003	By letter

Tom McNally	Former MP. Now Lord McNally	27 November 2002	London
Brian Nicholson	TGWU former Chairman; Londoners for Labour; Labour First	6 March 2002	Dockers' Club, London
The late Gerry O'Brien	Former Labour Party Regional Officer, Solidarity	16 March 2002	Pitlochry
Martin O'Neill MP	Solidarity	17 September 2003	By telephone
Tony Page	Advisor to Gerald Kaufman MP	21 March 2002	London
Jenny Pardington	TGWU; TULV	2 February 2002	Cardiff
Joyce Quin	Former MP	Spring 2004	House of Commons, London
Reg Race	NUPE official and subsequently MP for Wood Green	6 May 2004	By telephone
Giles Radice	Former GMWU official; subsequently MP and Manifesto Group Chairman; Solidarity, St Ermins Group. Now Lord Radice	7 October 2002 and 26 November 2003	House of Lords, London
George Robertson	Former MP. Manifesto Group Secretary; Solidarity. Now Lord Robertson of Port Ellen	30 April 2003	By e-mail
Roger Robinson	Labour Party staff	29 November 2002	Oxford
Chris Savage	Solidarity	30 January 2003	London
Sherpas	Political advisors to the Shadow Cabinet, 1979–83: Tony Page [EricVarley MP], David Cowling [Peter Shore MP], Richard Heller [Denis Healey MP], Patrick Cheney [Denis Howell MP]	21 March 2002	St Martin's, London
Mrs Peter Shore	Widow of Peter Shore MP	14 February 2002	By telephone
Bill Sirs	ISTC; St Ermins Group	21 October 2002	By letter
John Spellar MP	EETPU; St Ermins Group; Solidarity; Londoners for Labour. One time MP for Birmingham Northfield. Now MP for Warley West	21 May 2003	London
Bryan Stanley	POEU; St Ermins Group	24 January 2003	Borehamwood
Neil Stewart	Neil Kinnock's office	14 March 2002	Farringdon, London

Matt Tee	Tatchell Campaign Team, Bermondsey	16 April 2002	Kentish Town
Bill Thomas	National Union of Labour and Socialist Clubs	16 March 2002	Pitlochry
Mike Thomas	Former MP. Manifesto Group	2 July 2002	Reform Club, London
Richard Tomlinson	CLV; Solidarity; Co-operative Party	28 January 2003	London
Alan Tuffin	St Ermins Group; UCW	18 April 2002	TUC, London
Charlie Turnock	St Ermins Group; NUR	28 May 2003	St Albans
John Wakefield	Manifesto Group Research Officer	7 February 2003	Kentish Town
Peter Walker	Red Wellies Club (Discussion Group)	10 November 2001	Millbank, London
David Warburton	Forward Labour; GMWU; TULV	7 December 2001	Rickmansworth
David Watkins	Former MP. Labour First	14 April 2004	Commonwealth Club, London
Mike Watts	Labour Party staff	7 May 2002	Kentish Town
Ken Weetch	Former MP. Manifesto Group Treasurer; Solidarity	3 April 2003	Kentish Town
James Wellbeloved	Former MP. Manifesto Group	3 April 2002	Tower Bridge, London
Phillip Whitehead	Former MP. Manifesto Group. Now Member of the European Parliament	9 January 2003	Kentish Town
Clive Wilkinson	CLV Chairman; Solidarity	17 April 2002	Canary Wharf, London
Alan Lee Williams	Former MP. Manifesto Group	3 April 2002	Tower Bridge, London
Ken Woolmer	Former MP. Secretary, Solidarity. Now Lord Woolmer	12 June 2003	House of Lords, London
Ian Wrigglesworth	Former MP. Manifesto Group Secretary; CLV. Now Sir Ian Wrigglesworth	4 November 2002	London
Phil Wyatt	John Silkin Deputy Leadership Campaign	11 December 2001	London

With only one or two exceptions, the interviews were all recorded and have been transcribed. The recordings and full transcriptions will be lodged at the Labour History Archive at the John Rylands Library, Manchester University.

Bibliography

Archives

EETPU Archives
Labour Party Archives (Labour History Archive at the John Rylands Library, Manchester University)
Labour Solidarity Campaign Archives (University of Hull)
Manifesto Group (Labour History Archive at the John Rylands Library, Manchester University)
PLP Archives (Labour History Archive at the John Rylands Library, Manchester University)
Radical Centre for Democratic Studies Archives (private collection)
St Ermins Group archives (by kind permission of Roger Godsiff MP)

Personal papers

David Bean papers
Nick Butler papers
Lord (David) Clark of Windermere papers
Jim Daly papers
Bob Eadie papers
Sandy Feather papers
John Grant papers (by kind permission of Mrs Pat Grant)
John Gyford papers
Lord (Roy) Hattersley papers, University of Hull.
Alan Haworth papers
Mike Parker papers
John F. Spellar papers
Charles Turnock papers
David Webster papers
Ian Wrigglesworth papers

Books and articles

Bell, Stuart, *Tony Really Loves Me*, Spen View Publications, 2000.
Benn, Tony, *The End of an Era: Diaries 1980–90*, Hutchinson, 1992.

Bing, Inigo (ed.), *The Labour Party: An Organisational Study*, Fabian Society, 1971.

Blick, Andrew, *People who Live in the Dark*, Politico's Publishing, 2004.

Boothroyd, Betty, *Betty Boothroyd: The Autobiography*, Century, 2001.

Bosanquet, Nick and Peter Townsend (eds), *Labour and Equality: A Fabian Study of Labour in Power, 1974–79*, Heinemann, 1980.

Bradley, Ian, *Breaking the Mould? The Birth and Prospects of the SDP*, Martin Robertson, 1981.

Brivati, Brian L. 'The Campaign for Democratic Socialism 1960–1964', PhD Thesis, Queen Mary and Westfield College, University of London, 1992.

Broad, Roger, *Labour's European Dilemmas: From Bevin to Blair*, Palgrave, 2001.

Bullock, Alan, *Ernest Bevin: A Biography*, ed. Brian Brivati, Politico's, 2002.

Chapple, Frank, *Sparks Fly! A Trade Union Life*, Michael Joseph, 1984.

Claven, Jim, *The Centre is Mine*, Pluto Press, Australia, 2000.

Cole, John, *The Thatcher Years: A Decade of Revolution in British Politics*, BBC Books, 1987.

Crewe, Ivor and Anthony King, *SDP: The Birth, Life and Death of the Social Democratic Party*, Oxford University Press, 1995.

Crick, Michael, *The March of Militant*, Faber and Faber, 1986.

Crosland, Susan, *Tony Crosland*, Jonathan Cape, 1982.

Cunningham, George, 'Was Tony Benn the true winner against Healey?', unpublished, 1983.

Daly, Gerald J. 'The crisis in the Labour Party 1974–81 and the origins of the 1981 schism', PhD thesis, University of London, 1992.

Daly, Jim, 'Let ALL the members vote!', *Socialist Commentary*, October 1976.

Donoughue, Bernard, *The Heat of the Kitchen*, Politico's, 2003.

Egan, Dominic, *Irvine: Politically Incorrect?*, Mainstream Publishing, 1999.

Evans, John, 'One member one vote democracy in the Labour Party', *Labour Club News*, April 1987.

Fielding, Steven, *The Labour Party: Continuity and Change in the Making of 'New' Labour*, Palgrave, 2003.

Flanders, Allan, *Trade Unions and Politics; London Trades Council 1860–1960 Centenary Lecture*, London Trades Council, 1961.

Golding, John, 'The fixers: the rise and fall of Benn and Heffer', unpublished, 1988.

Golding, John, *Hammer of the Left*, Politico's, 2003.

Goss, Sue, *Local Labour and Local Government*, Edinburgh University Press, 1988.

Gould, Philip, *The Unfinished Revolution*, Little, Brown, 1998.

Grant, John, *Blood Brothers*, Weidenfeld & Nicolson, 1992.

Gray, Joseph, *Labour Leader*, August 1978.

Gyford, John, *The Politics of Local Socialism*, George Allen & Unwin, 1985.

Haines, Joe, *The Politics of Power*, Coronet Books, 1977.

Harris, Andy, 'CLPD slams CLV "democracy" fraud', *London Labour Briefing*, 3 June 1980.

Harris, Robert, *The Making of Neil Kinnock*, Faber and Faber, 1984.

Hatfield, Michael, *The House the Left Built*, Victor Gollancz, 1978.

Hayter, Dianne, *The Labour Party: Crisis and Prospects*, Fabian Society, 1977.

Hayter, Dianne, 'NEC needs rank-and-file', *Labour Weekly*, 7 September 1979.

Hayter, Dianne, 'What if Benn had beaten Healey in 1981?', in Duncan Brack and Iain Dale (eds), *Prime Minister Portillo and Other Things That Never Happened*, Politico's, 2003.

Hayter, Dianne, 'The fightback of the traditional right in the Labour Party, 1979 to 1987', PhD thesis, University of London, 2004.

Healey, Denis, *The Time of My Life*, Michael Joseph, 1989.

Heffernan, Richard and Mike Marqusee, *Defeat from the Jaws of Victory: Inside Kinnock's Labour Party*, Verso, 1992.

Hemming, Christopher, 'Labour's "penny-farthing" machine: was Labour's local organisation better than the Wilson spin suggested?', unpublished, 2002.

Hobsbawm, Eric, *Interesting Times: A Twentieth-Century Life*, Allen Lane, 2002.

Howell, Denis, *Made in Birmingham: The Memoirs of Denis Howell*, Queen Anne Press, 1990.

Jones, George, 'A left house built on sand', *Socialist Commentary*, November 1978.

Jones, Jack, *Union Man: An Autobiography*, Collins, 1986.

Kavanagh, Dennis (ed.), *The Politics of the Labour Party*, George Allen & Unwin, 1982.

Kellner, Peter, 'Widespread balloting gives Hattersley landslide', *New Statesman*, 7 October 1983.

Kendall, Walter, *The Revolutionary Movement in Britain, 1900–21: The Origins of British Communism*, Weidenfeld & Nicolson, 1969.

Kennet, Wayland, *Rebirth of Britain*, Weidenfeld & Nicolson, 1982.

Kogan, David and Maurice Kogan, *The Battle for the Labour Party*, Fontana, 1982.

Laybourn, Keith, *A Century of Labour: A History of the Labour Party 1900–2000*, Sutton Publishing, 2000.

Liverpool Black Caucus, *The Racial Politics of Militant in Liverpool: The Black Community's Struggle for Participation in Local Politics 1980–1986*, Runnymede Trust, 1986.

May, Eddie, 'The mosaic of Labour politics, 1900–1918', in Duncan Tanner *et al.* (eds), *The Labour Party in Wales, 1900–2000*, University of Wales Press, 2001.

McSmith, Andy, *Faces of Labour: The Inside Story*, Verso, 1996.

Meacher, Michael, 'Breaking the block vote', *New Statesman*, 13 November 1981.

Middlemas, Keith, *Power, Competition and the State*, Macmillan, 1990.

Minkin, Lewis, *The Labour Party Conference*, Manchester University Press, 1980.

Minkin, Lewis, *The Contentious Alliance: Trade Unions and the Labour Party*, Edinburgh University Press, 1991.

Minkin, Lewis, *Exits and Entrances: Political Research as a Creative Art*, Sheffield Hallam University Press, 1997.

Minkin, Lewis, *Domination and delivery: The politics of Blair's party management*, Manchester University Press, forthcoming.

Mitchell, Austin, *Four Years in the Death of the Labour Party*, Methuen, 1983.

Mitchell, Austin, 'Party people: review of Dictionary of Labour biography', *The House Magazine*, 4 November 2002.

O'Brien, J., E. Preston and B. Winter, *Who Rules: Annual Conference versus the Parliamentary Party*, Independent Labour Publications, 1979.

Owen, David, *Time to Declare*, Penguin Books, 1992.

Panitch, Leo and Colin Leys, *The End of Parliamentary Socialism*, Verso, 2001.

Pearce, Edward, *Denis Healey: A Life in Our Times*, Little, Brown, 2002.

Pimlott, Ben and Chris Cook (eds), *Trade Unions in British Politics*, Longman, 1982.

Radice, Giles, *Friends and Rivals*, Little, Brown, 2002.

Radice, Giles, *Diaries 1980–2001: The Political Diaries of Giles Radice*, Weidenfeld & Nicolson, 2004.

Rentoul, John, *Tony Blair, Prime Minister*, Time Warner, 2001.

Richards, Paul, 'Why study Labour History?', *Labour History*, autumn 2003.

Rodgers, Bill, *Fourth Among Equals*, Politico's, 2000.

Russell, Meg, *Building New Labour: The Politics of Party Organisation*, Palgrave, 2005.

Seyd, Patrick, *The Rise and Fall of the Labour Left*, Macmillan Education, 1987.

Shaw, Eric, *Discipline and Discord in the Labour Party*, Manchester University Press, 1988.

Silkin, John, *Changing Battlefields: The Challenge to the Labour Party*, Hamish Hamilton Ltd, 1987.

Sirs, Bill, *Hard Labour*, Sidgwick & Jackson, 1985.

Sked, Alan and Chris Cook, *Post-War Britain: A Political History, 1945–1992*, Penguin, 1993.

Sofer, Anne, *The London Left Takeover*, Self-published, 1987.

Stewart, Michael, *Life & Labour: An Autobiography*, Sidgwick & Jackson, 1980.

Sutchbury, Oliver, 'Reform of party organisation', in Inigo Bing (ed.), *The Labour Party: An Organisational Study*, Fabian Society, 1971.

Tatchell, Peter, *The Battle for Bermondsey*, Heretic Books, 1983.

Thatcher, Margaret, *The Downing Street Years*, Harper Collins, 1993.

Townsend, Peter and Nick Bosanquet (eds), *Labour and Inequality*, Fabian Society, 1972.

Turnock, Charles, 'Labour needs 30 miracles', unpublished, 1987.

Turnock, Charles, 'Mersey militants', unpublished, 1987.

Turnock, Charles, 'Rigorous route by rail and river', unpublished, 1995.

Warde, Alan, *Consensus and Beyond: The Development of Labour Party Strategy since the Second World War*, Manchester University Press, 1982.

Webb, N. and R. Wybrow, *The Gallup Report 1981*, Sphere, 1982.

Webster, David, *The Labour Party and the New Left*, Fabian Society, 1981.

Weighell, Sidney, *On the Rails*, Orbis Publishing, 1983.

Westlake, Martin, *Kinnock*, Little, Brown, 2001.

Whitehead, Phillip, *The Writing on the Wall: Britain in the Seventies*, Michael Joseph, 1985.

Whiteley, Paul, *The Labour Party in Crisis*, Methuen, 1983.

Wilson, Frank L., 'The sources of party change: the social democratic parties of Britain, France, Germany and Spain', in Kay Lawson (ed.), *How Political Parties Work*, Praeger, 1994.

Young Fabian Group, *The Mechanics of Victory*, Fabian Society, 1962.

A Better Way, published by the Signatories, 1979.

Labour Party publications

Consultation Working Party, *Party Franchise*, 1987.

Reports of the 1975 to 1986 Annual Conferences of the Labour Party.

Underhill, Reg, *How the Labour Party Works*, 1975.

Published by the EETPU

'Elitism and democracy', *Political Bulletin*, August 1983.

'Leadership election', *Political Bulletin*, 25 July 1988.

Political Bulletin, Issue 27, July 1989.

'The Electoral College', *Political Bulletin*, 23 November 1987.

Published by Labour Solidarity

Bristol Labour Solidarity, 1983.

Labour Solidarity, March 1981 to February 1987.

Student Solidarity News, October 1985 to March 1986.

Other publications

1983/84 and 1984/85 Annual Reports of Campaign Group of Labour MPs.
Broad Left Alliance Journal, October 1982.
Clause IV, The Journal, December 1984, Spring 1985 and July 1987.
Labour Club News, National Union of Labour and Socialist Clubs, April 1987.
Labour Leader, ILP, August 1978.
Labour Victory, CLV, May 1977 to October 1979.
London Labour Briefing, June 1980.
Witch Hunt News, January 1986, March 1986, May 1986 and June/July 1986.

TV programmes

A Week in Politics, Channel Four, 13 February 1983 and 11 June 1983.
BBC TV News, 2 April 1981.
The Battle for Labour, 30 October 2002, BBC 4.
The Wilderness Years, BBC, 1995.

Name index

Note: 'n.' after a page reference indicates the number of the note on that page.

Lightning Source UK Ltd.
Milton Keynes UK
UKOW06f0611260216

269155UK00001B/39/P